BRAHMA
IN THE WEST

Vol.1.
P 243

धमाइंबिष्यनामुव: BRAHMA

Engraving of Brahma from William Jones's
On the Gods of Greece, Italy, and India

BRAHMA
IN THE WEST

William Blake
and the Oriental Renaissance

David Weir

State University of New York Press

Published by
State University of New York Press, Albany

Printed in the United States of America

Cover photo: Engraving of the accusers of Socrates, plate 93, William Blake,
Jerusalem, the emanation of the giant Albion, copy D, London, 1804.
Typ 6500 49F, Department of Printing and Graphic Arts, Houghton Library,
Harvard College Library.

For information, address State University of New York Press,
90 State Street, Suite 700, Albany, NY 12207

Production by Diane Ganeles
Marketing by Fran Keneston

Library of Congress Cataloging-in-Publication Data

Weir, David, 1947 Apr. 20–
    Brahma in the West : William Blake and the Oriental renaissance / David Weir.
        p. cm.
    Includes bibliographical references (p.) and index.
    ISBN 0-7914-5817-2 (alk. paper) — ISBN 0-7914-5818-0 (pbk. : alk. paper)
        1. Blake, William, 1757–1827—Knowledge—Mythology. 2. Blake, William,
1757–1827—Knowledge—India. 3. Blake, William, 1757–1827. Four Zoas. 4. Blake,
William, 1757–1827—Religion. 5. Brahmā (Hindu deity)—In literature. 6. English
poetry—Indic influences. 7. Orientalism in literature. 8. Hinduism in literature. 9.
Mythology, Hindu. I. Title.

PR4148.M83 W45 2003
821'.7—dc21
                                                                        2002030965

10 9 8 7 6 5 4 3 2 1

What is the Life of Man but Art & Science?

—*Jerusalem*, plate 77

In memory of
David Geoffrey Weir
(1973–1991)

Contents

Figures

Acknowledgments

We who dwell on Earth can do nothing without Others they are to us as Muses were in Antient Days. Of these whose Love and Labour have helped to guide my own unsteady Hand in making this unworthy Work are those immense intelligences of Astor Place. There sweet Science & gentle Art advance together and of those Spirits Brian Booth and Boshra Al-Saadi are honoured most for bringing light to dark Designs. Then comes Nancy of that Northern Zone where opens Ellegate into Great Presses of Albany expanding through Eternity. In the Mills of Balthazar labour too great Mosso and Maher, Brothers of the Vine serving Eno continually. And to Camille in Beulah soft and mild I can never be too thankful O What Wonders are the Children of Men.

Permission to reproduce plates 53, 78, and 93 (Typ 6500 49F) from copy D of *Jerusalem, the emanation of the giant Albion,* Department of Printing and Graphic Arts, Houghton Library, Harvard College Library; and to reproduce an untitled drawing by William Bell Scott after a lost drawing by William Blake, *William Blake: Etchings from His Works* (London: Chatto and Windus, 1878), Print Collection, Miriam and Ira D. Wallach Division of Arts, Prints and Photographs, The New York Public Library, Astor, Lenox and Tilden Foundations, is gratefully acknowledged.

Abbreviations

AR   *Analytical Review, or History of Literature, Domestic and For-*
      eign, on an Enlarged Plan. Edited and published by Joseph John-
      son. 28 vols. London, 1788–98.

BG   *The Bhăgvăt-Gēēta, or Dialogues of Krĕĕshnă and Ărjŏŏn.* Trans.
      Charles Wilkins (1785; rpt. Delmar, NY: Scholars' Facsimiles &
      Reprints, 1959).

E   David V. Erdman, ed., *The Complete Poetry and Prose of William*
      Blake, newly revised edition (Garden City, NY: Anchor, 1982). All
      references to Blake's writings in poetry or prose are to this edition.
      Texts other than those indicated below, such as Blake's letters and
      marginalia, are referenced by *E.* Specific works by Blake are refer-
      enced in Erdman using the following abbreviations:

      BT   *The Book of Thel*
      SI   *Songs of Innocence*
      SE   *Songs of Experience*
      MHH   *The Marriage of Heaven and Hell*
      AP   *America a Prophecy*
      EP   *Europe a Prophecy*
      SL   *The Song of Los*
      U   *The Book of Urizen*
      M   *Milton a Poem in 2 Books*
      J   *Jerusalem: The Emanation of the Giant Albion*
      FZ   *The Four Zoas*

      Specific passages in Blake's engraved works are referenced by plate
      and line number (e.g., *BT* 1.6), or by plate number and the word
      Prose for prose passages in the engraved works (e.g., *MHH*
      21.*Prose*). The manuscript poem *The Four Zoas* is referenced by
      chapter number (i.e., "Night" number) followed by manuscript
      page number followed by line number (e.g., *FZ* 1.4.3–4).

Introduction

The belief that William Blake was an untutored naif is by now a naïve notion. In truth, the poet read widely and tutored himself in an eclectic but impressive range of knowledge, from Plato to Locke, Swedenborg to Newton, Paracelsus to Paine. Arbitrary pairings such as these suggest an opposition of mystical tradition and enlightenment thought, with Plato's idealism, for example, ascendant over Locke's empiricism. But Blake did not think as we do, and our categories cannot contain his. If Blake was a Platonist, his idealism was a highly sensuous sort not to be found in Plato. The sensuous nature of Blake's idealism and his insistence on the "Minute Particulars" (*J* 91.21) of existence might seem to make Locke somehow allowable, but, in fact, the philosopher is consistently demonized by the poet for his denial of innate ideas. At the same time, however, Blake's republican politics surely owes something to Locke's doctrine of natural rights.

Whether he knew it or not, Blake participated in the liberal ideology of Locke by way of Paine, whose vigorous advocacy of individual liberty evidently permitted the poet to overlook the deism in Paine that he so despised in Newton. Indeed, Newton's mechanistic conception of nature was, for Blake, vastly inferior to the code of correspondences that allowed Swedenborg to make everything natural a pathway to a spiritual world. When that code was codified into a prescribed set of beliefs, however, then Swedenborg became no different from Newton—the authoritarian head of a cult, albeit spiritual rather than rational. For this reason Blake preferred the cosmology of Paracelsus to that of Newton. This brings us back to the poet's paradoxical acceptance of Tom Paine, who might have been rejected on the same basis as Newton was, because the political pamphleteer no less than the natural philosopher was a member of the deistic "cult" of reason. For Blake, reason in defense of liberty was no vice, but it was as an explanation of nature. Hence the arbitrary pairing of Paracelsus and Paine is not so arbitrary after all: both mystical cosmology and rational politics gave imagination room to operate.

The point here is not so much to stress Blake's indebtedness to particular figures but rather to suggest the curious compatibility of contradictory traditions in Blake's poetry. The compatibility results, in most

1

cases, from the poet's sense that representatives from various traditions might share a similar ideology, a common consciousness. In political terms, this ideology falls within the leftist spectrum of republicanism and libertarianism; in religious terms, it occupies the band between Dissent and antinomianism. As E. P. Thompson and others have shown, these political and religious traditions were tightly interwoven in Great Britain from the Civil War onward, especially among the tradesman class to which Blake's family belonged.[1] In this context, John Milton was to Blake as much a model for republican politics and Protestant dissent as he was for the poetic method of sublime allegory. Likewise, the importance to Blake of a mystic like Jacob Boehme rests, in part, in the tradition of Dissent that makes mystical insight and individualist politics mutually reinforcing. The dual tradition of libertarian politics and dissenting religion can be heard in one of Blake's most famous lines, when the character Los proclaims: "I must Create a System, or be enslav'd by another Mans" (*J* 10.20). The politics of this pronouncement is easy enough to hear: avoiding enslavement to a system that one has had no part in forming is of a piece with the Painite practice of individual liberty. The resonance of religion is perhaps harder to detect, but it is there in *system,* a word that is consistently used in the eighteenth century to describe a set of religious beliefs and practices, or a "comprehensive body of doctrines" *(OED).* The usage, for example, appears in the title of a mythographic study by Jacob Bryant that Blake read, *A New System; or, An Analysis of Ancient Mythology.* Thus, when Blake has his mythic alter ego Los assert the need for an individual system he makes a political statement that has religious implications.

The complicated relationship of politics, myth, and religion in the strange career of William Blake is the subject of this book, whose general assumption is that Blake's mythic system was the product of those same historical forces that had brought conventional Christianity into question by the end of the eighteenth century. Principal among these forces are republican politics and dissenting theology, both of which ramify throughout Blake's poetry in surprising and sometimes perplexing ways. All of this is familiar enough to students of Blake: everyone knows that he belonged to a revolutionary generation and participated in its political ideals, even as he put forth a mixture of dissenting opinions. But the dual context of politics and theology that plays through Blake's system also informs a broader metamorphosis of religious thought in the eighteenth century, and animates especially the great English awakening to Indic culture that occurred in the midst of Blake's artistic career. Indeed, Blake was witness to the series of discoveries that later writers described under the rubric of "the Oriental Renaissance,"

a phrase implying that the Sanskrit texts brought to light by William
Jones in the service of the East India Company in Bengal occupy a place
of importance equivalent to the Greek texts translated by Marsilio
Ficino for the Medicis in Florence. It is a stunning claim, and one that
may seem less credible now than it would have in the nineteenth century,
at a time when romantic writers understood the Oriental Renaissance to
have "marked the close of the neoclassical age just as the Classical
Renaissance had marked the close of the medieval age."[2] Blake is hardly
one with the romantic writers, but he anticipates many of their political
and cultural concerns. He gave expression to republicanism in poetry
well before Wordsworth did, and he explored the Oriental Renaissance
far in advance of Coleridge or Shelley. At the same time, however, Blake
looked backward to an earlier age of strange sects and theological pecu-
liarities somehow kept alive in the London of his youth. This specifically
British tradition combines with French republicanism and world
mythology (Hindu, Classical, and Scandinavian, mainly) to make
Blake's system what it is—the elaborate expression of a sense of political individualism so eccentric and extreme as to make the poet a sect of
one and to effectively blur the distinctions between politics, myth, and
religion. In fact, the poet's work is unified by the strain of individualist
ideology that descends from the mix of sectarianism and republicanism
that attended the English Civil War, so that, ultimately, Blake's poetic
mythology can be understood as a religious transformation of libertarian politics. This general thesis finds support in the particular way that
Blake assimilated Eastern mythology—the newly discovered literature of
Hinduism—into his own poetic system.

　　Blake was not alone in understanding politics, myth, and religion
in ideologically interchangeable terms. The eighteenth century was the
great age of mythography when the religions of the world were
described, compared, and criticized. The basic debate in the many
mythographic studies of world religions that appeared in Blake's lifetime
was whether the faith of the Hebrew patriarchs was the fount from
which all other religions flowed, albeit in corrupt form, or whether the
Hebrew patriarchs received their faith from some still more ancient
source. In a sense, Blake manages to have it both ways. The patriarchs
take pride of place in one way, but in other ways the ancient faith of the
Israelites is no more original than that of the Egyptians or the Hindus.
This is so because Blake believed that *all* religion was a codified corruption of poetry, or rather, of the vital, energetic vision of the world the
Poetic Genius makes possible. This much is clear from plate 11 of *The
Marriage of Heaven and Hell,* so seminal to Blake's basic myth from the
early 1790s onward. Around this time the strange names of Blake's

mythic figures begin to appear: first Luvah in *The Book of Thel* (1789), then Urthona, Orc, and Urizen in *America* (1793), then Los and Enitharmon in *Europe* (1794), together with a host of secondary figures— Oothoon, Theotormon, Bromion, Rintrah, Palamabron, and so on. There can be no doubt that Blake believed in these creatures of the imagination because he believed so strongly in imagination itself. Blake's emendations to his Laocoön engraving, done late in life, express nonetheless the Everlasting Gospel that drove him to create early on: "The Eternal Body of Man is The IMAGINATION. / God himself / that is . . . JESUS" (*E* 273).

If Jesus is imagination, and if *system* is allowed to resonate with its eighteenth-century meaning, there is reason to read the famous words of Los in *Jerusalem* as the poet's own: "I must Create a System, or be enslav'd by another Mans / I will not Reason and Compare: my business is to Create" (*J* 10.20–21). Mythographers such as Jacob Bryant compared Egyptian, Persian, Greek, and Roman systems in order to reason in favor of the Hebrew prophets, who provided, in turn, the foundation for Christianity. Joseph Priestley compared the polytheistic Hindu system to the Mosaic faith and reasoned in favor of monotheism, which provided, in turn, the basis for Unitarianism. As different as Blake is from Bryant and Priestley, he has in common with them the mythographic approach to religion. He differs from them, however, in that his system is creative, not comparative. But Blake's creative mythography, that is, his poetic system, would not have been possible without the precedent of comparative mythography. The comparatists helped Blake to understand that all religions are one; his radical Protestantism allowed him to invent his own; and his republican devotion to liberty provided the impulse to invention.

Comparing Blake to the comparatists can be a rewarding exercise; indeed, the idea that the poet was as much a mythographer as Jacob Bryant or Joseph Priestley makes him seem far less eccentric or idiosyncratic and much more in touch with his times. Blake's knowledge of mythography probably dates from his days as a teenage apprentice to James Basire, when he is likely to have engraved plates for Bryant's *A New System, or, An Analysis of Ancient Mythology* (1774).[3] In his *Descriptive Catalogue* of 1809 Blake mentions Bryant in the context of the "British Antiquities" that he represented in his lost painting of *The Ancient Britons,* a depiction of the "three general classes of men" who have survived *"the last Battle of King Arthur."* This last battle *of* Arthur seems really to have been a battle *within* Arthur, a contest that occurred in the distant past when "the Sun of Britain s[e]t." Blake's mythological nightfall reverses the Scandinavian myth of the twilight of the gods and paradoxically gives birth to divine forces that take the human forms of *"the Strongest Man, the Beautifullest Man, and the Ugliest Man."* These are the three classes of men who possess the earth in Arthur's absence "and remain for ever unsubdued, age after age," at least until *"Arthur shall awake from sleep, and resume his dominion over earth and ocean."* In Arthur's absence, during his sleep, the Druids begin to have dominion, and their history is written in the Bible: "Adam was a Druid, and Noah; also Abraham was called to succeed the Druidical age, which began to turn allegoric and mental signification into corporeal command, whereby human sacrifice would have depopulated the earth" (*E* 542–43). Blake's syntax is a little slippery here, but the meaning seems to be that the practice of *actual* human sacrifice ended with Abraham, whose son Isaac did escape the knife but did not escape the allegoric sacrifice of humanity on the altar of moral law or "corporeal command," the law that governs "the world of vegetation and generation" subsequent to Arthur's sleep. The condition of allegorical Druidism or repressive moral law results, in part, because of the disintegration of Arthur into the three classes of men, whose meaning Blake elaborates:

> The Strong man represents the human sublime. The Beautiful man represents the human pathetic, which was in the wars of Eden divided into male and female. The Ugly man represents the human reason. They were originally one man, who was fourfold; he was self-divided, and his real humanity slain on the stems of generation, and the form of the fourth was like the Son of God. (*E* 543)

Strength, beauty, and ugliness, then, or sublimity, pathos, and reason added together produce a fourth, an addition of "real humanity" that results in oneness, an integrated form that makes humanity divine and the divine human—"like the Son of God." "How he became divided," Blake adds, "is a subject of great sublimity and pathos. The Artist has written it under inspiration, and will, if God please, publish it; it is voluminous, and contains the ancient history of Britain, and the world of Satan and of Adam" (*E* 543).

Here in his description of this fantastic lost painting Blake provides the basic outlines of his great myth. What the artist has already written "under inspiration" we now know in its early form as *The Four Zoas* and later as *Jerusalem: The Emanation of the Giant Albion,* for Albion and Arthur are, at base, the same allegorical figure: "The giant Albion, was Patriarch of the Atlantic, he is the Atlas of the Greeks, one of those the Greeks called Titans. The stories of Arthur are the acts of Albion, applied to a Prince of the fifth century" (*E* 543). One of the things Blake would have learned as a boy from reading Bryant's *New System* as he engraved plates for it was that the same god might have many names. Albion, Arthur, and Atlas are different but equivalent terms for the same thing. Blake calls Albion the "Patriarch of the Atlantic," meaning the Atlantic flood that overwhelmed Atlantis, which makes him not unlike Noah, except that Albion belongs to a period of far greater antiquity than the Asiatic patriarch, who was, after all, part of the Druid disintegration of things after the fall of Arthur.

This is the crucial point where Blake departs from Bryant, a traditional mythographer who accounts for the various pagan gods as corrupt manifestations of the original patriarchal religion practiced by Noah and disseminated by his sons after the deluge. Here is Bryant's explanation of pagan mythology: "The history of the Patriarch was recorded by the ancients through their whole theology: but it has been obscured by their describing him under so many different titles, and such a variety of characters. They represented him as Thoth, Hermes, Menes, Osiris, Zeuth, Atlas, Phoroneus, Prometheus: to which list a further number of great extent might be added."[4] Blake's misreading or misremembrance of Bryant's account of the spread of religion in the *Descriptive Catalogue* is highly instructive: "The antiquities of every Nation under Heaven, is no less sacred than that of the Jews. They are the same thing as Jacob Bryant, and all antiquaries have proved. How other antiquities came to be neglected and disbelieved, while those of the Jews are collected and arranged, is an enquiry, worthy of both the Antiquarian and the Divine" (*E* 543). Nothing could, in fact, be further from Bryant's purpose, which is clear enough from the title page announcing "an Attempt . . . to divest Tradition of Fable; and to reduce the Truth to its Original Purity" (Bryant, 1: title page).

There is much in Bryant that is of value to an understanding of some of the details of Blake's poetry, such as the principle of creation by process of emanation that first appears in *The Four Zoas*—"Some of the ancients thought that the soul of man was a divine emanation; a portion of light from the Sun. Hence probably it was called Zoan from that luminary" (Bryant 1: 38)—and it is possible that this passage also furnished Blake with the term *Zoa* itself.[5] Critics have pointed out that Blake seems to have named his character Tharmas after Thamuz or Thaumus in Bryant, and picked up the name Luban from the *New System* as well.[6] But sometimes Blake's borrowings seem less important than his misunderstandings. His remark on Bryant shows that what Blake called "antiquities," and we call mythology, the poet was prepared to accept as true in the same sense that the Bible is true and that all inspired writing is true—including Blake's own. Blake, in other words, was constitutionally inclined to believe the antiquities of any nation, so long as they were authorized by the Poetic Genius. In principle, then, there is no reason why Blake should not have been receptive to the antiquities of Asia that were coming to light in his lifetime. Indeed, there is every reason to believe that Blake took an interest in Eastern mythology and incorporated elements of it into his own system, just as he did elements from biblical, classical, and Scandinavian mythology. As we shall see, the politics of empire put British republicans on the side of Indian liberty, even as English divines interpreted the Hindu faith in a way that made it amendable with religious dissent. This convergence of political and theological interests in India occurred in circles so close to Blake that the poet's participation in them is virtually certain. That the convergence occurred within the context of a tradition of mythography suddenly given new life by the fresh discovery of Indian antiquities makes Blake's involvement all the more likely.

Typically, the mythographer subjected religious systems outside the Western tradition to either Christian or rationalist criteria to show, in the first instance, that Christianity was the one true faith, or, in the second instance, that all religions were equally ridiculous in the light of reason. But Blake differs from both Christian and enlightenment mythographers in that he does not intend to affirm traditional Christianity or to replace religion with rationality; rather, he means to replace institutional religion with individual mythology. In other words, Blake truly is a creative mythographer who values religion as an individual means of understanding and organizing human experience. In this respect his poetry differs from the prose of the enlightenment mythographers, such as the comte de Volney, whose *Ruins* (1791) compares the religions of the world only to point out their inconsistencies and absurdities. By contrast, Blake means for his system to be systematic, consistent both with that condition outside of history that he called Eternity and with history itself. *The Song of Los* (1795) is Blake's first attempt to make the system systematic, to consolidate his ramifying myth and set it into some kind of sequence. This much is clear from the two parts of the poem titled "Africa" and "Asia," the first of which forms the background of *America*, the second the sequel to *Europe*.

In broad terms, the patchwork sequence connects ancient religion and modern politics: "Africa" recounts the collapse of poetry into priestcraft, *America* the successful resistance of that process on one side of the Atlantic, *Europe* the anxieties of the struggle on the other, and "Asia" a somewhat equivocal victory of humanity over the forces of Church and King. In a sense, the cycle begins and ends in Asia, even though the first part of *The Song of Los* is titled "Africa":

Adam stood in the garden of Eden:
And Noah on the mountains of Ararat;
They saw Urizen give his Laws to the Nations
By the hands of the children of Los.
Adam shudderd! Noah faded! black grew the sunny African
When Rintrah gave Abstract Philosophy to Brama in the
     East:

(*SL* 3.6–11)

Thus, religion in the form of Abstract Philosophy is dispatched first to "Brama in the East." In this way Blake manages to accommodate several competing mythographic accounts of the origin of religion. By making Adam and Noah contemporaries in Eternity rather than successive figures in a biblical lineage, he aligns himself with those mythographers who attributed the origin of religion to the Hebrew patriarchs. But by locating both Eden and Ararat in Africa, Blake gives the nod to those who favored Egypt as the preferred point of origin of those "forms of dark delusion" (*SL* 3.17) that blacken humanity with religious ritual and moral law. Finally, by making Brahma the first recipient of Urizen's laws, conveyed to the East by Los's corrupted son Rintrah, Blake accommodates Hinduism as the most recent candidate (circa 1795) for the most ancient faith.

    The reference to Brahma in *The Song of Los* shows that Blake was able to incorporate the latest mythographic material into his own evolving system. As we shall see, the allusion to Brama in the East is neither the first nor the last acknowledgment of Hindu mythology in the poet's work. Blake's openness to the Hindu system helps to show that his own elaborate mythology was, for him, a religious system that had the same status as any of the other world religions that were coming to light during his lifetime, but with one important difference: Blake's system is not intended to compel belief in others. To do so would have been for Blake to position himself as yet another priest of a mysterious cult, a position completely untenable with the political principle of radical individualism he espoused. Blake's system is not, therefore, a religion, but it is religious; and Blake himself is not a spiritual authority, but he is a spiritual author, someone who earnestly believed in the Protestant power of conscience as a guide to behavior and of inspiration as an impetus to art. In his annotations to Bishop Watson's *An Apology for the Bible* (1797), when the Bishop writes that "in obeying the dictates of his conscience" a man will *"on all occasions act right,"* Blake adds, "Always, or the Bible is false" (*E* 613).

Here the Bible is the authority for obeying the dictates of conscience, but not even the Bible occupies this privileged position in a subsequent annotation to Watson: "The Bible or Peculiar Word of God, Exclusive of Conscience or the Word of God Universal, is that abomination which like the Jewish ceremonies is for ever removed & henceforth every man may converse with God & be a King & Priest in his own house" (*E* 615). The political implications of religious conscience could not be clearer, and Blake assuredly brought the same sense of radical individualism to the question of poetic inspiration, as the preface to his epic poem *Milton* shows: "The Stolen and Perverted Writings of Homer & Ovid: of Plato and Cicero. which all Men ought to contemn: are set up by artifice against the Sublime of the Bible. but when the New Age is at leisure to Pronounce; all will be set right: & those Grand Works of the more ancient & consciously & professedly Inspired Men, will hold their proper rank, & the Daughters of Memory shall become the Daughters of Inspiration" (*M* 1.*Prose*). In this passage the doctrine of inspiration may be informed by the common mythographic claim that the poems of the Greek and Latin writers were merely copies of lost "Asiatic" originals. In addition, the millenarian context of the "New Age" implies that Blake's own poem represents a recovery of the same visionary power that animated the "Grand Works" of the "Inspired Men" of the past. It follows that Blake's poetry is a contribution to a continuing canon of inspired works that include not only the Bible, but also the prose *Edda*, say, and the *Bhagavad Gita,* both of which Blake knew in the mythographic context in which they first appeared.

The idea that all works of inspired art form a continuing canon of visionary or spiritual scripture was phrased in archetypal terms years ago by Northrop Frye: "In this world the Word of God is the aggregate of works of inspired art, the Scripture written by the Holy Spirit which spoke by the prophets. Properly interpreted, all works of art are phases of that archetypal vision."[7] Recourse to archetypes outside of history, however, is not necessary to make the point that Blake believed his poetry to be a continuation of holy scripture in general and biblical prophecy in particular. Jon Mee has shown that Blake was not alone in thinking of the Word of God as an ongoing process of revelation: in the 1790s other religious enthusiasts believed that the books of the Bible were still being written, and would continue to be written so long as inspiration obtained. This claim was made by the visionary Richard Brothers in *A Revealed Knowledge of the Prophecies and Times* (1794), a work written in the style of biblical prophecy that has something in common with Blake's *Europe,* published in the same year. As Mee puts it, both "Blake and Brothers . . . offered to supplement and even replace the received prophetic canon with their own visionary experience."[8]

The Bible, then, was not unique, and was far from being the sole repository of spiritual truths. Many spiritual systems were available for examination by the rational mythographer in the latter half of the eighteenth century, and many more were possible for the inspired bard. Blake's poetry draws on both these traditions: yes, his mythological system is the product of a genuine belief in inspiration, but the form that the inspiration took is drawn from or modeled on a number of sources in addition to the Bible. And while the Bible remains the single most important source for Blake's mythology, there are many elements of that mythology that seem genuinely alien to the Bible as it is commonly understood. For example, a crucial component of Blake's system is the conception of history as a cyclical process, but the notion of historical recurrence is really foreign to the eschatological scheme of the New Testament that punctuates linear time with apocalypse and removes reality from history altogether. Now Blake certainly entertains the millenarian notion of an apocalyptic end of history which is well within a tradition of Biblical commentary, but it is hard to see how the concept of historical recurrence that leads up to Blake's apocalypse is based on the Bible.[9]

I am not the first to suggest that Blake's poetry owes something to religious systems outside the Western tradition. For many years now a fairly large contingent of critics has insisted on a relationship between Blake's work and Hindu mythology. In 1924 S. Foster Damon claimed that Blake was "in accord with Eastern mysticism: Urthona is Dharma; Urizen, Karma; while both Tharmas and Luvah are included in Maya."[10] Five years after Damon's monumental study, Denis Saurat's *Blake and Modern Thought* (1929) explored certain parallelisms to "The Hindoos" by listing "essential elements of the Blakean myth" common also to "Indian religion":

> the primitive hermaphrodite, or giant containing all the
>   world
> his separation into beings and especially
> his separation into Male and Female
> the refusal of the female, her flight
> the pursuit by the male, his conquest of the female
> the origin of all species from their union.[11]

Saurat's comments are more valuable than most because he attempts to ground the analogies he makes in the literature about India published in

Blake's lifetime. He makes no attempt, however, to show that Blake might actually have had specific opportunities for exposure to that literature.

The lone work of Hindu literature that the poet assuredly knew something about is the *Bhagavad Gita,* and in 1947 Northrop Frye observed that "Blake was among the first of European idealists to link his own tradition of thought" with the Indian classic, taking the account of the lost drawing of "Mr. Wilkin translating the Geeta" (*E* 548) in Blake's *Descriptive Catalogue* of 1809 as evidence for such a link. Frye also noted, but did not explore, the possibility that Blake's conception of three classes of human beings—Angels, Devils, and Elect—"may have come from the 'Gumas' of the *Bhagavadgita.*"[12]

In 1961 Frye extended the Hindu context to a more general Oriental philosophy and made the astonishing claim that "terms from Blake and Mahayana Buddhism [could] be used interchangeably." He came to this conclusion by way of his brilliant student Peter Francis Fisher, whose early death prevented a full exploration of the connections he noted between Blake and Eastern traditions in his posthumously published but incomplete book, *The Valley of Vision.*[13] The most extensive examination of Blake in connection with esoteric Eastern traditions is Kathleen Raine's 1968 study, *Blake and Tradition,* in which she asserts that Blake "rightly supposed that those learned in the kind of thought of which his own poetry is an expression would have read Plato and Plotinus, the Hermetica and the alchemists, the Bible and the Bhagavad-Gita."[14] This tendency to assume that Blake's knowledge necessarily comprises whatever the critic has read in forming his or her interpretation is taken to fantastic lengths by Charu Sheel Singh in *The Chariot of Fire: A Study of William Blake in the Light of Hindu Thought* (1981). At one point Singh cites a book published in 1978 as evidence for a "Hindu" image in a poem dated 1783.[15] Evidently, chronology is a real liability whenever there are "consciousnesses" to be compared. A recent study of *The Four Zoas* by Kathryn Freeman, for instance, says that "Eastern nondualism . . . provides an analogue" for understanding the "ever present state" of "undifferentiated consciousness" that Blake allegedly represents, a state that can be understood in terms of "[t]he nondualism of Keshir Shaivism, an ancient Indian philosophy."[16]

I do not dispute the general drift of these critics' claims: that elements of Blake's poetic myth are not easily explained by reference to the more familiar strains of the Western tradition—the Bible, say, or classical literature. Indeed, the long tradition of Blake scholarship that locates Asia in Albion suggests to me that at least some of that scholarship exists for a reason. Like Coleridge and Shelley after him, Blake was assuredly affected by some of the Indian literature that appeared in literary and political circles in the last fifteen years or so of the eighteenth century, even though he can only be said to be on the periphery of such circles. What I object to in most of the previous scholarship on the subject is not the argument for Eastern influence on an English poet, but the way in which the argument is made. To my mind, there are a number of problems with the way the case for Blake and Brahma has been made thus far. Too many critics either reason from analogy and textual parallels alone or, worse, argue from archetypes. Matching up a bit of Blake with a swatch of Coomaraswamy, say, shows only that one writer reminds the critic of another.[17] Reading Blake in archetypal terms means mainly that the poet's contradictions and inconsistencies can be smoothed over by categories and schemata derived from Carl Jung. This procedure is doubly problematic: not only do archetypal readings take Blake outside of history, they ignore the disturbing historical context of the late 1930s that produced Jung's predilection for archetypes in the first place.

But the main problem with both analogical and archetypal commentary is the assumption that Blake thought in the 1790s as we do now. The tendency has been to situate Hindu religion in the context of western esoteric traditions, such as Neoplatonism and hermeticism, and then to read any reference to Hinduism in Blake as confirmation of his place within those mystical traditions. But Blake's sense of Hindu religion—whatever it was—would have been strongly colored by radical politics and comparative mythography, and he would not necessarily have understood the new literature that reached London from the East in the late eighteenth century as strictly "mystical."

Finally, the most serious problem with earlier scholarship on Blake and Hinduism has been a real failure to investigate the sources of Indian mythology that the poet would have most likely known—or known about. So far, the only primary source we can be certain Blake knew something about is Charles Wilkins's 1785 translation of the *Bhagavad Gita*, which Blake mentions in 1809. Whether he actually read the *Gita* is not clear, but we need not suppose that Blake got his knowledge of India solely from translations of Hindu literature. In addition to translations of original Sanskrit works by Wilkins and others, a wealth of material was available to Blake in the form of the new mythographic studies that had begun to include the culture of "Hindostan" or "Indostan" in the progression of ancient civilizations that had shaped the modern world of the late eighteenth century.

Even a cursory look at Blake's system suggests similarities with Hindu mythology, and this fairly early in his poetic career. In *The Book of Thel,* when Blake's overly innocent heroine asks, "why fades the lotus of the water?" (*BT* 1.6), the image evokes India rather than the

English countryside. In *Europe,* when the poet speaks to the Fairy who dictates the poem, he sounds like Arjuna questioning Krishna: "Then tell me, what is the material world, and is it dead?" (*EP* iii.13). Later in the same poem Blake evokes a sense of time more Eastern than Western when he describes the "infinite / Shut up in finite revolutions" (*EP* 10.21–22). Blake would not require recourse to the *Bhagavad Gita* to inquire about the reality of the material world, but he might in order to set that world into cyclical, recurrent motion. Another obvious element of comparison is the acceptance of sexuality in both the Blakean and Hindu systems. The "obscene image of the lingam" and the seductiveness of the Devi were often singled out by French and English commentators as instances of the vulgarity of the Indians,[18] but Blake would certainly have thought otherwise of the frank expression of sexuality in Hinduism because he celebrated sexual love so strongly in his own poetry: "The lust of the goat is the bounty of God" (*MHH* 8.23). In this case there is no reason to think that Blake was influenced by Hinduism: his anti-Puritanical attitudes are doubtless rooted in some species of religious dissent that understood religious prohibitions against sexual pleasure as one more instance of an institutionalized moral code that conscience had every right to override. But if the Hindus looked with favor on sexual pleasure, then Blake would have looked with favor on the Hindus. And he would have been that much more likely to see what else they had to offer.

Charles Wilkins's claim in his "Translator's Preface" to the *Bhagavad Gita* that the "Brāhmǎns . . . are Unitarians" (*BG* 24) might also have encouraged curiosity about the East—not because Blake was himself a Unitarian, but because some of his fellow dissenters were. More important, Blake's fellow dissenters were under attack—physically, in some cases—by the same agents of Church and King that were operating in India half a world away. Blake and the Indians had a common enemy in state religion, and those same counter-revolutionary forces that had lost an empire in America had found another one in India. This is quite literally the case: Lord Cornwallis may have surrendered America at Yorktown in 1781, but he secured India for England at Mysore in 1792. The historical context goes a long way toward explaining the mix of republicanism, mythology, and mysticism in Blake. The same context also explains a similar mix in the translation, transmission, and reception of Indic culture from East to West in the late eighteenth century.

Republican politics, creative mythography, and dissenting theology are the three principal strains of Blake's work that are rather maddeningly interrelated in the poems of his maturity. Often the politics and the theology cooperate in the making of the myth, but just as often they interfere with each other and end up making the myth indecipherable. Much of Hindu mythology, also, first appeared in London in the dual context of republicanism and Dissent, although the strange claim that the Hindus were somehow Unitarians soon gave way to the equally odd notion that they were Platonists. The attenuation of Blake's radicalism and antinomianism into an elaborate mythology that can with some justification be termed "mystical" has its parallel in a similar tendency for Hinduism to be understood early on in republican and dissenting terms, and then later to be treated as the Eastern cognate of Western idealism. These parallels and analogies are not fortuitous, and they cannot—and should not—be explained as the operation of archetypes; rather, they exist because Blake's creative mythography developed in the same context as the discovery and interpretation of Hindu mythology. In the history of Blake criticism a kind of competition has developed between those critics who insist on reading Blake as a radical writer within history and those who want their Blake to be a mystical poet promoting some "perennial philosophy" outside of history.[19] I suggest that the tension between radicalism and mysticism in Blake criticism recapitulates an actual tension in Blake's career that was not, in fact, limited to Blake but was also evident in the British reception of Hindu mythology during the same period.

The tension between radicalism and mysticism is only part of a larger set of relationships that contribute to the complexity of Blake's myth and the difficulty of understanding it in simple terms. What makes the myth both difficult and eccentric is the combination in it of apocalyptic, biblical language; dissenting, antinomian rhetoric; radical, republican polemic; and esoteric, mystical discourse. These four types of language have provided the impetus to the major schools of Blake criticism. The competition among these schools no doubt derives from the contradictory mixture of discourses in Blake's poetry itself. The mystical Blake makes his first appearance in the theosophical circles frequented by William Butler Yeats and other members of the Celtic Twilight at the end of the nineteenth century. For the most part, the poet remains trapped in the theosophical fog until David Erdman saves him from mysticism by grounding the myth in republican politics. Then, Harold Bloom rescues Blake from political allegory by aligning him with Milton and biblical tradition. Next, Kathleen Raine reacts by removing Blake from both local politics and familiar tradition to situate him in the ether of esoterica. And E. P. Thompson brings Blake back down to earth and into the antinomian fold, a dissenting tradition that can, nonetheless, include radicalism, the Bible, and even esoterica—so long as the myth is omitted.[20]

One of the things I mean to do in this book is supplement earlier presentations of Blake as both a republican and an antinomian author with the argument that mythography has political and religious dimensions that complement both radicalism and Dissent.[21] The difficulties of Blake are such that the compartmentalization of the poet into Dissenter, Radical, Miltonist, and Mystic are inevitable and ultimately helpful. But Blake, for all his contradictions, was after all one person who was somehow capable of sustaining continuities among these four traditions that have latterly been transformed into separate, single-minded approaches to the poet. In Blake's time, and in Blake's work, the religious, political, literary, and mystical strands were much more tightly interwoven than their subsequent disentanglement suggests. The mythographic tradition of the eighteenth century likewise provided a rich texture of religion, politics, literature, and mysticism, and the infusion of Hinduism into that tradition enlivened and complicated the meaning of mythology just as Blake began his artistic career.

Separating the strands in Blake's myth runs the risk of misrepresenting the importance of any one of them to the exclusion of the others, so it is important to recognize relationships among them. Seeing the links, for instance, between biblical apocalypse and dissenting theology in Blake's sensibility is easy to do because the links were already formed in Blake's own time. Many Antinomians were also Millenarians who looked to see their dissent from moral law verified by the end of the rule of the Beast and the beginning of the thousand-year reign of Christ on earth. At one point in 1801 Blake thought he was on the verge of the millennium when he wrote to his friend John Flaxman, the sculptor: "I rejoice to hear that your Great Work is accomplish'd. Peace opens the way to greater still. The Kingdoms of this World are now become the Kingdoms of God & his Christ, & we shall reign with him for ever & ever." It goes almost without saying that the apocalypse that abrogates the need for dissent and ushers in the age of art is of a piece with recent political events: "I hope that France & England will henceforth be as One Country and their Arts One, & that you will Ere long be erecting Monuments in Paris—Emblems of Peace" (E 717–18). But the peace that makes Blake so optimistic here was to be short-lived. The treaty between the British and French forged at Amiens in March 1801 lasted less than fourteen months. These events prompted Blake to complete and then to abandon his "long Poem descriptive" of "the Spiritual Acts" that occurred during his three-year residence in Felpham (E 728). His return to London coincides with the evident decision to revise the grandiose revolutionary narrative of The Four Zoas, with its coded references to the machinery of political and military power, into the more personal examination of the operations of poetic power that is *Milton*. It is fairly easy to get from *Milton* to mysticism, and to argue that the poet's pilgrimage from revolutionary ardor to aesthetic introspection, and thence to the grand vision of *Jerusalem* simply follows the track of the times. If in his early years Blake has something in common with Paine, Priestley, Wollstonecraft, and Joseph Johnson, in his later years he comes to resemble those great revolutionary artists and thinkers of his age who moved from radical republicanism through political disillusionment and into mysticism, introspection, and even madness: Wordsworth, Beethoven, Goya.

Not surprisingly, previous studies of Blake and Hindu mythology have dwelt on the late, post-revolutionary work of the poet, or, rather, have taken that work as the visionary evidence of an undifferentiated and ahistorical consciousness that can comprehend the esoterica of both the East and the West. I approach the problem of Blake and Brahma differently, and try to describe the poet's relationship to Indic culture in three separate but related contexts: the political, the mythographic, and the theological. In each of these three cases, I seek to situate Blake in relation to the historical reality of Hinduism as it was understood in the late eighteenth century, so that the British experience of Indic culture and Blake's poetic development may emerge as products of the same historical circumstances. Thus, this is a book that tries to do for Blake's mythology what has already been done for his politics and religion—to set it in relation to the poet's times.

The emphasis on historical context means that the reader will encounter more documentation than interpretation in the pages to follow. This is not a book intended to provide startlingly new and unusual readings of Blake's poetry. By contrast, my purpose is to use the "Oriental Renaissance" to show that Blake's poetry is not so unique and idiosyncratic as it seems, but is, rather, an understandable product of the historical context that brought political radicalism, mythographic analysis, and religious dissent together at the same time. If Blake's poetry is read as the expression of this curious confluence, what we think we know about Blake may not change a great deal, but how we think we know it might.

Thus Blake's mythic system is here understood as the product of historical conditions, but the complicated cultural transactions that occurred as a result of those conditions make the matter of Blake and Brahma difficult to describe as an issue of simple influence. Certainly there are instances where it is highly likely that Blake borrowed an image or an idea from a particular source first-hand. But, in general, the presence of Indic elements in Blake's system cannot always be explained in so obvious a fashion as, say, the influence of Swedenborg. Rather, the influence of the Hindu system on the Blakean one appears to have been mediated by those political, mythographic, and theological traditions that already held the poet's attention. Thus, the first chapter of this book discusses the republican circles in which Hindu literature was initially presented in late eighteenth-century London and shows how close Blake was to those circles. In this exposition Blake disappears from the discussion for pages at a time, but I believe it is important to establish the political conditions under which Indian affairs were debated and discussed because those conditions provided the context for the discovery and dissemination of Hindu mythology by Blake's contemporaries. The poet enters the picture more clearly in chapter 2, which shows how the political and theological conditions that marked the appearance of Brahma in the West also marked the mythographic tradition that Blake inherited: contemporary accounts of Hinduism provided the poet with a precedent for his mythic system and supplied him with a wealth of material that he could use to make that system richer. Chapter 3 explains how the theological contexts that were employed to interpret the Hindu faith conformed in certain key respects to Blake's dissenting system. Thus, the progression of the chapters is intended to show first how Blake would have been drawn to Hinduism for political reasons; second, how the parallels between the poet's myth and the Hindu system provide evidence of actual influence; and, third, how this influence played out in theological terms, as certain Christian interpretations of Hinduism found their way into Blake's composite mythology.

If Blake seems more mystical than mythical as his poetic career progresses, the same might be said of the British understanding of Hinduism over the same period. This mysticism, however, is highly complicated by the process that produced it, and the last thing I want to suggest is that Blake turned to Brahma out of some fellow-feeling for the mysterious East. On the contrary, Blake did not need to be mystical to be interested in India. From a republican perspective, the Hindus were on the right side of revolution in the 1790s, and so was Blake. Only when it became evident that empire would outlast the kind of liberty that conscience claimed as its birthright did Blake entertain Eternity in the full sense that we find in the late epics. Only when the millennium failed to materialize did Blake's vision become visionary, but even then, whatever is mystical in Blake is historical first.

CHAPTER 1

Politics

"The Tyger" is one of two or three poems by William Blake that everyone knows, or, at least, knows about. The familiarity of the poem is evidently linked with its obscurity, for those who know about the poem may not necessarily know what the poem is about. The unwritten rules of interpretation dictate that because "The Tyger" is a poem it cannot be about a tiger: the beast in the jungle must therefore be a symbol of something else, or something Other. Surely the thing that burns in the night is not a tiger, but desire: "Tyger Tyger, burning bright / In the forests of the night" (*SE* 42.1–2). Or perhaps the tiger is the evil evidence of an impossible theological conundrum in which innocence is forever locked into a relationship with its contrary: "Did he who made the Lamb make thee?" (*SE* 42.20). It may be, also, that the poem is about poetry—a self-referential exercise in which Blake claims that only a human being could command the creative energy to make something as complex and contradictory as "The Tyger": "What immortal hand or eye, / Could frame thy fearful symmetry?" (*SE* 42.3–4). The implicit answer is that no immortal could, but a mortal artist might, because Blake did. Another meaning may be that the tiger which burns so brightly represents the fires of revolution lighting up the night of continental tyranny, an interpretation consistent with the flames of Orc that burn away mystery and empire elsewhere in Blake's poetry. But this last interpretation begs an obvious question: Why would an English poet choose an image from India to represent a revolution in France? In fact, just about any interpretation leads the reader to wonder why an English poet would be thinking about an Indian tiger anyway.

Because trade with India had been a fact of British life since the early seventeenth century, we should not be surprised to learn that there were tigers in London during Blake's lifetime. Two were kept at the Tower of London, and Blake could have seen one exhibited at Leicester House near Green Street where the poet resided after his marriage to Catherine in 1782.[1] "The Tyger" was written ten years later, and it is tempting to think that Blake's symbolic beast was inspired by one of two real tigers, either the one he saw around the corner from his home in Green Street or another one in India that he never saw but would certainly have heard

19

about in the same year he wrote the poem. In December 1792 the only son of a British general named Sir Hector Munro died after he was attacked and mauled by a tiger in western India. General Munro had earlier defeated the notorious Muslim leader Tipu Sultan in a battle in the same region where his son was killed, so there was a certain awful irony about the younger Munro's death in the wake of his father's victory—a fearful symmetry, you might say. Blake would have known about the attacks—both the British general's upon the Indian prince and the Indian tiger's upon the English youth—because news from India was not hard to come by in 1790s London. Indeed, the tiger attack was such a sensational event that it immediately took hold in the public imagination and gained a secure place in English popular culture when it was commemorated in the form of the cheap domestic artware known as chimney ornaments.[2] Whether Blake's poem also commemorates the tiger attack is hard to say, but there is no denying the emblematic value of tigers in Great Britain (whether literal or symbolic) to show the involvement of India in the English empire.

How might this information affect interpretation of this famous poem? For one thing, it helps to explain the strange dualism of poem and picture: the tiger in the text is a fearful, mysterious beast that prompts the poet to ask how so much power could ever have been given form at all; by contrast, the image of the tiger that accompanies the poem represents the creature as rather tame, sheepish even. Many critics think this tiger looks more like a lamb,[3] and it could very well correspond to the caged beast that Blake saw at Leicester House as a young newlywed, while the barely imaginable tiger of the text suggests the animal in India that killed the General's son. Certainly the creation of this kind of unbound energy has its risks—what immortal would dare to do such a thing?—and if the tiger is an emblem of India then perhaps the creation of a colonial empire has its risks as well, all the more so because the hands and eyes of the Englishmen in India were merely mortal. More than one British general must have looked into the forests of the Indian night and wondered where the tiger Tipu lay concealed.

"The Tyger" may be a rather oblique reference to the English presence in India, but elsewhere Blake is more direct in suggesting relationships between Great Britain and its Indian empire. We have already noted that *The Song of Los* is a mythographically complex comparison of world religions in the context of state authority, with Blake describing some primordial moment when original vision gives way to religious system. But the poet may also be using this mythographic moment to describe his own age as well. The historical allegory that makes Blake's mythic figure Rintrah the agent of British authority (usually understood as William Pitt) squares with reality.[4] Thus the poet's meaning may also include a contemporary reference to the use of imperial authority to impose British political and religious systems on a native Indian population. Rintrah really did give "Abstract Philosophy to Brama in the East" (*SL* 3.11). By 1795, when *The Song of Los* was written, England was well on its way to consolidating its empire in the East, and any number of Englishmen in India were already enjoying the kind of commercial despotism that led a later writer to say that they had become "Sultanized."[5]

But for all the Sultanized Englishmen in India, there were a few who had become "Brahmanized" instead. Some members of the Asiatic Society in Bengal were so receptive to and respectful of native traditions that they were, in effect, culturally colonized by the very society they had been sent by "Rintrah" to regulate and, to some extent, put aside their own "Abstract Philosophy" for "Brama." This generous reading of British imperialism is, to be sure, limited to only a few enlightened scholars, but certainly the interests of William Jones and Charles Wilkins went beyond the purely commercial concerns of most members of the East India Company. Jones, after all, used his position as a jurist to help establish a system whereby legal disputes in India would be adjudicated by Indian laws, and Charles Wilkins used his skills as a printer to fabricate the first movable Devanagari typeface to make the printing and distribution of Sanskrit texts possible. Blake's own sense that Wilkins had "gone native" is suggested by that part of his 1809 catalog description of his drawing of *The Bramins* where he admits to some confusion about Indian garb: "I understand that my Costume is incorrect, but in this I plead the authority of the ancients, who often deviated from the Habits, to preserve the Manners, as in the instance of Laocoon, who, though a priest, is represented naked" (*E* 548). The drawing, in other words, probably represented Wilkins in some kind of Indian costume that accorded with Blake's idea of the "manner" of a Brahmin, even though he had no sense of what such a costume would actually look like.

That he was corrected in his pictorial representation of Indian costume implies that Blake was in contact with someone who knew how the costume should have appeared. Whoever this person was, he (or, less likely, she) would have been able to impart additional information about India to Blake. The possibility exists that the informant might have been Wilkins himself, who had returned to England in 1786 and was active in circles very close to Blake. In the same year that Blake advertised his drawing of *The Bramins* Wilkins was in contact with one Moses Haughton, who was doing a series of engravings for Edward Moor's *The Hindu Pantheon*, published in 1810. The Blake connection is the poet's friend and fellow artist Henry Fuseli, who employed Haughton on a regular basis to engrave many of his own compositions.[6] Haughton, in turn, had Wilkins supply the names of the Hindu deities written in Sanskrit using the new Devanagari fonts. This daisy chain linking Blake to Wilkins in the year 1809 does not identify Blake's informant on the correct mode of Hindu costume definitively, but it is one more piece of suggestive evidence—together with the drawing of Wilkins itself—that can be used to justify the claim that Blake had some understanding of Hindu mythology by the time he was working on *Jerusalem*.

But Blake would not have had to wait until 1809 for India to enter his consciousness. Over the last quarter of the eighteenth century Indian affairs were a constant concern of the King's ministers and the statesmen in Parliament.[7] The London *Times* published regular reports in columns devoted exclusively to news from India, and quite a few British periodicals reviewed and summarized new books about India at some length. Blake would not have been able to avoid the talk about India in the 1790s among the dissenters and republicans he saw from time to time, especially toward the end of the decade, when republicanism reached into India itself in the person of that same Tipu Sultan whom General Munro had defeated in 1792. The tiger attack on the General's son, however sensational, was only a small part of the meaning of India for English radicals in the late eighteenth century. Those who supported the Revolution in France, as Blake did, would have understood the importance of India to the engine of empire and the exercise of imperial power, both at home and abroad. Blake's knowledge of India would have come to him first in the form of political controversy surrounding the East India Company and by way of reports in the radical press of the Hindu literature that was reaching London around the same time. The argument of this chapter, then, is that Blake's understanding of mythology was inextricably linked with revolutionary enthusiasm because the myths of India could only have been communicated to him in a republican context.

I

The East India Company was formally incorporated on 31 December 1600 after a group of London merchants had raised £30,000 capital and petitioned Queen Elizabeth for a charter. Between 1601 and 1613 the Company undertook twelve voyages for the purpose of securing a British-controlled source of spices (to flavor salt-cured meat) in the face of rising prices from Dutch and Portuguese suppliers. The earliest voyages were made to the spice islands of the East Indies, trade being established with India proper only after the destruction of the Portuguese fleet in 1612. After Elizabeth, James I renewed the Company's charter indefinitely. Royal sponsorship abated temporarily with the overthrow of Charles I, Oliver Cromwell's initial inclination being to end the Company's monopoly privileges altogether. He was persuaded otherwise, however, and the Company's enterprises in India actually expanded during the Protectorate. With the Restoration came even greater privileges and more territory. Charles II had married the daughter of the king of Portugal and received the island of Bombay as part of her dowry. When Bombay proved unprofitable as a royalist possession, the king handed it over to the Company for use as a new port for English ships, formerly docked at Surat. He also granted the Company extraordinary political powers through a series of new charters, including the power to make governmental appointments and administer justice; to wage war and negotiate peace with the native princes; and to acquire new territories and defend existing ones against rival colonial adventurers.[8] Nevertheless, the Company's exclusive privileges in India were not always honored. In 1698 a *second* British East India Company was given royal sanction when the crown required fresh funds to restore a depleted war chest. Queen Anne consolidated the two companies in 1709, and the newly unified East India Company once again held an exclusive charter to do business in the East (Robert, 76).

By the beginning of the eighteenth century, then, the Company's unusual position as a commercial entity with monopoly privileges and independent powers of government over a native population was firmly established. England had superceded Holland and Portugal as a colonial force in India, with trading posts secured in Surat, Bombay, Madras, and Calcutta. But new threats emerged from the French and from the native Indian princes. In 1746 Joseph François Dupleix, Governor-General of French India, successfully attacked the British fort at Madras, where an unassuming twenty-year-old clerk named Robert Clive was stationed. Clive escaped to Cuddalore, site of another English settlement, and joined up with Major Stringer Lawrence; together they launched a counterattack on the French settlement at Pondicherry. The British and French negotiated their way out of continued hostilities at this time, and Madras was returned to English control, but the episode was the harbinger of numerous military engagements to come between England and France in India over the second half of the eighteenth century. No less than the Caribbean Islands, India was to be the colonial staging ground for conflicts between the two countries, especially during the Seven Years War and, later, throughout the French Revolution and the Napoleonic era.

The situation in India was further complicated by the decline of the old Mogul dynasty in Delhi, which was no longer able to exercise authority over native princes. To protect their own interests the princes began to alternate allegiances with the rival East India Companies of the French and the English, often playing one off against the other. The ensuing vacuum of political power was eventually filled by the British under the spectacular military leadership of Clive that made him a national hero when news of his exploits reached London. Clive had secured the mercantile empire in India by force, but his strengths as a military leader were not well-suited to the peaceful administration of the Company's concerns. That task fell to Warren Hastings, who had impressed Clive during the fighting in Bengal and was appointed to the Calcutta Council in 1761 (Robert, 78–79, 85). Here is the point where the story of the East India Company begins to intersect with the career of William Blake, since it was Hastings who encouraged Charles Wilkins to translate the *Bhagavad Gita*. Of equal importance, however, is the role Hastings played—unwillingly, to be sure—in helping to keep India in the foreground of the political consciousness of English radicals in the 1790s.

In 1772 Warren Hastings was named Governor-General of Bengal, a title that was changed to Governor-General of India the next year (Robert, 85). The change of title was mandated by the Regulating Act of 1773 that brought India more directly under parliamentary control but stopped short of full regulation: the Company still enjoyed a considerable measure of independence, which the traders and administrators took full advantage of to amass enormous private fortunes at the expense of the native population. The process of regulation was completed only in 1784 with the passage of Pitt's India Bill, which placed clear limitations on the Company's governmental and economic powers. The India Bill provided for a Board of Control that made the Company fully accountable to Parliament, a development that did not jibe with the autocratic nature of Hastings, who was caught in the middle of the transition and was not really prepared for such a sweeping change in the administration of the Company's commercial interests. All of the changes were mandated by recent events of considerable importance to the Crown. The loss of the American colonies with the surrender of Lord Cornwallis at Yorktown in 1781 shifted the focus of British imperial power eastward and made clarification of the relationship between England and the East India Company a serious political concern.[9] The India Bill also served a more immediate political purpose by giving George III's supporters an opportunity to undermine a ministry that the King disliked and wanted overthrown (Sutherland, 366). The power struggle did not completely end with the formation of a new ministry acceptable to the King and passage of the East India Bill in 1784.

The animus against an earlier administration out of favor with the King had a kind of afterlife in the impeachment of Warren Hastings that began in February of 1788. The attack against Hastings was mainly conducted by Edmund Burke in the form of humanitarian outrage against the treatment of Indians during Hastings's tenure as Governor-General. Basically, Burke made Hastings the scapegoat for all the disorder and exploitation that had occurred during his direction of the Company. Prior to the passage of the 1784 bill, officials of the Company were free to plunder villages and overtax the local princes, abuses that Hastings himself had pointed out as damaging to British interests.[10] On some occasions Hastings had behaved with gross disregard for the lives of Indians, as when he had Nand Kumar, a member of the Brahmin caste, hanged for the minor offense of forgery (Robert, 87). He had also wounded Burke's friend Philip Francis in a duel in 1780, so seriously that he had to return to England, where he supplied Burke with information to use against Hastings. Although Hastings had resigned as Governor-General and had returned to England in 1785, he still maintained a position of importance in the Company, and so Burke led the effort to impeach him three years later. Burke's humanitarian rhetoric, however moving, seems to have been uttered mainly for party purposes, since "he showed far more interest in exposing abuses and attacking individuals than in working out a constructive policy of reform" (Sutherland, 367–68). Burke also viewed Indian society through the lens of his own ideology of natural law, understanding the caste system in India, for example, "as a noteworthy example of the natural order of things under God" (Bearce, 16). The prosecution of Hastings, then, was a way of defending the stable institutions of society, whether in England or in India: "In Asia as well as in Europe," Burke averred, "the same law of nations prevails, the same principles are continually resorted to, and the same maxims held and strenuously maintained. . . . India is enlightened in that respect as well as Europe" (quoted by Bearce, 17). The proceedings against Hastings dragged on until 1795, when he was finally acquitted of the charges against him. Clearly, Hastings was no angel, but his vindication in 1795 could be seen as a failure of the Crown. At the very least, Hastings had not always been a willing instrument of empire, and he did take a strong interest in Indian culture by encouraging the formation of the Asiatic Society and by taking concrete steps to ensure that Islamic and Hindu laws were administered in India.[11]

Whatever else he was, Hastings was no puppet of Church and State, and it is easy to see how English radicals who took an interest in

Indian affairs would have preferred him to the governors-general who succeeded him. Moreover, the shamelessly partisan involvement of Edmund Burke assured that Hastings would find support among English Jacobins and also among more moderate factions. In the radical press Burke was criticized both for his opposition to the French Revolution and for his dogged attempt to impeach Hastings. A pamphlet in support of the French published by an anonymous "Member of the Revolution Society" in 1790, for example, focuses more on Burke's efforts to impeach Hastings than on his indictment of the Revolution. *A Letter to the Right Hon. Edmund Burke, in Reply to his "Reflections on the Revolution in France"* is noteworthy for its linkage of religious dissent, revolutionary sentiment, and support of Warren Hastings. The *Analytical Review* comments that the author of the pamphlet, "[t]hough himself a Churchman, . . . pays a handsome compliment to the Dissenters; and attributes Mr. B.'s [i.e., Burke's] dislike to that body to personal motives. He questions the truth of Mr. Burke's statement respecting the affairs of France, which he suspects to be as much overcharged as his representations on Indian affairs" (*AR* 8 [Sept.–Dec. 1790]: 415). The reviewer follows this comment with a quote from the pamphlet itself:

> Since the publication [of Burke's *Reflections*], it was the subject of conversation between two gentlemen of considerable talents—the one had been in France during the summer; the other for many years in India.— The first declared, that he should pay no credit to what you had said of Mr. Hastings, because he could convict you of many errors in your French accounts—the other expressed equal distrust of the facts mentioned in your book, because he knew your ignorance of a country he himself had long resided in. (*AR* 8: 415)

The argument is hardly elegant, but the point is clear: Burke's ignorance of France is matched by his ignorance of India. Also clear is the writer's sense of a radical relationship between revolution on the Continent and support of Hastings, which the *Analytical Review* considers to be weighted too heavily in favor of the former Governor-General: "The author is led to a vindication of Mr. Hastings, which indeed would have been a better title for the pamphlet than that which it now bears" (*AR* 8: 415). That this vindication also included "a handsome compliment to the Dissenters" shows that interest in India was interconnected with political liberty and religious freedom in the radical press during the 1790s.

Time and again, Warren Hastings is held up as a model governor whose political behavior provides the basis for judging that of his adversaries, Burke and Pitt. A notice in the *Analytical Review* of a pamphlet published in 1794 typifies the radical attitude that understood Hastings's handling of Indian affairs to be vastly superior to Pitt's ministry of British concerns. *The Merits of Mr. Pitt and Mr. Hastings, as Ministers in War and Peace, impartially stated* has nothing but praise for Hastings's tenure as Governor-General:

> England sent out a powerful fleet, and as many British troops as she could spare, from the pressing demands made upon her from other quarters. But she left Mr. Hastings *to find resources as he could, for supporting seventy thousand men in the field.* He did find resources, and he concluded a separate peace with Madagee Sindia, which was signed and ratified in october, 1781. The Maratta peace was concluded in may, 1782, and ratified the january following. The peace in Europe was proclaimed in India in june, 1783, and the peace with Tippoo Sultaun was signed in march, 1784. Mr. Hastings quitted India in february, 1785, leaving that great continent universally in peace; the provinces under his own immediate government, in the highest state of prosperity, and the general resources increased from *three millions* sterling a year to *five*. (*AR* 18 [Jan.–April 1794]: 212)

Against Hastings's record of peace and prosperity the author contrasts the record of Pitt "as a war minister" and "affirm[s] that all [his] great designs . . . have miscarried" (*AR* 18: 213). The author also claims of Hastings (rather improbably) that "[n]ot one of the millions, *in whose name he was so solemnly impeached,* has preferred a single complaint against him." The absence of Indian complaint against Hastings is attributed to a high moral sense thoroughly lacking in Mr. Pitt. The kind of morality exhibited by Hastings and "so admirably laid down for India, is by no means calculated for a *more northern latitude,*" as Pitt's wartime policies show. The reviewer editorializes over this last point in the kind of bold language that was soon to become impossible in the British press: "Mr. P. bullies Denmark, Florence, and Genoa, neutral and independent nations, without murmur, and almost without remark" (*AR* 18: 213). The author of the pamphlet offers one backhanded compliment to Pitt when he says that the minister's Indian policies were at their best when Burke opposed them: "[I]t is a very curious circumstance, that as long as Mr. Pitt was exposed to the almost daily invectives of Mr. B., *success attended him.* India flourished under that system which Mr. B. calls 'most corrupt and oppressive.' . . . But from the time that Mr. B. became the *panegyrist* of Mr. Pitt, the minister has been *unfortunate* in every important measure of his administration" (*AR* 18: 214). In other words, so long as Hastings was allowed to govern Bengal without interference from Parliament, Pitt's policy in India was successful. Burke's character assassination of Hastings and his praise of Pitt are interconnected—to the detriment of British interests in India, not to mention the Indians themselves. By way of conclusion the writer for the *Analytical Review* opines that "Mr. Burke's conduct is deemed justly obnoxious" (*AR* 18: 214). Examples of this sort could be multiplied to show how Hastings was idealized as a model governor in the radical press.[12] The major reason for this political idealization is, no doubt, the political reality of the governors-general who succeeded Hastings.

From 1786 to 1793, and again briefly in 1805, the Governor-General of the East India Company in Bengal was that same Lord Cornwallis who had so recently failed to defend the British empire in America. To say that England found the empire in India that it had lost in America may be oversimple, but strictly speaking there was no British empire in India until Cornwallis established it, because it was not until 1786 that the full intent of Pitt's India Bill began to be felt. Prior to Cornwallis, the governors-general in India had been agents of a state-chartered commercial monopoly, but they had not been officers of the state itself. Newly empowered as a state official, Cornwallis went to India for the purpose of making administrative reforms, but he did not attempt the preservation of traditional Indian institutions (as Hastings, despite Burke's arguments to the contrary, had tried to do). Rather, Cornwallis encouraged the formation of British institutions based on British principles. For example, he established a system of land tenures and revenues in the hope of creating an aristocratic, landowning class of Indian gentry: "Cornwallis believed that a British-type landlordism would ensure general prosperity. If the upper classes were prosperous, then, he felt, the whole population of merchants, artisans, and peasants would benefit" (Bearce, 45). Cornwallis also began the dismantlement of the legal system based on the Indian laws that Hastings had instituted and replaced it with a system that followed British practices in law enforcement and adjudication. Although Cornwallis was under strict orders from Pitt's lieutenant Henry Dundas not to become involved in military affairs in India, he could not resist the temptation to return to military command when in 1790 the forces of Tipu Sultan threatened the area of Travancore, territory under the Company's control, in the name of Indian independence.[13]

Tipu Sultan of Mysore had allied himself with France well before resumption of Anglo-French hostilities in 1793. During the war of 1778–83, Charles Bussy, the French representative in India, had enlisted Tipu's support against the British, and even though the Indian leader had signed a treaty with the English in 1784, he continued to cooperate with Bussy's secret intrigues against British power in India (Misra, 6, 8). In 1787 Tipu wrote to the French governor of Pondicherry, urging him to maintain a state of military readiness in case an opportunity for revenge against the British presented itself. The next year he communicated directly with the court of Louis XVI to solidify the alliance between France and Mysore, with the ultimate aim of removing the English from India. With the outbreak of revolution in France, Tipu no longer felt the need to coordinate his actions with those of local French authorities and so initiated hostilities himself (Misra, 17, 20–23). Cornwallis succeeded in putting down the threat in 1792 by securing the region of Mysore, where Tipu had ruled since 1782, and by capturing Tipu's two young sons and holding them hostage. Cornwallis wrote to Dundas that he had been forced into action by "the ungovernable ambition and violence of [Tipu's] character," but assured his superior that the Indian leader would be incapable "for many years to come" of causing "any material disturbance to the British possessions in India" (quoted by Gardner, 134). In this he was mistaken.

After Cornwallis left India in 1793, events in France that same year inspired Tipu to emulate the revolution there. He began calling himself "Citizen Tipu" and hired French mercenaries to help him train his army for another attack against the English (Gardner, 138–39). Tipu's preparations for war were not impeded by the governorship of Sir John Shore, Cornwallis's successor, who faithfully obeyed orders from England to follow a policy of non-interference in Indian affairs. When Shore failed to put down the mutiny of his own military officers, who understood Tipu's activities as a threat to British interests, the Company recalled Shore to London and sent Lord Wellesley to India to replace him.[14] By 1798 Tipu had devoted considerable efforts to enlist the support of French republicans to fight for Mysore, but without great success (Misra, 35, 37). Nonetheless, Wellesley felt that the threat posed by Tipu was serious, largely because of Napoléon's plans to sweep through Persia and into India after his expected conquest of Egypt. Indeed, a letter from Bonaparte written to Tipu in 1799 said as much and showed that British concerns about a Napoleonic "liberation" of India were well-founded (Misra, 41). The threat ended when Tipu was killed by the British East India force, led by Wellesley, in the Fourth Anglo-Mysore war of 1799 (Gardner, 146).

These events show that anyone who supported the revolution in France would be likely to oppose British imperialism in India. Indeed, one of the problems Wellesley faced during his tenure as Governor-General was the support registered for the French in Indian newspapers edited by English Jacobins, which created the need for a campaign of censorship. At least one editor was ordered out of India altogether because of his republican sentiments (Misra, 43). The war against

France and the exploitation of India were related in a real way because
revenues from the East India Company, now controlled by Parliament,
could be used to finance the war. Although the East India Company was
not a profitable enterprise when Parliament took control of its operations in 1784, several reforms made the Company much more solvent
and stable in succeeding years. Cornwallis reduced corruption by ending
the privilege that the Company's agents had long enjoyed of conducting
private trade within India. Pitt's Commutation Act of 1784 resulted in
enormous increases in the Company's trade in tea from China, financed
by the sale of Indian cotton in Canton (Nightingale, 6, 9, 23). By April
1793 Henry Dundas, President of the Company's Board of Control, was
claiming vast revenues from the India trade as an argument for renewal
of the Company's charter (*AR* 17 [Sept.–Dec. 1793]: 210). When war
with France was declared earlier in 1793 Dundas had been made Min-
ister-in-Charge of the War Department, a position that complemented
his role with the East India Company. As G. S. Misra explains, "Dundas
was completely engrossed in the war with France, and committed himself whole-heartedly to the adoption of measures to preserve British
power and trade in the east" (Misra, 35). Misra also observes that the
interests of the East India Company were well served when the articles
of peace were ratified at Amiens in 1801, since Lord Cornwallis was
party to the negotiations and "was fully conversant with all the leading
points respecting British interests in India" (Misra, 50). There is no
question, then, that the development of the Indian empire and the war
against France were deeply related.

   These political circumstances require emphasis here because they
provide the context in which the first translations of Sanskrit texts and
the mythographic analysis of Hindu religion based on them appeared in
London during the 1790s. The chances are quite good that Blake came
into contact with the work of Wilkins and Jones at this time; if so, he
would most likely have responded to it sympathetically through a radical political perspective. We can gain some sense of what this perspective would have been like by examining the pages of the *Analytical
Review*, published by Blake's friend and sometime employer Joseph
Johnson.[15] This is not to say that Blake's attitudes toward India would
have been identical to those expressed in the *Analytical Review*; however, Johnson's sympathy with religious dissent, his support of the
French Revolution, his criticism of Pitt's ministry, and his antagonism to
the Crown itself chime with Blake's antinomianism and republicanism.
Johnson was genteel in comparison with the eccentric Blake, but the two
men did share certain ideological assumptions. The sentiments expressed
in the *Analytical Review*, then, can be read as an approximation of

Blake's radical attitudes, albeit conveyed in a different register. And because Indian affairs received extensive coverage in the *Analytical Review*, Blake's relationship with Johnson means that the political controversies surrounding the East India Company and the cultural discoveries of the Asiatic Society would likely have been known to him. This connection between Blake and Brahma is quite significant because it occurred at the same time that the poet began to form his mythic system. Around 1789 or 1790, Hindu mythology was not exactly in the air of all of republican London, but it was in the neighborhood where Blake made his living. In fact, in Blake's case the chances are that the literature of Hindostan was not only in the air—it was in his hands, fresh from Johnson's press.

II

Joseph Johnson began publication of the *Analytical Review* in 1788. The journal's origins were due largely to Johnson's support of religious dissent and his close association with Joseph Priestley, whose Unitarian tracts and theological studies Johnson published on a regular basis. The title of the journal signals its Unitarian origins: unlike the more enthusiastic sects of dissenters, the Unitarians were rationalists who sought to investigate scripture on "the *analytic* plan of interpretation."[16] Thus the journal made religious enquiry part of its purpose, but it also reviewed books and pamphlets published outside of England, as Paul Henry Maty had done in *A New Review*, which ceased publication in 1786. The same year saw the cessation of Priestley's *Theological Repository*, a journal meant as "a *theatre of religious controversy*" and "free enquiry" (*AR* 2 [Sept.–Dec. 1788]: 304). The *Analytical Review*, then, took up the agendas of both these earlier journals, but it was clearly more than the sum of the two. The dissenting background of the publication and the Continental perspective taken over from *A New Review* were important ideological biases that only intensified as the government of Burke and Pitt became more reactionary and repressive. By the end of 1793, with Pitt committed to war against France and liberty on the wane in England, the tone of the *Analytical Review* was marked less by religious dissent than by political radicalism, and its perspective was not only Continental but also international.

The journal chronicled discoveries and discussions at the Asiatic Society on a regular basis at a time when cultural curiosity about India was interwoven with political anxiety over empire. Support of French republicanism was sometimes explicitly linked to criticism of Indian affairs, as in the review, quoted above, of a reply to Edmund Burke's *Reflections on the Revolution in France* in which Burke's prosecution of Warren Hastings is cited in a roundabout way as evidence of his mistaken political attitudes. The endorsement of Hastings appeared in the *Analytical Review* in the last issue of 1790; in that same issue Johnson printed a review of a French publication titled *De l'Inde, &c.*, translated as *On India; or Thoughts on the Means which France ought to employ with Respect to its Possessions in Asia.* Significantly, the author of this work counsels against empire "and advises"—in the words of the reviewer—"that France be not desirous of territorial acquisitions." The review closes with a quotation in which the French author urges removal of the English, not so that France can assume the imperial role in its place, but to restore India to the Indians:

> How should the princes of India interest themselves in our success, if we drive out the English only to put ourselves in their place? The true conquerors of that wealthy part of the world will be they, who, having taken from their rivals the dominions they have usurped, shall restore them to the princes who ought to possess them, under no conditions but that of stipulating a trade in their favor. (*AR* 8 [Sept.–Dec. 1790]: 358)

Here, the argument is based not on republican principles but on commercial concerns, which was precisely the argument used three years later by the Foxite Whigs against Pitt's petition to renew the East India Company's charter in 1793.

The *Analytical Review* paid close attention to the parliamentary debates over the East India Company's application for a twenty-three-year renewal of its charter. In April 1793 Henry Dundas argued on Pitt's behalf in favor of continuing the Company's "exclusive privilege" of trade with India, even though he acknowledged that "no writer on commercial economy" would agree in principle with limitations on free trade, just as "no writer upon political economy . . . has as yet supposed that an extensive empire can be administered by a commercial association" (*AR* 17 [Sept.–Dec. 1793]: 210). Even though he acknowledged the economic and political irregularities of the East India Company, Dundas urged renewal of the charter on the basis of the immense economic benefits involved. He noted, for example, that the ships of the East India Company employed some 7,000 men, and that "raw materials imported from India, for the use of the home manufactures" were a source of even more employment. In addition, "various articles of British produce and manufacture annually exported to India and China, in the company's ships, amounted to upwards of a million and a half sterling." The private fortunes accumulated in India, Dundas went on, and "remitted home through the medium of private trade . . . formed an addition to the capital of the nation" estimated at "a million per annum," at least (*AR* 17: 210). He concluded the speech by making a direct link between the commercial interests of the East India Company and the imperial interests of Great Britain: "A British legislature have to reflect, that our commercial revenues are immense, that whatever can preserve them, is preserving and adding to the greatness of empire" (*AR* 17: 212).

The *Analytical Review*'s account of Dundas's speech seems fairly straightforward, with little criticism of the government's position on the value of empire. What follows, however, is a report of the reply to Dundas made by Philip Francis, also on April 23, in which Francis protests against "the proposed continuance of the government in the hands of a company of merchants" (*AR* 17: 213), arguing that commercial and governmental interests had best be kept separate. Francis denied one of the principal claims made by the supporters of the East India Company, that the condition of the indigenous population had improved under the Company's administration, asserting instead that "provinces . . . still under the control of the native princes" are better governed: "[D]o you think you can stand a comparison with any of the Indian governments, which are real and effective?" There can be no doubt that the *Analytical Review* seconds this assessment, as the anonymous reviewer editorializes over the Francis pamphlet: "[I]t affords but a melancholy prospect to every man who has the welfare of his fellow-creatures at heart, as it conveys an idea, that our conquests and acquisitions tend but to add to the sum of human misery" (*AR* 17: 214). The reports on the East India charter controversy are followed immediately by a lengthy review of *Les Préjugés Detruits (Prejudices Destroyed)* by J. M. Lequinio, a member of the National Convention of France and a self-proclaimed "Citizen of the Globe." Lequinio, we are told, "has always distinguished himself by a fervid attachment to the cause of liberty." Readers of the *Analytical Review* would surely have made some kind of connection between the republican cause in France and British imperialism in India, and some of Johnson's more enthusiastic readers could well have applied to India the ringing admonition quoted from Lequinio's republican diatribe: "Men, dare to think! nations, arise! tyrants, disappear!" (*AR* 17: 215).

Johnson's reviewers never adopted the rhetoric of a Lequinio, but always maintained the analytical tone. Nonetheless, the criticism of the empire in India was complete, and often more pointed than that of principled parliamentarians like William Fox. In *The East India Charter considered,* Fox points out the advantages of free private trade over state monopoly: "Mr. Dundas well knows that experience will warrant no intercourse between nations, but the intercourse of fair and legitimate commerce. . . . He knows that private adventurers offered to *treble* the *exports* of the company" and to supply the government with certain commodities "much under the company's price" (*AR* 17 [Sept.–Dec. 1793]: 335). Fox's comments are prefaced by a paragraph that makes the *Analytical Review*'s position on commercial monopoly and political empire remarkably clear:

> The caustic is as necessary in some cases of political, as of animal disease. Few seem to require it more, than the exhausted excrescences of chartered monopoly. And we know few political surgeons better capable of administering it, than the spirited and intelligent writer of this pamphlet. In a bold vein of sarcasm, he expresses his admiration of the facility with which a British council gives laws to distant regions; of the munificence, with which immense asiatic nations are conveyed by royal charter to certain men, women, and children, of various nations, called the *honourable* the East-India company; and of the wisdom so seasonably exerted to secure this extraordinary dominion, at a time when it has been found, by experience, that distant dominions stand on a very slippery foundation. (*AR* 17: 334)

Such passages show how intensely felt the political and moral implications of the East India Company charter were among London radicals in 1793.

The argument that Blake's "London" refers indirectly to the debate over the charter is strengthened when we know how important that debate was to Johnson and his colleagues at the *Analytical Review*. Early drafts of the poem show that Blake canceled the rather ordinary word *dirty* and replaced it with *charter'd* (*E* 796) in the first quatrain:

> I wander thro' each charter'd street,
> Near where the charter'd Thames does flow.
> And mark in every face I meet
> Marks of weakness, marks of woe.

> (*SE* 46.1–4)

Given the political atmosphere surrounding the debate over the East India Company, Blake could easily have thought of the streets of London as "charter'd" in the same sense that the streets of Calcutta were.[17] In *The Marriage of Heaven and Hell*, Blake had already signaled his opposition to empire in vaguely allegorical but still forceful terms: "Empire is no more! and now the lion & wolf shall cease" (*MHH*.27.*Prose*). Already in "London" the republican energy is beginning to wane, and it is not too much to say that Blake understood his own experiences as somehow similar to those of fellow victims of empire in the distant dominions ruled by the Crown.

In "London," Blake comes as close as he ever does to making a direct public protest, albeit in poetic form, against Pitt's government. Likewise, Joseph Johnson through the medium of the *Analytical Review* circa 1793 is quite fearless in his criticism of some of the ministry's policies—in all areas, not just in those concerning India. After 1795, Blake fell silent for many years, and even though he continued until the end of his life to claim that he was a practitioner of "Republican Art" (*E* 783), his politics became so thoroughly interwoven with his obscure mythology that the poet's career as a radical author—such as it was—was effectively over after the Lambeth prophecies. The *Analytical Review,* also, became politically muted after 1795, and it is instructive to contrast the tone of the journal's intense criticism of Indian affairs toward the end of 1793 with the cautious concern of, say, 1796. In the October issue of that year, the *Analytical Review* commented on the East India Company's treatment of "the *Nawab Visier's* dominions" in fairly non-committal terms: "[T]wo . . . questions remain to be answered, anterior to any interference on our part: 1. Have we the right to take the *entire* government of his country from the vizier? and 2. Would the inhabitants be less oppressed, and less plundered, under our own management?" (*AR* 24 [July–Dec. 1796]: 425).

The same attenuated tone sounds through in another review, also from 1796, of a fictitious *Translation of the Letters of a Hindoo Rajah* by Eliza Hamilton. The reviewer politely disagrees with the author's opinion "respecting the happy change which the long-suffering hindoos have experienced under the dominion of Great Britain." The reviewer also hedges on the subject of Hamilton's attitude toward the recently acquitted Hastings, saying that the compliments that are paid to the former Governor-General "will be adjudged by the reader, either as just, or the grateful language of private obligation or friendship, according to his own preconceived opinions on the subject." Despite this kind of caution, the writer still manages to convey some opposition to empire, making the radical attitude evident if not urgent:

> Many, it may be, will be rather inclined to believe, that, however mitigated in some respects by the tolerant principles of the british legislature, on the subjects of law and religion; these injured people have merely *changed masters,* and one species of oppression for another. The interference of foreign states in the internal government of nations is generally equivocal in its motives, and always mischievous in its tendency. (*AR* 24 [July–Dec. 1796]: 429)

However attenuated the radical voice of the *Analytical Review* had become later in the decade, two key facts remain. First, all or most of the information about India that appeared in the pages of Johnson's journal appeared alongside—and often within—a thoroughly republican perspective. Second, the *Analytical Review* made that information accessible and available to Blake.

These facts overturn two mistaken assumptions that have dominated discussions of Blake's relationship to Hindu mythology: one, that the India of Blake's time was already then what it is to many people today—a fount of mysticism; two, that Blake somehow had free access to some of the rarest and most obscure books ever published. The truth is that the *Analytical Review* was one of the few—perhaps the only— places where Blake could have come across material about Hindu mythology at precisely that point in his poetic career when he began to formulate his own mythology. Moreover, the India that Blake encountered was fraught with political controversy. The political conditions under which Hindu mythology arrived in England immediately valorized that mythology as "republican," as least for a radical reader like Blake. In the early 1790s, the mythology of Brahma was politicized even before it was understood, and something similar might be said of Blake: that his poetry is political because it takes mythological form.

III

The mythology of India was most likely conveyed to Blake through the medium of the *Analytical Review*. Indeed, Johnson's journal was one of the most important sources of information about the new scholarship on Indian culture produced by the Asiatic Society of Bengal. That Society was formed early in 1784 on the model of the learned societies of Europe, with the crucial difference that its field of inquiry would be confined to "the geographical limits of Asia."[18] Warren Hastings encouraged the formation of the Society but declined the invitation to serve as its first president, a title conferred on Sir William Jones instead. Jones is best known today as one of the founders of the modern science of comparative linguistics because of his observation, made in 1786, that Sanskrit, Greek, and Latin share so many linguistic features that all three must "have sprung from some common source, which, perhaps, no longer exists."[19] Already a master of classical languages and a noted translator of Persian when he arrived in India in 1783 to serve as a jurist, Jones soon realized the necessity of knowing Sanskrit in order to adjudicate cases based on Hindu laws (in accordance with Governor-General

Hastings's wishes). At first, Jones had hoped to rely on Charles Wilkins for scholarly investigations involving Sanskrit and on learned Indian pundits for translations of the Hindu laws. When he realized that the pundits were providing unreliable translations and manipulating the law for personal gain, Jones began to study Sanskrit himself and soon became so expert in the language that he claimed to "jabber" in it "every day with the *pundits.*"[20] Jones's knowledge of Sanskrit and his enlightened attitude toward Hinduism made reasonably reliable information about Indic culture available in English for the first time, and the Asiatic Society he helped to found provided a forum for the dissemination of that information.

The importance of Jones and the other members of the Asiatic Society becomes evident when their activities are compared to earlier attempts at making Indian culture known to the West. The Jesuit missionary Roberto de Nobili (1577–1658) mastered Sanskrit well before Jones and Wilkins, but he used his considerable linguistic abilities and his reputation as the "Brahman Jesuit" to promote an "original" version of the Vedas that echoed Christian beliefs. The French translation of this work, known as *L'Ezour Vedam,* succeeded in duping even so acerbic a skeptic as Voltaire into thinking the spurious text authentic.[21] In the case of honest efforts to understand Hindu literature, such as John Marshall's translation of the *Bhagavat Purana* (completed in 1677), no forum existed to bring the knowledge to wider notice. Marshall was an employee of the East India Company whose interest in Indian studies was not tainted by Christian bias, but his work was known only in manuscript, if at all (Kejariwal, 18). The separate instances of de Nobili and Marshall help to show how special the set of circumstances was that arose for the first time at the end of the eighteenth century with the founding of the Asiatic Society: a knowledge of Sanskrit, an enlightened perspective on religion, a community of sympathetic scholars, and a learned society where this knowledgeable, enlightened community could meet and exchange ideas.

These conditions allowed for the production of new knowledge about the culture of India, but they did not, by any means, assure that the knowledge would reach the shores of England. In his first discourse to the Asiatic Society in 1784 William Jones had proposed that the papers read at the meetings of the Society be printed in the form of an "*Asiatick* miscellany" for the benefit of "the literary world" (Jones, *Asiatick Researches* 1: xv). This plan was not realized until 1788 with the publication of the first volume of the *Asiatick Researches.* By that time Jones's original title for a publication of the proceedings of the Society had been usurped by Francis Gladwin, who published two volumes of the *Asiatic Miscellany* privately in Calcutta in 1785 and 1786. Even though Gladwin was a founding member of the Asiatic Society, Jones distanced himself from the *Asiatic Miscellany*, calling the book a collection of "scraps" and "mere translations" (quoted by Kejariwal, 54). Despite its unofficial status, Gladwin's *Asiatic Miscellany* does mark the initial publication of several influential works by William Jones, including "A Hymn to Narayena," which provides an account of a Hindu creation myth possibly of some importance to Blake (see chapter 3). It seems unlikely, however, that Blake could have gotten his hands on a copy of the *Asiatic Miscellany* at the time of its publication, even if he had been interested in doing so.

The early volumes of the *Asiatick Researches* were also scarce: only seven hundred copies of the first volume were sent to England, many for private circulation among officials of the East India Company (Kejariwal, 54). Such a book—or, at least, the information in it—would never have found its way into the hands of a tradesman like Blake without the fortunate intercession of Joseph Johnson. Blake's employer printed many long excerpts from the volumes of the *Asiatick Researches* shortly after they were published in book form. He also felt that the new knowledge arriving from the East was of sufficient importance to merit reviews of second editions and compilations of previously published material. An example of the latter practice is a notice from a 1794 issue of the *Analytical Review* announcing the publication of a compilation of selections from the first two volumes of the *Asiatick Researches,* titled *Dissertations and miscellaneous Pieces relating to the History and Antiquities, the Arts, Sciences, and Literature of Asia* (1792). The reviewer comments on the need for such a volume: "Although a great many interesting articles . . . are of course omitted in the present compilation, yet, as but few persons, from the scarcity and high price of the originals, can obtain them, it must be acceptable to the public" (*AR* 18 [Jan.–April 1794]: 112). This comment helps to show that even though the original books may have been scarce, the appeal of the Indian material in the *Asiatick Researches* to the British literary sensibility in Blake's time was considerable. If the interest in India is manifested more clearly in Coleridge and Shelley than in Blake, this may be due, in part, to the greater availability of the *Asiatick Researches* later on in less expensive, more accessible editions. For example, pirated versions began to be published in 1798 (Kejariwal, 54), an event that might stand alongside the appearance of *Lyrical Ballads* in a re-written account of British literary history. In any case, the publications of the Asiatic Society were not immediately available in their original form to most English readers, let alone to someone like Blake at the lower strata of the tradesman class.

But the material in those publications was available, albeit in abbreviated form, when Joseph Johnson excerpted it for articles in his *Analytical Review*. There is also the tantalizing possibility that Blake might actually have seen some of the original volumes of the *Asiatick Researches* after they had been reviewed by Johnson's readers.

This possibility is strengthened by the likelihood that one of the readers Johnson employed to write reviews of the *Asiatick Researches* was Blake's friend Henry Fuseli. Reviews of the premier volume containing the transactions of the Asiatic Society were spread over several issues of the *Analytical Review*. The first of these appeared in 1789 with an explanation of how the Asiatic Society was formed "on the plan of the Royal Society at London, under the patronage of the Governor-General and Council of Bengal" (*AR* 5 [Sept.–Dec. 1789]: 202). The reviewer also explains how Sir William Jones came to be president of the society only when Warren Hastings himself declined the honor, and after this Jones's elegant opening discourse is printed in its entirety. Following the discourse is a list of the titles of all twenty-six of the articles contained in the first volume, including "On the Gods of Greece, Italy, and India," one of Jones's most important mythographic essays. For our purposes, however, the most significant part of the notice is its closing paragraph: "Of these curious articles, we mean to give, in our future numbers, a particular account; having been favored with the use of a copy of the work by a friend, immediately on its arrival." The review is signed with the initial "F." (*AR* 5: 206). Almost certainly, "F." stands for Fuseli,[22] and "F." has a copy of the first volume of the *Asiatick Researches* in his possession. It is not at all far-fetched to suppose that Fuseli would have shared the volume with his friend Blake, late in 1789 or early in 1790. The reason for making this supposition is the historical fact of Fuseli's and Blake's long-lasting friendship and their artistic collaboration on several books published by Joseph Johnson over the period 1788–91. During this period Blake executed engravings of designs provided by Fuseli for Lavater's *Aphorisms* and *Essays in Physiognomy* (both published 1789), and for Erasmus Darwin's *The Botanic Garden* (1791).[23]

The arrival of the first volume of the *Asiatick Researches* in London late in 1789 and the *Analytical Review*'s summaries of all twenty-six articles in it throughout 1790 coincide not only with Blake's collaboration with Fuseli but also with one of the most significant phases of his poetic development. *The Marriage of Heaven and Hell* was most likely begun in 1790, as plate 3 suggests: "As a new heaven is begun, and it is now thirty-three years since its advent: the Eternal Hell revives" (*MHH* 3.*Prose*). The passage is usually understood as an autobiographical reference:

Blake was born in 1757, and thirty-three years later, in 1790, he breaks with the New Jerusalem Church, founded by Emmanuel Swedenborg, who claimed that the last judgment "was commenced in the beginning of the year 1757."[24] The context of *The Marriage of Heaven and Hell* is mainly millenarian and antinomian, with those two separate but related species of religious dissent combining with republican politics in the "Song of Liberty" that concludes the work. "The Song of Liberty," along with the "Preludium" to the work, is also the harbinger of the vast mythological system to come: Rintrah and Urthona are named outright, and while Orc and Urizen are not, their attributes are given (respectively, "the new born terror" and "the starry king" [*MHH 25.Prose*]), thereby indicating that Blake's system already exists in some early, embryonic stage in the mythological material that brackets the proverbs and prose polemics of *The Marriage of Heaven and Hell*. Many things combined around 1790 to urge Blake along on his curious poetic career: the waning interest in Swedenborg and the rise of republicanism, certainly; the discovery of Hindu mythology, probably. With the New Jerusalem Church behind him and the French Revolution before him, Blake in 1790 was especially receptive to new ideas, and Fuseli was most likely there to introduce him to some of the latest mythographic discoveries from the East.

The Marriage of Heaven and Hell offers direct evidence of Blake's awareness of some kind of "Oriental" sensibility in the "Memorable Fancy" of Blake's dinner with the prophets Isaiah and Ezekiel:

> Then Ezekiel said. The philosophy of the east taught the first principles of human perception some nations held one principle for the origin & some another, we of Israel taught that the Poetic Genius (as you now call it) was the first principle and all the others merely derivative, which was the cause of our despising the Priests & Philosophers of other countries, and prophecying that all Gods would at last be proved. to originate in ours & to be the tributaries of the Poetic Genius, it was this. that our great poet King David desired so fervently & invokes so patheticly, saying by this he conquers enemies and governs kingdoms; and we so loved our God. that we cursed in his name all the deities of surrounding nations, and asserted that they had rebelled; from these opinions the vulgar came to think that all nations would at last be subject to the jews. (*MHH* 12–13. *Prose*)

The purpose of the passage is evidently to illustrate in specific terms the general process that is described in the preceding plate. Plate 11 details how an enlarged, poetic perception of human reality was gradually reduced by religion into the narrow, ritualized practice of "[c]hoosing forms of worship from poetic tales." This plate also tells us that "[t]he ancient poets animated . . . whatever their enlarged and numerous senses could perceive" (*MHH* 11.*Prose*); since the next plate claims that "[t]he philosophy of the east taught the first principles of human perception," there would seem to be some relation between the principles of the East and the practices of the poets. The philosophy of the East, then, occupies a place of privileged priority over the prophets of Israel, who employed the Poetic Genius to promote their God over others and so misled the vulgar. Again, this is a specific instance of a religious "system" in action, as plate 11 says: "some took advantage . . . & enslav'd the vulgar."

Early in 1790, the fourth review of the first volume of the *Asiatick Researches* appeared in the *Analytical Review* and was devoted exclusively to Sir William Jones's long essay "On the Gods of Greece, Italy, and India." Like plate 11 of *The Marriage of Heaven and Hell*, Jones's essay is concerned mainly with the origins of religion, as the reviewer notes:

> All mythology, our author observes, may be traced to four principal sources. 1st. Historical or natural truth, perverted into fable. 2d. A wild admiration of the heavenly bodies. 3d. The magic of poetry, "whose business is to personify the most abstract notions, and to place a nymph or genius in every grove." 4th. The metaphors and allegories of moralists and metaphysicians. . . . (*AR* 6 [Jan.–April 1790]: 313)

The third source in the list bears comparison with the first sentence from Blake's plate 11: "The ancient Poets animated all sensible objects with Gods or Geniuses, calling them by the names and adorning them with the properties of woods, rivers, mountains, lakes, cities, nations, and whatever their enlarged and numerous senses could perceive" (*MHH* 11.*Prose*). Personifying abstract notions with nymphs or geniuses is not exactly the same as animating sensible objects with gods or geniuses, with the difference inhering in the meaning of poetry. Jones thinks of poetry as a primitive misunderstanding of reality; Blake, by contrast, conceives of poetry as an original, vital insight that gives human meaning—and human form—to the world at large. In fact, Blake's explanation is really a kind of contrary account of the origins of religion that understands Jones's "abstract notions" as the error that results when the original poetic energy is perverted into worship by the priests. What Blake and Jones have in common, however, is more important than their differences over the nature of poetry. Both are concerned, quite simply, to locate the origins of religion outside the Bible. Jones describes a myth that antedates the Bible, and Blake creates one. Fuseli's review of Jones's essay in the first volume of the *Asiatick Researches* is almost certainly a direct source for Blake's ruminations about "the philosophy of the east" in *The Marriage of Heaven and Hell*. But it is also more than that: Jones's essay "On the Gods of Greece, Italy, and India" provides a model for the kind of syncretic system Blake created by showing how thoroughly interrelated the various religions of the world really were. Here was the scholarly substance—the actual mythographic material—to support the assertion Blake had made as early as 1788: "The Religions of all Nations are derived from each Nations different reception of the Poetic Genius which is every where call'd the Spirit of Prophecy" (*E* 1).

The *Analytical Review* continued to provide extensive coverage of mythographic books and essays about the "Religions of all Nations" throughout the 1790s. One of the most interesting of these, because of its possible influence on Blake, is the review of an essay by Francis Wilford, another member of the Asiatic Society and a close associate of William Jones. Wilford's essay on "Egypt and other countries adjacent to the Cali River or Nile of Ethiopia, from the ancient books of the hindus" appeared in the third volume of the *Asiatick Researches* (published in 1792), and was reviewed by the *Analytical Review* in the May–August volume of 1794. The reviewer is skeptical of any claim that the Hindu myths might be more ancient than those of Egypt or the Bible, especially as concerns the deluge:

> It has been observed, that, as Moses was instructed in all the learning of the egyptians, probably the account of the creation and universal deluge might have been taken from their traditions. If the hindus drew their legends from the same source, they have preserved, as far as we are hitherto acquainted with their writings, very little that has any resemblance to the mosaic account of the former of these events: but with regard to the latter, their accounts are manifestly derived from the same origin. (*AR* 19 [May–August 1794]:124)

This comment from mid-1794 anticipates Blake's poetic treatment of the question of origins in *The Song of Los* in 1795. The reviewer singles out for comparative commentary the creation and the deluge, just as Blake does when he emphasizes Adam and Noah at the beginning of his account of the dissemination of religion throughout the world. And, like the reviewer of Wilford's article, Blake implies that the religion of Brahma originated in "Africa," that is, Egypt. In addition, the discussion of Wilford's article in the *Analytical Review* helps to make sense of Blake's use of the phrase "Abstract Philosophy" to describe the particular variety of religion that Rintrah conveys to Brahma, because the critic refers the reader to Bishop Berkeley to explicate the mysteries of Brahminism. "[W]hatever may appear, and may not appear in the mind, know that to be the mind's *maya* (or *delusion*)"—so runs a passage from a Hindu text that the reviewer compares to Berkeley's philosophy: "Dr. Berkeley's system agrees with this, so far as the notion that all objects are a delusion of the mind" (*AR* 19: 123). Blake reasons along similar lines when he refers to religious commandments as "forms of dark delusion" (*SL* 3.17). At the very least, *The Song of Los* can be said to capture in condensed form some of the same concerns about the origin and meaning of Hinduism that Blake's contemporaries explored in more discursive terms.

Where Blake differs from his contemporaries is in the respect he shows for what he calls "poetic tales," that is, the myths themselves, apart from the religious rites in which the myths are couched. He would certainly have agreed with the *Analytical Review*'s comments on the Brahmin cast: "it is no matter of surprize that priestcraft has so large a sway [in India]; when we reflect how small a time it is since all Europe was duped by similar artifices" (*AR* 19: 129); but he would just as certainly have shown far greater respect for the original poetic tales that provided the priests with religious material. The writer for the *Analytical Review* understands Hindu mythology merely as so many outlandish legends, but Blake would have taken a different attitude entirely. The reason for supposing this is that several points of Hindu myth that are singled out for their absurdity bear a close resemblance to the features of Blake's myth. For example, the "general destruction occasioned by the sleep of Brahma, whence his creatures in different worlds were drowned in a vast ocean" compares with the sleep of Albion and the general destruction caused by the chaos of Tharmas's waters. Likewise, when the critic observes that "a god in Hindostan" can "show his power of destruction" with impunity because "destruction is only a change of form" (*AR* 19: 124), we are reminded of the changing forms of Urizen and Luvah in their endlessly destructive "wars of Eternal Death" (*FZ* 1.22.15). This pattern appears again and again: one of Blake's contemporaries offers an enlightened critique of religion that accords with Blake's hatred of priestcraft, but in the process of making the critique the writer describes religion in mythographic terms that correspond to some aspect of Blake's developed system. The conclusion that follows from such connections is that Blake's exposure to Hindu mythology in the early 1790s through the medium of enlightened writers such as Volney, William Jones, and the contributors to Joseph Johnson's *Analytical Review* provided the poet with a stock of mythic images and ideas to add to those he gleaned from more traditional sources.

This is not the same as saying that Indian myth had an Indian meaning for the eccentric English poet. The nature of the influence of Hindu myth on William Blake, however it is measured, is always mediated, and modified in the process. The political and theological contexts through which Hinduism made its entrance into England account for Blake's initial interest in Eastern myth, certainly, but those contexts also condition the meaning of that myth. This point should be borne in mind as we review those mythographic works available to Blake when he formed his own mythic system in the early 1790s. Blake had no opportunity for any kind of direct, unmediated exposure to Hindu myth; he had multiple opportunities for exposure to Hindu myth as it was transmitted to him through the mists of language and thought well removed from the culture that produced the myths in the first place. A second point to keep in mind is basic to the relationship of creation and comparison. Comparative mythography always sets one system against another; Blake's creative mythography does the same thing. The comparatists, however, are quite explicit about the systems they compare, and are careful to explain the meaning of one system in relation to another. Blake, by contrast, asks us to infer the meaning of his eccentric system without the advantage of knowing precisely the alternative systems he has set his own against. The effort of inference is never easy, but, at least, by comparing Blake to the comparatists we can come to understand how much mythology meant in the 1790s. The Hindu system was charged with political and theological meaning for Blake's contemporaries, and much of that meaning ramifies into Blake's system as well.

CHAPTER 2

Mythography

The meaning of Indian myth was often bound up with republican and dissenting sympathies in the last decade of the eighteenth century: this much is clear from the way the myths were represented in Joseph Johnson's radical review. If the myths of Hindostan were set against the Church of England and the government of Burke and Pitt, then surely myth itself might be understood as a means of resisting orthodoxy and advancing republicanism. Mythology did not have this kind of meaning for Paul Henri Mallet when he introduced the world to the *Northern Antiquities* of Scandinavian mythology in 1770, nor did it when Jacob Bryant made his *Analysis of Ancient Mythology* in 1774. But in 1789, when the *Asiatick Researches* arrived in England, political and religious controversy surrounded the myths of India. The previous chapter argues, in brief, that Blake's system received significant impetus from the transformation in the meaning of mythology that occurred when Hinduism entered the consciousness of radical republicans. This general impetus to myth, however, is not enough to sustain the claim that Blake's mythology has its genesis in the British reception of Hinduism. Additional evidence is needed to show Blake's indebtedness to Hindu myth, and the purpose of the present chapter is to provide that evidence.

Much of the evidence for Blake's knowledge of Hindu mythology is circumstantial and suppositional, but a number of compelling facts point to that knowledge. A biographical detail worth noting (because it has never been noted before) is quite remarkable in its implications: most of the people with whom Blake enjoyed his longest personal and professional relationships had serious creative and intellectual interests in Indian affairs. In addition to Johnson and Fuseli, William Hayley, John Flaxman, and Ozias Humphry—three of the poet's closest friends and supporters—were at one time or another actively involved in projects inspired by India. Hayley wrote an elegy upon the death of William Jones in 1795 and Flaxman did a drawing of the great orientalist the same year. Prior to making Blake's acquaintance Humphry had spent several years in India, where he had painted a series of miniatures of local princes.[1] Humphry's credentials as an orientalist are further certified by the appearance of his name on a list published in the 1798 reprint of the first volume of the *Asiatick Researches* under the heading "Members of the Asiatick Society."[2] He is also one of the few people known to have received a special invitation to Blake's 1809 exhibition of *The Bramins* and other works.[3] Any one of these men could have supplied Blake with information about Indian myth, either in conversation or by providing copies of the books about Hindu mythology that began to appear in increasing numbers over the last decade of the eighteenth century, as the original publications of the Asiatic Society were republished, summarized, interpreted, or otherwise disseminated to an ever broadening audience.

Precisely which sources were available to Blake is extremely difficult to determine. For this reason I have limited my discussion of possible sources to those that can be connected to Blake using the double criteria of personal affiliation and textual comparison: with one exception, all of the sources I discuss were known to one or more of Blake's associates and contain phrasing or ideas that allow comparison of the poet's work with Hindu mythography. The sources in their order of presentation in this chapter are as follows: *The Ruins; or, a Survey of the Revolutions of Empires* (1791), by the comte de Volney; "On the Gods of Greece, Italy, and India" (1788), by Sir William Jones; *The History of Hindostan* (1796–98), by Thomas Maurice; "Enquiry into the Religious Tenets and Philosophy of the Brahmins" (3d ed., 1798), by William Julius Mickle; *A Comparison of the Institutions of Moses with those of the Hindoos and other Ancient Nations* (1799), by Joseph Priestley; and, finally, *The Hindu Pantheon* (1810), by Edward Moor. Of these texts, the only one that cannot be connected to Blake either directly or through one of his associates is Thomas Maurice's *The History of Hindostan*. But this book was so widely known that the probability of Blake's familiarity with it may be reasonably assumed; besides, Maurice's books were always reviewed and summarized by Joseph Johnson. Johnson was also the publisher of the English edition of Volney in 1792 and of Moor's *Hindu Pantheon* in 1810. These two books, published almost twenty years apart, are related to the early and late phases of Blake's mythic career: Volney's republican rhetoric is consonant with *The Marriage of Heaven and Hell* and Moor's presentation of the Hindu pantheon inspired some of Blake's designs for *Jerusalem*. But Blake plays havoc with chronology, and the other sources cannot be connected so neatly to specific works. My supposition is that Blake's interest in Jones would have occurred in the mid-1790s at the time of the orientalist's commemoration in Hayley's elegy and Flaxman's drawing. Maurice follows Jones because he thought of himself as Jones's successor, and his copious accounts of Hindu mythology are contemporary with Blake's work on

The Four Zoas. Priestley's comparison of Mosaic and Hindu religion also contains material that bears comparison with passages from *The Four Zoas.* The original edition of William Julius Mickle's disquisition on the Brahmin philosophy is not contemporary with *The Four Zoas,* but the third edition, published in 1798, is, and this is the edition that Blake is most likely to have known. Thus I have made a rough attempt to align the sources with the progression of Blake's career, but, in truth, it is impossible to say precisely when Blake encountered such-and-such a source, whether he encountered it first hand or through some secondary channel (such as a remark by Johnson or a comment by Hayley), and so on. The larger point to keep in mind is that an extraordinary profusion of mythic material was available to Blake in the form of various mythographic representations of Hinduism as he formed and reformed his own mythic system.

I

The Marriage of Heaven and Hell claims that "[t]he philosophy of the east taught the first principles of human perception" (*MHH* 12.*Prose*). The statement is made in the context of "A Memorable Fancy" in which the prophet Ezekiel explains how "the vulgar came to think that all nations would at last be subject to the jews" simply because of the claim "that all Gods would at last be proved to originate in ours" (*MHH* 12–13.*Prose*). While we are not told precisely what "the first principles of human perception" are, it is clear that the Jewish claim to origins is compromised by the prior principles of the East. In Blake's time, the realization that the Hindu religion might be of greater antiquity than the ancient Hebrew faith helped to undermine the authority of the Bible. This attitude toward biblical authority was energetically encouraged by the comte de Volney, whose *Ruins* may have added to Blake's understanding of Hindu myth as early as 1792, when the first English translation of Volney's book was published by Joseph Johnson. If the route to India runs through radicalism, Blake could have gotten there through Volney as readily as through the excerpts of the *Asiatick Researches* that Johnson published in his radical review. And even though India was just another Pandora's box of superstition for the French philosophe, Blake with his poet's eye may have seen things differently.

Constantin-François Chasseboeuf comte de Volney (1757–1820) belonged to the younger generation of philosophes who succeeded Voltaire and Diderot in their critique of revealed religion. Unlike his

great precursors, however, Volney's attitude toward the God of Christianity was not agnostic but atheistic, and his tone tends toward the
polemical rather than the skeptical. In his lifetime he achieved a reputation as an orientalist for an account of his journey to Egypt, Palestine,
and Syria that was published in 1787. He also traveled in America and
took both a scientific and a political interest in the new republic, an
interest reciprocated by Thomas Jefferson and Joel Barlow, whose translation of Volney's *Ruins* was published in 1802. Volney completed this
powerful indictment of religion and endorsement of republicanism in
revolutionary Paris in 1791.

The work caught the attention of radical sympathizers in Great
Britain almost immediately, and an anonymous English translation was
brought out by Johnson in 1792. Johnson's text of *The Ruins; or, a Survey of the Revolutions of Empires* was published in a second edition in
1794 and a third in 1796. This was the standard English version of the
work until it was superceded in 1802 by the Jefferson–Barlow translation,
on which Volney himself assisted.[4] In addition, excerpts from *The Ruins*
were printed in the form of pamphlets and broadsides from late 1792 on;
the full text was also widely available in pocket-sized, undated editions. E.
P. Thompson calls the book "more positive and challenging, and perhaps
as influential, in English radical history as Paine's *Age of Reason.*"
Thompson also says that by the mid-1790s "the cognoscenti of the London Corresponding Society—master craftsmen, shopkeepers, engravers,
hosiers, printers—carried *[The Ruins]* around with them in their pock-
ets."[5] Blake, the son of a hosier and an engraver by trade, was not a member of the Corresponding Society, but he consorted with those who were
and was probably as radical as any of them in the early 1790s. He was
also periodically employed by the publisher of *The Ruins* and may even
have seen some of the sheets of Johnson's 1792 edition in press, since he
was working for Johnson on Stedman's *Narrative of Surinam* the same
year.[6] The context could not be more conducive to the supposition that
Blake was one of those radical tradesmen who had Volney in his pocket.

The Ruins would certainly have appealed to the Blake of 1792–95
because of Volney's republicanism and his insight into the operations of
state religion. According to Volney, religion in its modern form originated when "[t]he art of governing" became "nothing more than that of
subjecting the many to the few" and the condition of political subjection
provided the basis for superstition:

> [B]ecause [the people] had tyrants upon earth, they supposed there to
> be tyrants in heaven; and superstition came in aid to aggravate the dis-
> asters of nations.

Hence originated gloomy and misanthropic systems of religion, which painted their Gods malignant and envious like human despots. To appease them, man offered the sacrifice of all his enjoyments, punished himself with privations, and overturned the laws of nature. Considering his pleasures as crimes, his sufferings as expiations, he endeavored to cherish a passion for pain, and to renounce self-love; he persecuted his senses; detested his life; and by a self-denying and unsocial system of morals, nations were plunged in the sluggishness of death.[7]

There are many passages like this one in *The Ruins* whose basic themes ramify through *The Marriage of Heaven and Hell* and Blake's Lambeth prophecies: gods made in the image of despotic men; religion reinforcing tyranny and empire; the senses limited and pleasure constrained; humanity reconciled to suffering; love and brotherhood lost to morality and law. Indeed, plate 11 of *The Marriage of Heaven and Hell* has been singled out for promoting attitudes "quite close to the argument of Volney":[8]

The ancient Poets animated all sensible objects with Gods or Geniuses, calling them by the names and adorning them with the properties of woods, rivers, mountains, lakes, cities, nations, and whatever their enlarged & numerous senses could perceive.

And particularly they studied the genius of each city & country. placing it under its mental deity.

Till a system was formed, which some took advantage of & enslav'd the vulgar by attempting to realize or abstract the mental deities from their objects: thus began Priesthood.

Choosing forms of worship from poetic tales.

And at length they pronounced that the Gods had orderd such things.

Thus men forgot that All deities reside in the human breast. (*MHH* 11.*Prose*)

The ideas and even the language of this plate resemble parts of Johnson's edition of *The Ruins*. For example, chapter 22 of the book, on the "Origin and genealogy of religious ideas," describes how primitive man "in the infancy of his reason . . . animated with his understanding and his passions the great agents of nature" (*Ruins*, 229). This process produced an idea of God "originally as various and manifold as the forms under which he seemed to act: each being was a Power, a Genius, and the first men found the universe crowded with innumerable Gods" (*Ruins*, 229). As Thompson observes, the ideas here are close to those in the first paragraph of plate 11, and the similitude continues with another passage from Volney from which Blake could have drawn the idea that religious systems are abstracted from animated objects in nature: "Thus the Deity, after having been originally considered as the sensible and various actions of meteors and the elements; . . . then as the complex powers of Nature, in her two principal operations of production and destruction; . . . became at last a chimerical and abstract being" (*Ruins*, 276–77).

The difference between Volney and Blake is the point of origin for the process of abstraction that both writers chart: Volney's chimerical Deity starts out as primitive man's misunderstanding of nature, and nature thus misunderstood does resemble Blake's world of rivers and lakes animated with Gods and Geniuses. In Blake, however, the animist world of the past that has since degenerated into abstraction was self-consciously created—or, at least, named and adorned—by the "ancient Poets." A priest differs from a poet because he corrupts the myths the poet has made and turns them into religious rituals, "[c]hoosing forms of worship from poetic tales." Blake's idea that priests mystified poetic explanations of reality by systematizing them into a set of religious beliefs is similar to the standard explanation of religion offered by Volney and other enlightened mythographers, such as John Toland. Blake's sense of enlightenment, however, applies only to the present age, not to the past. In this respect Blake differs from the atheist Volney and the deist Toland, a difference that requires some explanation. In *The Eighteenth Century Confronts the Gods*, Frank Manuel summarizes Toland's explication of Egyptian idolatry, and the summary can stand here as a model of Enlightenment mythography:

> Wise men in Egypt had innocently named a planet after one of their gracious monarchs. With the passage of years the ignorant people came to believe that their deceased ruler was not buried beneath the earth, but was somehow present in another form in the heavenly body which bore his name. From the idea of immortality to idol-worship of the fancied immortal was an easy transition. For Toland paganism thus had its source in rational error and misunderstanding; the wicked priests only later capitalized on a human weakness.[9]

This line of argument differs from Blake's in one crucial detail. Whereas Toland encourages an enlightened response to *both* the primitive age of innocence *and* the later age of priestly corruption, Blake accepts the earlier age as a genuine period when primitive explanations of nature were not the result of human weakness but of poetic strength.

This general pattern appears again and again; that is, Blake sustains the Enlightenment sense that contemporary religious beliefs are corruptions of primitive understanding, but he diverges from Enlightenment mythography in his acceptance of primitive understanding as a more imaginative, vital, and human explanation of reality than anything reason can offer. Blake agrees with the basic premise that religion was acquired at a certain point in history, but he disagrees with the image of primitive man that most mythographers propounded. Indeed, the mythographic thesis was that primitive man was driven toward religion because he lacked reason and so suffered from "the limitations of his perception."[10] Blake, by contrast, thought that primitive man had the benefit of expanded senses and enhanced perceptual abilities. In the picture of primordial man, what the Enlightenment mythographer construed as a liability Blake saw as an asset.

To return to Volney with this important distinction in mind, *The Marriage of Heaven and Hell* and *The Ruins* do have many details in common. Volney mentions a Japanese "Sintoist [who] denies that the soul can exist independently of the senses" (*Ruins*, 168); Blake says "Man has no Body distinct from his Soul for that calld Body is a portion of Soul discerned by the five Senses" (*MHH* 4.*Prose*). Volney asserts that it is "the deceit of mankind" to "have pretended that God made man in his own image" because men "have really made God in theirs" (*Ruins*, 84); Blake claims that "[a]ll deities reside in the human breast" (*MHH* 11.*Prose*). There are even some explicit mythic resemblances. At the beginning of *The Ruins*, Volney's melancholy narrator is suddenly transported aloft and presented with a view of the whole earth by the Genius who is presently to offer a global account of religion: "Instantly, penetrated as with celestial flame, the ties that fix us to earth seemed to be loosened; and lifted by the wing of the Genius, I felt myself like a light vapour conveyed in the uppermost region. There, from above the atmosphere, looking down towards the earth I had quitted, I beheld a scene entirely new" (*Ruins*, 25). In one of the "Memorable Fancies" of *The Marriage of Heaven and Hell*, Blake plays the role of Volney's Genius when he seizes an orthodox angel and flies into space: "I by force suddenly caught him in my arms, & flew westerly thro' the night, till we were elevated above the earths shadow" (*MHH* 19.*Prose*). These examples could be multiplied at some length, so it seems quite certain that Blake read *The Ruins* and put Volney's mythographic critique of religion to his own purposes.

The basic insight that Volney reinforced some of Blake's own ideas about the history of religion needs to be tempered with the understanding that the poet's acceptance of the philosophe's assessment of the present state of religion does not mean that he accepts his rationalistic premises. In fact, Blake would have found in Volney a wealth of material that could have been of great use to him as a creative mythographer:

he would have found, in other words, not only a criticism of "forms of worship," but also an account of a vast number of "poetic tales," including those of India. Chapter 22 of *The Ruins* does contain a number of passages that can be matched up with some of the more polemical plates of *The Marriage of Heaven and Hell*. What I am suggesting here, however, is that Blake read Volney for poetics as well as polemics, and found in the philosophe's critique of religion some useful materials for his own mythic system. For example, Volney uses the Hindu gods Chib-en and Brama, that is, Siva and Brahma, to illustrate the religious system that he calls "Worship of two principles, or dualism." Like many mythographers before him, Volney gives astrological origins for a number of religious beliefs and practices, as here: "[t]he astronomical priests . . . supposed nature to contain two contrary powers always struggling with and resisting each other" (*Ruins*, 254). With "the Zodiac and the constellations disposed in a circular order," the priests "presented [the] halves in diametrical opposition; the winter hemisphere was adverse, contrary, opposite to, being the Antipodes of, that of summer. By the continued metaphor these words were converted into a moral sense; and the adverse angels and Genii became rebels and enemies. From that period the whole astronomical history of the constellations was turned into a political history; the heavens became a human state where everything happened as it does on the earth" (*Ruins*, 255). The transfer of meanings here, from natural opposites to moral and political contraries, may lie behind Blake's exploration of dualism and contraries in *The Marriage of Heaven and Hell*.

Also of interest is what happens to Volney's contraries when they are converted into gods. A "benign god," like Brahma, "received a worship of joy and love; whence are derived all religious acts of a gay nature, festivals, dances, banquets . . . ; in a word, everything that delights the senses and the soul." A "malign god," such as Chib-en (Siva), "on the contrary, received a worship of fear and pain; whence originated all religious acts of the sombre kind, tears, grief, mourning, self-denial, blood-offerings, and cruel sacrifices" (*Ruins*, 257–58). To be sure, "Brama" and "Chib-en" are only the Indian names by which these opposing gods are known, but that in itself is an important mythic principle soon to be exploited by Blake, who names his god of love and joy Luvah, his (fallen) god of self-denial and sacrifice Urizen. The point here is that Blake may have read Volney's *Ruins* in 1792 or 1793 for its enlightened criticism of religion, but he would have picked up a variety of useful mythographic details along the way. These details probably complemented those that Blake had already come across by way of Fuseli or Johnson around 1790 and so added to the store of information about India he already possessed.

Volney presents any number of mythic formulations that might have furnished Blake with some of the basic elements of his own evolving mythology, such as the principle of contrary gods. The philosophe's succinct exposition of "Braminism, or the Indian System" conveys the idea that two contrary principles necessitate a third: "the Indian system . . . , refining after Zoraster upon the two principles of creation and destruction, introduced an intermediate one, that of conservatism, and upon their trinity in unity, of Brama, Chiven, and Bichenou [i.e., Vishnu], accumulated a multitude of traditional allegories" (*Ruins,* 282–83). In *The Marriage of Heaven and Hell,* the third principle is "progression," but later in Blake's poetic career the Zoa Urthona or the prophet Los occupies an intermediate position between the forces of Luvah and those of Urizen in order to conserve or preserve humanity. Moreover, the gods—or Zoas—in Blake's myth are contrary for a reason: they have become dislocated from their proper regions in Eternity. Luvah belongs in the East but has fallen to the South; Urizen's eternal domain is the South but he has fallen into the zone of Urthona, the northern Zoa (see *FZ* 7.74.14–19, 28.29). In Blake, the spatial dislocation of the Zoas from their proper places is a metaphor for the disruption of their appropriate roles in Eternity; the mythic disruption, in turn, is an allegorical reflection of the overvaluation or undervaluation of certain key human capacities in the society of Blake's time.

From Blake's perspective, reason is overvalued at the expense of imagination—Urizen is adored as though he were Luvah and Urthona is neglected as a result. These types of shifts and dislocations are also evident in the Hindu pantheon as Volney presents it. In *The Ruins,* Volney says that the Hindu gods Vishnu and Siva are supposed to have one function but perform another:

> Bichenou, . . . though preserver of the world, has passed a part of his life in malevolent actions. Sometimes you see him under the hideous forms of a boar and a lion tearing the entrails of mankind; sometimes under that of a horse, soon to appear upon the face of the earth, with a sabre in his hand, to destroy the present inhabitants of the world, to darken the stars, to drive the planets from their spheres, to shake the whole earth, and to oblige the mighty serpent to vomit a flame which shall consume the globes. (*Ruins,* 166)

Volney provides a note to this passage explaining what would have been obvious to Blake—that Vishnu's destructive power can be compared to "the four horses of the apocalypse" (*Ruins,* 344n. 14). The apocalyptic power of the Hindu god here, together with the image of the fiery serpent, makes Vishnu not unlike Orc, perhaps, but what is most important is that the great preserver of Hindu myth is here made to perform the role of his contrary Siva. Likewise, Siva performs a function contrary to his designated one of destruction:

> Chiven, the destroyer of all things, the God of desolation, . . . nevertheless has for his emblem the instrument of production [i.e., the phallus]; he is the most detestable of the three, and he has the greatest number of followers. Proud of his attribute and character, his partizans in their devotions express every sort of contempt for the other Gods . . . ; and imitating the inconsistency that characterises him, they profess modesty and chastity, and at the same time publicly crown with flowers, and bathe with milk and honey, the obscene image of the Lingam. (*Ruins,* 166–67)

Volney has little to say about Brahma, but he does note that the god is "a figure with four heads" who is "the Creator of the universe" (*Ruins,* 165). Blake may have found inspiration here for the four-fold giant Albion who, like Brahma, *is* the creation he creates through the action of the four Zoas.

Elsewhere in *The Ruins* Volney offers a summary of the Hindu creation myth, or at least one version of it, that includes the highly suggestive Blakean detail of an "infinite, eternal . . . Being" who, "desirous at length to manifest himself, separated the faculties of male and female which were in him, and operated an act of generation" (*Ruins,* 200). Blake's patriarchal myth makes the Eternals androgynous, except for the isolated case of Albion, who in his fallen form divides into the four male Zoas and also produces the female emanation named Jerusalem. The Zoas, in turn, likewise produce female consorts through a process of emanation. This division into male and female is one feature of the Fall, which results in the necessity of generation. Near the end of *The Four Zoas,* after Albion is re-created in fallen form, the Eternals observe "[t]he female form now separate." They shudder "at the horrible thing" and say "to one another this is Sin / This is the Generative world" (*FZ* 9.133.6, 8–9). So both Blake's Albion and Volney's Brahma perform an act of generation subsequent to a separation of male and female faculties.

Volney's *Ruins* remains a mine of mythic material as yet not fully explored by Blake scholars. The historical context of the early 1790s and the evident textual and conceptual echoes that connect *The Ruins* to *The Marriage of Heaven and Hell* justify the argument that Volney might be a major source for some of the general features of Blake's poetic system, including those that resemble Hindu myths. Volney's *Ruins,* however, belongs to a mythographic tradition that did not enjoy the benefits of the discoveries of the Asiatic Society in full. Volney does express his gratitude to Warren Hastings for his part in sponsoring "at Calcutta a literary society and a printing press," but, at the same time, he complains of the "exclusive spirit" of the Society, meaning that its productions are not widely available, "the number of copies printed of each book being such as it is impossible to purchase them even in England." He names the *Asiatic Miscellany* as a book that is particularly scarce. He also says that, of "the sacred books of the Hindoos, all that are yet in our hands are the Bhagvat Geeta, the Ezour-Vedam, the Bagavadam" and a few fragments of other texts appended at the end of the French translation of Wilkins's version of the *Bhagavad Gita* (*Ruins*, 350–1n. 31).[11] In other words, as of 1791 anyone desiring knowledge of the sacred texts of India would have had a hard time finding them, even in England, unless he happened to be an official of the East India Company, or, like Blake, had a friend who was reviewing the publications of the Asiatic Society. The situation Volney describes in 1791 was almost totally reversed by the end of the decade. As we shall see, this extraordinary proliferation of mythographic material does not simply coincide with the period of Blake's poetic development after *The Marriage of Heaven and Hell*—it contributes to that development and helps to account for the poet's predisposition to mythic expression in the first place.

II

In the last decade of the eighteenth century a substantial number of original mythographic studies of the Hindu gods appeared in response to the pioneering work of William Jones and other members of the Asiatic Society. In addition, publishers took advantage of the heightened interest in Hindu literature by bringing out new editions of previously published material, sometimes in pirated form. The evidence for Blake's awareness of these developments may never be established with certainty, but his poetry shows that he shares some general ideas—not to mention particular patterns of imagery and specific turns of phrase—with more than one mythographer. This fact alone is enough to argue that the poet participated along with many of his countrymen in the cultural curiosity about the myths of India that occurred in the 1790s. During this period no mythographer had more prestige than William Jones, so the case for the general influence of Jones on Blake can be made first by noting the high regard in which Jones was held by his contemporaries.

Even though Jones was conducting his inquiries into Hindu mythology half a world away, his mythographic investigations were well known in London, mainly through such periodicals as the *Monthly Review,* the *British Critic,* the *Critical Review,* and the *Analytical Review* (see chapter 1). The *Monthly Review,* for example, regularly reviewed and excerpted works by Jones; the journal devoted more than 100 pages to the first three volumes of the *Asiatick Researches* and printed extensive selections from Jones's translation of Kālidāsa's drama *Sacontala.*[12]

An indirect but compelling piece of evidence for Blake's possible knowledge of Jones concerns the poet's friends John Flaxman and William Hayley. When news of Jones's death in Bengal in 1794 reached London, Hayley published an elegy and Flaxman did a large-scale drawing of Jones in the act of gathering information from the pundits for his compilation of Hindu laws.[13] Although Blake later became estranged from both Flaxman and Hayley, the two men were among his few constant friends and supporters until 1805 or so.[14] In any event, Blake was on good terms with Flaxman when he did his picture of Jones, and the conclusion follows that Blake's drawing of Wilkins translating the Hindu scriptures was inspired by Flaxman's earlier drawing of Jones translating the Hindu laws. As for Hayley's *Elegy,* there is nothing inspiring about the poet's turgid versification of Jones's varied career and early death. But Hayley's effort is valuable to this discussion for another reason, for the *Elegy* has a number of notes appended to it that indicate Hayley's first-hand knowledge of Jones's Indian studies. The notes mention the first and third volumes of the *Asiatick Researches* and allude to Jones's essays "On the Gods of Greece, Italy, and India" and "On the Mystical Poetry of the Persians and Hindus." Hayley also praises Jones's translation of *Sacontala,* whose merits, he says, "I presume most English readers are familiar with . . . as it has lately been reprinted in a pocket volume."[15] The death of the great orientalist, then, was the occasion for the re-publication of some of his works in a format more readily available to the general reader. More important, Hayley's comments increase the likelihood that Blake would have known of Jones's work, if not by way of Hayley himself then through Flaxman, whom Hayley also employed.

Flaxman's drawing and Hayley's *Elegy,* both done in 1795, furnish further possible explanation for Blake's reference to "Brama" in the same year. If Blake was prompted by Flaxman or Hayley to look into Jones's mythography for himself, he would have found a wealth of mythic material in the celebrated essay "On the Gods of Greece, Italy, and India." Originally delivered as an address to the Asiatic Society in 1785, the essay was published in the first volume of the *Asiatick*

Researches in 1788 and widely excerpted in periodicals soon thereafter; it also appeared in pirated form in 1798 and in the thirteen-volume edition of Jones's work published in London in 1807. The essay opens by urging the view that all ancient religions—or "systems"—are similar: the "resemblance between the popular worship of the old *Greeks* and *Italians* and that of the *Hindus*" bears comparison with the "strange religions" of "*Egypt, China, Persia, Phrygia, Phœnice,* [and] *Syria,*" not to mention "the *Gothick* system, which prevailed in the northern regions of Europe."[16] We know that Blake would have been receptive to Jones's approach, since he believed that "[t]he antiquities of every Nation under Heaven . . . are the same thing" (*E* 543). Likewise, Blake would have agreed with Jones's claim that a major source "of all mythology" (Jones 2: 320) is poetry: "Numberless divinities have been created solely by the magick of poetry; whose essential business it is, to personify the most abstract notions, and to place a nymph or a genius in every grove and almost in every flower" (Jones 2: 321–22). As we have seen, the reviewer singled out this passage for special commentary in the September 1789 issue of the *Analytical Review*. The sense and even the diction of the passage are close to Blake's explanation of the way "[t]he ancient Poets animated all sensible objects with Gods or Geniuses" (*MHH* 11.*Prose*).

In addition, Jones's stunning claim that Moses might have "drawn his narrative through *Egyptian* conduits from the primeval fountains of *Indian* literature" (Jones 2: 325) finds a kind of cognate in *The Song of Los*. In that poem Brahma comes before Moses, receiving Abstract Philosophy in advance of the "forms of dark delusion" that comprise the Ten Commandments. It is true that Blake's invented genealogy is part of the negative lineage of the moral law, which is different from Jones's meaning. Elsewhere in his essay, however, Jones does allow that the Mosaic age is "less pure" than those that have gone before, namely "the *Diluvian,* or purest age" and "the *Patriarchal,* or pure, age" (Jones 2: 342). Blake also subscribed to these conventional divisions of biblical time, and as the author of more than one poem subtitled "A Prophecy" he would no doubt have understood Jones's description of the last age as having special relevance to his own times: "the *Prophetical,* or *impure,* age" necessitates "the vehement warnings given by the Prophets to apostate kings and degenerate nations" (Jones 2: 342). The points of resemblance between the enlightened Jones and the prophetic Blake show that both subscribed—albeit in rather different ways—to some of the same mythographic ideas.

Along with connections and similarities among different mythological systems, "On the Gods of Greece, Italy, and India" provides a number of hitherto unknown details about Hindu mythology, some of which resemble elements of Blake's basic myth and encourage the view that Jones's work may indeed have influenced the formation of that myth. For example, the destructiveness and chaos that surge through Blake's epic poems occur as a result of "the Sleeping Humanity" (*J* 5.30) of the giant Albion. The sleep of Albion makes it possible for Luvah to steal the horses of light from Urizen, from which event ensues the deluge, in the formless form of Tharmas, that overwhelms the sleeping giant. Jones's essay includes a translation from a Persian account of the *Bhagavat Purana* that describes a similar set of mythic events: "At the close of the last *Calpa*, there was a general destruction occasioned by the sleep of BRAHMA; whence his creatures in different worlds were drowned in a vast ocean. BRAHMA, being inclined to slumber, desiring repose after a lapse of ages, the strong demon HAYA-GRIVA came near him, and stole the *Vedas*" (Jones 2: 332). The theft of light in Blake's narrative is probably derived from the myth of Prometheus or, more likely, from the story of Phaeton and Helios. What Blake adds to the Greek myth is the strange combination of slumber and deluge, precisely the combination of elements conveyed in the Indic myth recounted by Jones.

Blake's myth also resembles the Hindu in that both require some agent of preservation to act in the absence of the god to guard the creation against outright ruin. In Blake the agent of preservation is Urthona (or his temporal avatar Los), the Zoa who protects the divine humanity of the giant Albion while he sleeps. In the *Bhagavat Purana* the agent of preservation who eventually recovers the Vedas stolen from the sleeping Brahma is named Heri, but Jones goes on to explain the preservative agency of Hindu mythology under the more familiar name Vishnu, who, along with the creator Brahma and the destroyer Siva, make up the so-called Hindu trinity. What Jones calls "[t]he three *powers, Creative, Preservative,* and *Destructive*" (2: 393) prefigures the Blakean dynamic that pits the sexual energy of Luvah against the destructive morality of Urizen, while strong Urthona preserves the world against the terrible contest of contrary powers. Add Tharmas, who takes the form of the flood after the fall or sleep of Albion, and the basic resemblance to the Hindu myth is complete. Jones's account of the Hindu myth differs from Blake's creative mythography, however, in that Jones is careful to point out the superiority of the Christian tradition rationally understood. Blake, by contrast, employs his own myth to criticize the organized, institutional religion of his day and to suggest a more imaginative and libertarian alternative. Indeed, the strict form of state religion that Blake objected to so strongly was precisely the spur that propelled the poet's interest toward Classical, Scandinavian, and Eastern mythology, and to understand that the antiquities of other cultures were as sacred as the antiquities of Christian tradition.

A generous understanding of the antiquities of Asia is not exactly evident in the work of William Jones's self-appointed successor, the churchman Thomas Maurice, whose *Indian Antiquities* and *History of Hindostan* commanded as much attention as the *Asiatick Researches* in 1790s London.[17] The *Analytical Review*, for example, summarized Maurice's *The History of Hindostan* at great length, concluding that "[h]e certainly hath discovered much both of industry and ingenuity in the conduct of the work; and to whatever degree of reputation his *Indian Antiquities* might entitle him, this new display of his talents is more highly deserving of praise" (*AR* 23 [April 1796]: 367). Of the *Indian Antiquities* itself, the *Analytical Review* had earlier commented that Maurice's tomes "well deserve a place in every public library, and in the library of every gentleman, who wishes to form an acquaintance with the affairs of India" (*AR* 22 [Sept. 1795]: 261). These remarks make clear the authoritative status of Thomas Maurice during the crucial decade of Blake's career, when he began to compress contemporary and eternal events into a single system of mythographic expression. No evidence for a historical connection between Blake and Maurice exists (aside from the tenuous link that both men were known to Joseph Johnson), so perhaps all that can be safely said about the two writers is that both were exploring mythic material outside the received tradition of biblical and classical literature around the same time. Still, Maurice is so completely on the other side of the political and religious issues so dear to Blake that it is tempting to think that the churchman's condescending treatment of the Indian system would have been a source of diabolical inspiration for the poet. Indeed, Maurice emerges as a kind of anti-Blake, and, as such, his work provides historical insight into the political and theological meaning of mythology in the last decade of the eighteenth century.

Maurice's voluminous examination of Hinduism is intended mainly as a vindication of Christianity against the dangerous mythographic discoveries of the atheistic French. He is particularly concerned about "Mr. Volney's impious attempt to mythologize the whole of the Christian system, by insisting that the history and miracles of Christ were borrowed from those of the Indian Chreeshna."[18] A point that Maurice never tires of making is that Hinduism so understood may have the result of "plunging Christian Europe into the horrors of atheistical France." Mythology, in other words, is a danger to what Maurice calls "the national code of faith" and, therefore, to the state itself: "Those who duly consider how intimately the established governments and the legal codes of Europe, and especially the jurisdiction of these kingdoms, are connected with the Christian code, will not be at a loss to see the drift and purport of arguments of this kind" (*HH* 2: v, vi–vii). This in 1798, in the second volume of *The History of Hindostan,* dedicated to William Pitt. What is clear in this instance is how threatening the myths of India are felt to be—so threatening, in fact, that they might destroy the British nation if they are not taken in hand and explained away. Here it is not difficult to imagine a contrary attitude on the part of Blake, who begins to mythologize with a vengeance around the same time that Maurice agonizes over the Hindu system. As a popularizer of Indian myth, Maurice consolidates and organizes a vast amount of material, but he says little that was not already known. For this very reason Maurice's *The History of Hindostan* is a useful compendium of Hindu mythology as it was represented in England during the time when Blake began to thicken his system with obscure and unusual mythographic details. Add to this Maurice's belief that the Hindu system helped to undermine the codes of state religion in France, and those details take on a powerful political resonance they might not otherwise have.

One of the most pervasive of these details is the creation myth involving "the Mundane Egg" (*M* 19.15), and it is instructive to compare Blake's treatment of this myth with that of Maurice and other mythographers. The myth of the mundane egg undergoes a number of permutations in Blake's poetry from its first expression in "Night the Second" of *The Four Zoas,* becoming closer to the Hindu version by the time of *Jerusalem.* The basic idea that the world was created either from an egg or in the form of one is quite common in the mythographic studies of the late eighteenth century that Blake was likely to have known, including the one he probably helped to illustrate, Jacob Bryant's *A New System.* In that earlier mythographic treatise, Bryant was intent on proving his thesis that all pagan mythology resulted from the corruption of the true religion of the Patriarchs that was spread across the earth by the sons of Noah after the flood. For this reason Bryant's account of the myth of the mundane egg is quite dismissive: "For an egg, containing in it the elements of life, was thought no improper emblem of the Ark, in which were preserved the rudiments of the future world" (Bryant 2: 321). Given this simplistic treatment of the myth, Blake was probably less impressed by Bryant's accounts of the mundane egg than by the plates illustrating it. One image in particular has been singled out as particularly Blakean, a serpent entwined about an egg underneath the heading "Ophis et Ovum Mundum" (*ophis* is Greek for "serpent," and the use of this word in conjunction with the Latin phrase for "mundane egg" has led some commentators to read the image in relation to the Gnostic sect of the Ophites, who regarded the serpent's impartation of knowledge to Adam and Eve as a positive benefit to mankind).[19]

Maurice paid attention to this same image in the first volume of *The History of Hindostan* (see fig. 1), but replaced Bryant's title with a much more descriptive one of his own: "The Agathodaimon, or good Genius symbolized by a serpent, circling in its genial embrace the MUN-DANE EGG." Maurice quotes copiously from the volumes of the *Asiatick Researches* for his account of the mundane egg, as in this translation of the opening of the *Laws of Menu* done by Sir William Jones:

> [T]he self-existent invisible God . . . [d]esiring to raise up creatures by an emanation of his own essence . . . first created the waters, and impressed them with the power of motion: by that power was pro-duced a golden egg, blazing like a thousand stars, in which was born Brahma, the great parent of all rational beings, THAT WHICH IS, the invisible cause, self-existing, but unperceived! That divinity having dwelt in the egg through revolving years, HIMSELF meditating upon HIMSELF, divided it into two equal parts; and from those halves he formed the heavens and the earth. (*HH* 1: 55)

Maurice goes into considerable detail "to prove that the notion of the mundane egg, floating upon the expanse of waters, was not peculiar to the Hindoos," citing, for example, "[t]hat famous representation . . . , encompassed by a serpent, and suspended aloft in the temples of Her-cules at Tyre," which is "well known to antiquaries" (*HH* 1: 69). The reference here is to the same image of the serpent-entwined egg in Bryant's *New System* that Maurice reproduces as well (fig. 1). In addi-tion, Maurice observes that the mundane egg competes with other cre-ation stories in Hindu myth, and attributes these "different and some-what discordant relations of the cosmogony" to the Indian belief "that there have been numerous and successive creations, dissolutions, and renovations of the mundane system" (*HH* 1: 65).

Maurice avers that the conception of creation as a continuing process is "by no means peculiar to the race of Hindostan" (*HH* 1: 65). The concept is, however, quite different from the notion of the creation in Genesis but not so different from the one in Blake's myth, which does involve successive creations, dissolutions, and renovations: first by Vala (or by Albion's emanation of Vala via Luvah), then by Urizen, and finally by Los. The passage from the *Laws of Menu* that Maurice quotes (first published in the *Asiatick Researches* of 1788; see Jones 2: 353), in which Brahma is called "the great parent of all rational beings," describes a process of creation that is quite similar to the one Blake

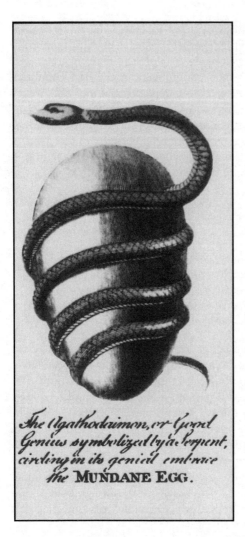

Figure 1. Engraving of the Mundane Egg from Thomas Maurice's *The History of Hindostan*

describes in *The Book of Urizen* (1794). Brahma meditates upon himself and creates the world by dividing it into equal parts, while Urizen, a "self-contemplating shadow," creates in the same fashion: "Times on times he divided" (*U* 3.21, 8). All that is missing is the explicit image of the egg itself, which is not named outright but is implied by the "Self-closd . . . abominable void" in which Urizen sits "Brooding secret" (*U* 3.2–7). As did Milton in *Paradise Lost*, Blake is rewriting the creation story in Genesis, but where Milton's God "Dove-like satst brooding on the vast Abyss" (I.21), metaphorically hatching the egg of the world, Blake's Urizen sits in it, like Brahma in the British translation of the Hindu myth. Blake's synthesis of Milton and Menu in *The Book of Urizen* is a good example of how comparative mythography can yield creative results.

Blake's treatment of the myth of the mundane egg undergoes a kind of evolution from its first shadowy appearance in *The Book of Urizen*, to a more elaborate version in *The Four Zoas*, and then to its final form in *Jerusalem*. In *The Four Zoas* the architect of the Mundane Shell is Urizen, who orders the construction of a mechanistic, limited world using the instruments of measurement: "The golden compasses, the quadrant & the rule & balance" (*FZ* 2.24.12). The purpose of the creation here is protective—"Build we a Bower for heavens darling in the grizly deep / Build we the Mundane Shell about the Rock of Albion" (*FZ* 2.24.7–8)— but its effect is dehumanizing: Urizen's mechanistic universe ends up "[p]etrifying all the Human Imagination into rock & sand" (*FZ* 2.25.6). The "Mundane Shell builded by Urizen's strong power" (*FZ* 2.32.15) is an image of the deistic natural philosophy Blake abhorred, a world governed by geometry and number, with "the stars of heaven":

> Travelling in silent majesty along their orderd ways
> In right lined paths outmeasurd by proportions of number
> > weight
> And measure. mathematic motion wondrous. along the
> > deep
> In fiery pyramid. or Cube. or unornamented pillar
> Of fire far shining. travelling along even to its destind end
>
> (*FZ* 2.33.22–26)

Here, it is easy to think of Urizen, like Brahma in the *Laws of Menu*, as "the great parent of all rational beings."

In *Milton*, the architect of the mundane egg is not Urizen but Los, and the world within that egg is not rationalistic or mechanistic but organic: "Los continual builds the Mundane Shell" around "the Ulro: a vast Polypus / Of living fibres down into the Sea of Time & Space growing" (*M* 34.31, 24–25). Here Los acts to preserve Eternity by separating the Ulro from it. By the time of *Milton*, then, Urizen's mechanistic universe is only one aspect or, perhaps, region of the mundane egg, as the illustration on plate 33 shows (fig. 2). Now the egg of the world is permeated by the energies of the other three Zoas in addition to Urizen's. The image on plate 33 is glossed earlier in the poem, on plate 19:

Four Universes round the Mundane Egg remain Chaotic
One to the North, named Urthona: One to the South, named
    Urizen:
One to the East, named Luvah: One to the West, named
    Tharmas
They are the Four Zoa's that stood around the Throne
    Divine!
But when Luvah assum'd the World of Urizen to the South:
And Albion was slain upon his mountains, & in his tent;
All fell towards the Center in dire ruin, sinking down.
And in the South remains a burning fire; in the East a void.
In the West, a world of raging waters; in the North a solid,
Unfathomable! without end. But in the midst of these,
Is built eternally the Universe of Los and Enitharmon. . . .

                             (M 19.15–25)

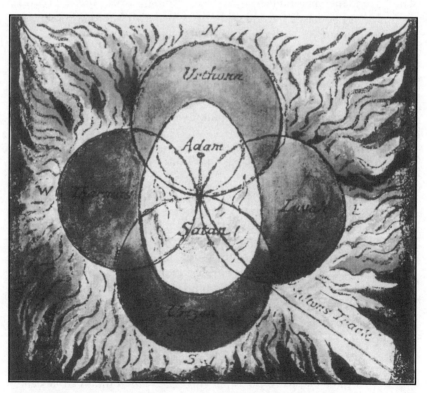

Figure 2. Engraving of the Mundane Egg from *Milton*, plate 33

Blake also adds two "poles" to the mundane egg named Adam and Satan, which he also terms, respectively, the limit of contraction and the limit of opacity. In *The Four Zoas,* these limits are imposed by "[t]he Saviour mild & gentle" as an act of divine mercy to proscribe the extent of the Fall: "Limit/Was put to Eternal Death" (*FZ* 4.56.17, 23–24). The mundane egg in *Milton,* then, is part of a fully elaborated metaphysical cosmogony that at first glance bears little resemblance to the mundane egg of Hindu mythology as it was represented in the late eighteenth century. The two eggs do go by the same name, however, and they do have in common the division of the primal egg into two halves (cf. Blake's "poles"). More importantly, both the Blakean and the Hindu eggs involve a myth that construes creation as a type of on-going preservation that is, at the same time, a transformation of divine forces into natural forms.

The creation myth of the mundane egg in *Jerusalem* maintains the uniquely Blakean elements of the myth as it appears in *Milton* but adds several new elements that may reflect additional Hindu influence. Some of Blake's most sublime language is used to describe the creation event in his final epic: "The Vegetative Universe, opens like a flower from the Earths center: / In which is Eternity. It expands in Stars to the Mundane Shell / And there it meets Eternity again, both within and without" (*J* 13.34–36). This passage is remarkable for a couple of reasons. First, the relationship between the mundane egg and the opening flower compares to the event that Maurice calls the "lotus creation" (*HH* 1: 65), which he interprets in biblical terms: "for what is Brahma floating on the chaos, and recumbent upon the sacred lotus, or water lily, but *the spirit of God moving upon the face of the waters?*" (*HH* 1: 54). Second, Blake's reference to Eternity as somehow both "within and without" the created universe suggests those Hindu creation myths describing Brahma as a divine force that simultaneously permeates the creation and remains outside of it. In *The History of Hindostan* Maurice comments on "the absurdity of a CREATED GOD, in Brahma, whom at the same time [the Hindus] still invest with the name and attributes of a CREATOR" (*HH* 1: 53). For Blake, however, the paradox of a created god with the power to create the universe he is a part of was clearly not absurd, as *The Book of Urizen* shows, when Urizen, after his birth from the side of Los, creates his children Thiriel, Utha, Grodna, and Fuzon (identified, respectively, with the four elements: air, water, earth, and fire; see *U* 6.4, 23.11–18).

Another feature of the mundane egg in *Jerusalem* brings us closer still to Hindu mythology, namely, the introduction of the "Veil of Vala" (*J* 42.81) that suggests, and may even have been derived from, the veil

of Maya so often described in accounts of Indian literature. Thomas
Maurice, however, may not be the most likely candidate as Blake's
source for this idea. In the *History of Hindostan,* Maurice concentrates
primarily on those aspects of Hindu mythology that can be dismissed as
mere extrapolations of astronomical observations, which means he is
simply not interested in philosophical questions about the nature of perception (references in Maurice to "Maya; or delusion" [*HH* 1: 556] are
allowed to pass without commentary). But the concept of Maya had
been thoroughly explained by Sir William Jones as early as 1785 in the
headnote to "A Hymn to Narayena"—where it is called "the *illusive
operation* of the Deity"[20]—and then again in 1788 in the first volume of
the *Asiatick Researches:*

> [T]he *Indian* Maʾyaʾ, or as the word is explained by some *Hindu* schol-
> ars, "the first inclination of the Godhead to diversify himself (such is
> their phrase) by creating worlds," is feigned to be the mother of uni-
> versal nature, and of all the inferior Gods; . . . but the word Maʾyaʾ, or
> *delusion,* has a more subtile and recondite sense in the *Vedanta* philos-
> ophy, where it signifies the system of *perceptions,* which the Deity was
> believed by . . . many truly pious men, to raise by his omnipresent spirit
> in the minds of his creatures, but which had not, in their opinion, any
> existence independent of mind. (Jones 2: 322–23)

Thus the concept of Maya was widely known by the time Blake wrote
Jerusalem. There, plate 42 tells us that "Los built the Mundane Shell,
/ In the Four Regions of Humanity East & West & North & South"
until the earth is covered with "the Net and Veil of Vala" (*J* 42.78–79,
81). Plate 59 adds that "the Veil of Vala" furnished Los with the material he used to fabricate "in process of time . . . the beautiful Mundane
Shell" (59.2, 7). The veil is a common poetic trope for deception or
delusion, and such is the case in *Jerusalem,* especially in plate 23,
which exploits the image of the Veil of Vala and treats the subject of
delusion at some length.

   Jerusalem plate 23 presents a confrontational scene in which
Albion berates his emanation Jerusalem, the allegorical figure of Liberty,
for wearing "the Veil of Moral Virtue" and producing the illusion that
human freedom can be regulated by moral law: "Lo here is Valas Veil
whole, for a Law, a Terror & a Curse!" (23.22, 32). The Veil of Vala
that forms the "substance" of the mundane egg is quite close in its general meaning to the veil of Maya in Hindu mythology. True, the meaning of Maya is not involved with the moral law as it is in Blake, which
may demonstrate, again, that the poet adapted the Eastern myth to suit
his own antinomian purposes. Still, there are passages in *Jerusalem*

where the Veil of Vala is very like the delusion of matter known as Maya, as in Chapter 4, where the "Daughters of Albion" (who are identified with Vala) weave "a beautiful Veil" that forms "the outside surface of the Earth / An outside shadowy surface superadded to the real Surface" (*J* 83.42, 45–47). The mix of images here—the mundane egg, the universe emerging from an opening flower, the deluding surface of matter figured as a veil—combine to form a pattern very like that of the Hindu myth. Almost certainly, Blake has borrowed the images from some account of Indic literature that was familiar to him.

The strange similitude of Blake's creative mythography and the scholarly mythography of Jones and Maurice seem less strange when contrasted with Joseph Priestley's theological inquiries into the Brahmin faith. Priestley covered some of the same mythographic ground that Jones and Maurice did, but he did so as a skeptical materialist, not a sympathetic comparatist or an anxious churchman. Priestley had a long-standing interest in oriental philosophy that ran from his *Disquisitions relating to Matter and Spirit,* published in 1777, to *A Comparison of the Institutions of Moses with those of the Hindoos and other Ancient Nations,* published in 1799. As the title of the later work suggests, Priestley used Hinduism mainly as a foil to the combination of Unitarian theology and scientific materialism he propounded. The philosophical divide between Blake and Priestley would seem to rule out any possibility of influence on points relating to Hindu mythology. On the other hand, Priestley was a dissenter who hated state religion as much as Blake did, and he was an avid proponent of republican politics, no less than Blake.[21] Unlike Blake, however, Priestley discriminated among the myths and antiquities of the various nations and found them lacking in comparison to the Mosaic account in the Bible, finding particular fault with Brahminism. There is an outside chance that Priestley himself could have conveyed his mythographic interest in the Brahmins to Blake directly, perhaps on some occasion when he left Birmingham to see Joseph Johnson in London. This is all highly speculative, as little is known about Blake's relationship to Priestley.[22]

Some time ago Priestley's treatise comparing Mosaic and Hindu institutions was identified as a possible source for an unusual creation myth in Blake's poetry. Both Kathleen Raine and Piloo Nanavutty single out the following passage from Priestley's study as an important source for Blake:

> The production of all things from the substance of the Divine Being is
> thus represented by some of the Bramins. Comparing the First Cause

to a spider, they say the universe was produced by that insect spinning
out of its own entrails and belly; so that it brought forth first the elements, and then the celestial globes, etc., and that things are to continue in this state until the end of ages, when this spider will draw into
its body the several threads which had issued from it, when all things
will be destroyed and the world no longer exist, but as in the belly of
the spider. (Priestley, 50)

Blake is supposed to have used this myth "[w]ith sardonic humor in his
depiction of Urizen, the Intellect divorced from the Emotions (Luvah)
and from Imagination (Los), blind to the Divine Vision, cold, hard, coer-
cive."[23] The depiction at issue is from *The Book of Urizen,* when religion
is introduced into the world in the allegorical form of a giant net spun
out of Urizen's tyrannic soul:

> And where-ever he wandered in sorrows
> Upon the aged heavens
> A cold shadow follow'd behind him
> Like a spiders web, moist, cold & dim
> The dungeon-like heaven dividing.
>
> (U 25.7–12)

This web, "stretch'd / From the sorrows of Urizens soul," becomes knot-
ted and "twisted like to the human brain": "And all called it, the Net of
Religion" (U 25.16–17, 21–22). There are several problems with the
critics' claim that Blake is "using" the myth provided in Priestley's book,
the most obvious of which is the fact that the so-called source was published in 1799, at least five years subsequent to *The Book of Urizen,*
printed by Blake in 1794. Another problem is the assumption that Blake
would need to look outside his own garden to find a spider's web to
serve as a metaphor for the constraints of religion.

    What is most interesting in the passage from Priestley is the way
the Hindu myth is somewhat patronizingly presented as a rather quaint
account of the origins of the universe, but one that does not compare
with the Unitarian, rationalist account Priestley prefers: a simple spider
is no match for "the Divine Being" or "the First Cause," not to mention
"elements" and "celestial globes." In fact, Priestley the scientist, with his
understanding of causality and elements, is really a kind of Urizen figure
himself. In *The Four Zoas,* the image of Urizen trailing a giant web
appears again, but with the meaning modified so that the net is no
longer religion but the rationalistic systems of science, with their "vast
instruments to measure out the immense":

> . . . in pride he wanderd weeping
> Clothed in aged venerableness obstinately resolvd
> Travelling thro darkness & whereever he traveld a dire Web
> Followd behind him as the Web of a Spider dusky & cold

(FZ 6.73.29–32)

If we are seeking to relate this passage from *The Four Zoas* to the passage in Priestley, at least it has the advantage of being written after *A Comparison of the Institutions of Moses with those of the Hindoos* was published,[24] as does the reference to Urizen's web at the end of "Night the Sixth":

> Then Urizen arose upon the wind back many a mile
> Retiring into his dire Web scattering fleecy snows
> As he ascended howling loud the Web vibrated strong
> From heaven to heaven from globe to globe. In vast excentric
>   paths
> Compulsive rolld the Comets at his dread command. . . .

(FZ 6.75.25–29)

Here Urizen really does appear as the spider of the Hindu myth, but he also behaves like the natural philosopher's primal cause as well, setting the comets and globes in motion through the vibrating action of the web. Where Priestley holds up the deistic account of creation as a standard by which to judge the Hindu account, Blake infuses the purely abstract concept of a primal cause with concrete imagery, a poetic maneuver that makes the august abstraction secondary to the homely notion of a spider's web. In addition, if Blake really did write with the passage from Priestley in mind, he did so in a much more complex manner than is usually supposed. Raine and Nanavutty assume that Blake merely picked up a reference to a Hindu creation myth in Priestley without, in effect, responding to Priestley—that is, without reacting to the context in which the myth is set. Blake may very well respond to the myth in Priestley, but he also responds to Priestley's response. Joseph Priestley's hostility to Hinduism does not, in itself, rule out the possibility that Blake would have seen mythic richness where Priestley saw only superstition and error. Criticism of Hindu myth for its "irrationality" in relation to the Bible could only have incited Blake's interest all the more.

This kind of contrary logic may also apply, in part, to the mythographic work that William Julius Mickle inserted into his translation of *The Lusiad,* Luiz Vaz de Camöens's epic poem about Vasco da Gama's conquest of India. In the case of Mickle, however, Blake could have found another justification for his interest in the translator's opinions: Mickle's *Lusiad* had been attacked by Voltaire, who was surely motivated by Mickle's own attacks against him in *Voltaire in the Shades* (1770), a critique of the deistic natural religion so despised by Blake. Any philosophical enemy of Voltaire would have been a philosophical friend to Blake, and the speculation that Mickle was of interest to the poet is supported by at least two pieces of textual evidence—one in a letter from Blake to Hayley, another in Mickle's "Enquiry into the Religious Tenets and Philosophy of the Brahmins." Blake refers to Camöens in a letter to Hayley of November 1800 when he apologizes for his tardiness in executing an engraving of Hayley's recently deceased son Tom: "Absorbed by the poets Milton, Homer, Camoens, Ercilla, Ariosto, and Spenser, whose physiognomies have been my delightful study, *Little Tom* has been of late unattended to" (*E* 714). The comment implies that Blake has been preoccupied with the *images* of the poets, but surely another meaning is that he has turned his attention to the epic tradition because he was working on his own epic at the time. No one would deny that Homer, Milton, and Spenser were important to Blake's elaboration of his myth in *The Four Zoas,* but that does not gainsay the possible relevance of Camöens's *Os Luciadas,* Ercilla's *La Araucana,* and Ariosto's *Orlando Furioso* as well. As noted, the edition of *The Lusiad* most available to Blake would have been Mickle's translation. Originally published in 1776, the book came out in a third edition in 1798. This edition contains the full complement of Mickle's extensive front matter and voluminous notes concerning India, along with the translator's long essay on the Brahmin philosophy, so when Blake read his Camöens he would have also gotten a good deal of information about Hinduism along with it.

The second piece of textual evidence that supports the probability that Blake knew Mickle's essay on the Brahmin philosophy comes by way of the light that the essay casts on one of the more obscure passages in Blake's poetry. In *Milton* Blake refers to "the Wicker Man of Scandinavia" that consumes "Jerusalems children" in flames (*M* 37.11–12); later in *Jerusalem* the Wicker Man likewise consumes his captives "in flames among the stars" (*J* 47.7–8). The reference in *Jerusalem* seems mostly about the sacrifice of British soldiers in the Napoleonic Wars: "Loud the cries of War on the Rhine & Danube, with Albions Sons, / Away from Beulahs hills & vales" (*J* 47.9–10). The reference in *Milton* is more obscure; there Milton himself in the form of "the Selfhood deadly" appears as the Wicker Man. In both instances, however, the meaning seems to relate to Blake's idea that any sacrifice of humanity is

a form of metaphorical Druidism, because the Druids of the north—i.e.,
Scandinavia—conducted rites of actual human sacrifice. The Wicker
Man in *Milton* is glossed by Harold Bloom as "a 'Druidic' figure possibly derived from Caesar's *Commentaries*" (E 926); Bloom has in mind
S. Foster Damon's note on the passage, which quotes from the *Commentaries* as follows: "Others use huge figures, whose wicker limbs they
fill with living men and set on fire, and the men die surrounded by
flames."[25] Obviously, the phrase "Wicker Man" does not actually
appear in this quotation, but it does in Mickle's discussion of the rites
and ceremonies of different religions that run counter to humanity:

> Yet what shall we think of the *Wicker Man!* A gigantic figure; the
> body, each leg and arm was a mast, to which an hundred or more
> human victims were bound with wicker. When there was a deficiency
> of malefactors, or prisoners of war, the innocent helpless were seized,
> that the horrid sacrifice might be complete. When all the rites were
> performed the sublime Druids gave the hecatomb to the flames, as an
> offering grateful to the gods, as the most acceptable insurance of the
> divine protection.[26]

Mickle uses the horrors of the wicker man to illustrate the dangers of
idolatry, a feature he finds rampant in "the religion of the Brahmins,"
and to show that "the most unworthy ideas of the Divinity . . . naturally
arise from idol worship" (Mickle 2: 201). In *Jerusalem* Blake writes of
"a Wicker Idol woven round Jerusalems children," and this, added to
the fact that both Mickle and Blake describe victims of war sacrificed to
the Wicker Man, make Mickle's essay on the Brahmins a highly likely
source for Blake's strange image. The "Enquiry into the Religious Tenets
and Philosophy of the Brahmins," then, can be taken as one more extensive—albeit mistaken—account of Hindu mythology that Blake probably knew firsthand.

Mickle's discussion of Hinduism is mistaken because he relies on
the work of John Holwell and Alexander Dow, both of whom based
their presentations on unreliable information and neither of whom knew
Sanskrit. But the question of reliability is really moot, and the fact
remains that Blake would have found in Mickle considerable confirmation of his own views about the way religion worked, together with a
great many details of Hindu mythology. Mickle's enquiry is clearly critical of what he calls the "Brahmin religion," but the criticism is directed
not so much toward the Brahmins in particular as it is toward the general problem of any religion dominated by priestcraft. In *The Marriage
of Heaven and Hell,* Blake describes the process whereby an original
poetic vision of the world becomes abstracted into religious doctrine to

be manipulated by priests. In *The Song of Los* he offers a wide-ranging account of the way many ancient poets, including Brahma, experience the ruin of vision and humanity caused by abstract philosophy and moral law. The "Enquiry into the Religious Tenets and Philosophy of the Brahmins" also describes a collapse of original vision into derivative, manipulative priestcraft. Mickle relies on Holwell to explain how the Brahmins "in process of time lost sight of the *divine original,* and in its place substituted new and strange doctrines" (Mickle 2: 231). Mickle then breaks the process down into several stages, as Blake did on plate 11 of *The Marriage of Heaven and Hell.* First, "the Gentoo [i.e., Hindu] Scriptures were translated from the language of angels and . . . reduced to writing"; then, the original text translated from the angelic language is paraphrased; next, the paraphrase is alluded to only in commentary; the commentaries, in turn, introduce "numberless ceremonies" and so ensure the "priestly power" of the Brahmin class, who oversee "the daily obligations of religious duties . . . imposed on every *Gentoo*" (Mickle 2: 232–33). Blake would surely have agreed with this explanation of the way "superstition, the sure support of preistcraft," turns people into "mere machines" (Mickle 2: 233). But he would also have understood, as *The Song of Los* implies, that Brahma was in possession of some original poetic vision long before the fall into idolatry, duty, and ceremony.

The points of general resemblance between Brahma's vision and Blake's that can be gleaned from a glance at Mickle's enquiry are not inconsiderable, but they can be—or have been—easily overlooked because they are so basic to Blake that they might be attributed solely to the poet's powers of invention. Take, for example, Blake's sublime sense of the vastness of time stretching back into eternity before the creation of man and after the fall of Albion. The way Blake conceives of time in, for instance, *The Book of Urizen,* with successive ages of great duration in which some phase of creation comes to pass, compares to the vast Hindu ages described by Mickle: "The time . . . is divided into four *Jogues,* or ages, which in reality are new creations of the universe" (Mickle 2: 185). All told, the four ages add up to a period of six million years. Blake, of course, measures human history by the conventional biblical figure of six thousand years, but before human history begins he imagines a period of astonishing duration that culminates in the creation, or rather, in a series of creations. Blake's expanded sense of time is one of those basic features of his mythic system that is so unlike anything in biblical or classical tradition that it begs comparison with Eastern myth.

Another feature of Blake's system that is quite unlike anything in the Bible or in Greek myth is the ability of the Zoas to experience death and recover from it, again and again. Mickle observes that the Hindu gods likewise "are always killing each other and springing up in some new *chimera*-form" (Mickle 2: 210), and in this they differ from the Greek gods, who may be wounded but cannot be killed. Most, but not all, of the Greek gods have female consorts, whereas the Hindu gods are unfailingly paired off with female Devi. Mickle claims that "[t]he Gentoo mythology provides every deity with a spouse. A god without a wife being, according to them, as preposterous . . . as a fire without heat" (Mickle 2: 221). Similarly, in Blake's myth no Zoa is complete without his female emanation, and it is indeed telling that in Blake the only "god without a wife" is Satan: "Son of Perdition terrible his form dishumanizd monstrous / A male without a female counterpart" (*FZ* 8.104.24–25). The Hindu system, again according to Mickle, provides its gods with contraries as well as counterparts: "*Birmah* is . . . appointed to create, *Bishnoo* to preserve, and *Sieb* to change or destroy" (2: 188). If the tension between Brahma and Siva is a partial model for the relationship of Urizen and Orc, Blake's inspiration could have been Mickle as easily as Volney or Jones. Mickle also mentions reincarnation, another feature of Indian myth that has no cognate in biblical or classical literature: "The less criminal spirits animate bees, singing birds, and other innocent creatures; while those of deeper guilt become wolves or tigers" (Mickle 2: 183). One of the more compelling of the "reincarnation" passages in *The Four Zoas* refers to the same creatures that Mickle does: at the close of one of the many battles in the poem, "those that remain / Return in pangs and horrible convulsions to their beastial state / For the monsters of the Elements Lions or Tygers or Wolves" (*FZ* 8.102.1–3). And in *The Book of Urizen*, the birth of Orc is achieved in stages that are quite suggestive of the cycles of reincarnation that Mickle describes. The spirit of Orc begins as a worm in the womb of Enitharmon and then becomes a serpent, until, at last, "Many forms of fish, bird & beast, / Brought forth an Infant form / Where was a worm before" (*U* 19.34–36).

Mickle's enquiry into the Brahmin philosophy may have been little more than a haphazard compilation of previously published accounts of Hinduism, but its value as a potential source of mythic material is in no way diminished thereby. Moreover, the book's re-publication in 1798 helps to show that interest in Indic culture was on the rise. The mythographic work of Blake's contemporaries has a kind of aggregate bearing on Blake's myth because no single author can be said to exercise exclusive individual influence over so particular a poet. In the 1790s, the crucial decade for the development of Blake's myth, the poet was surrounded by accounts of Indian affairs and Hindu mythology on all sides.

It was there in the pages of the *Analytical Review;* it was there in the daily papers as Hastings's fate was debated and the East India Company's charter was renewed; it was there in the theological discussions held by Priestley and other Dissenters; it was there in the pages of Volney that every radical tradesman knew by heart; it was there in the drawing of William Jones done by Flaxman and in the elegy penned by Hayley. Then, in the first decade of the nineteenth century the Hindu pantheon appeared again in the pages of a book engraved by a man living with one of Blake's best friends and published by another.

III

Blake refers to the "Geeta" in his *Descriptive Catalogue* of 1809, the same year that Moses Haughton engraved the plates for Edward Moor's *The Hindu Pantheon* (1810), a copious account of Hindu deities with the Sanskrit names of the gods affixed in Devanagari script by Charles Wilkins. Moor was good friends with Wilkins, both of whom were members of the Asiatic Society.[27] This connection does not, in itself, mean that Blake's interest in Wilkins led him to Moor's book, but it is one of several reasons for supposing that he knew *The Hindu Pantheon* well enough to model some of his designs in *Jerusalem* after Haughton's engravings and line drawings. The text of Moor's book also encourages the supposition that Blake might have taken an interest in it, since he would have found in Moor some of the same arguments against religion and priestcraft that he had articulated himself in *The Marriage of Heaven and Hell* and in "London" almost twenty years earlier. The first page of *The Hindu Pantheon,* in fact, explains religion in terms so close to Blake's that one is tempted to say that here it is the mythographer who has been influenced by the poet.

Moor begins by saying that the religion of the Hindus "may be divided . . . into *exoteric* and *esoteric*" forms. Exoteric religion "is preached to the vulgar" and consists merely of "gross idolatry and irrational superstition." The esoteric faith, on the other hand, contains "a considerable portion of unadulterated physical, and moral truths," which make it closer to poetry than religion:

> The doctrines thus divided, may be otherwise styled *religion* and *mythology*: the latter is perhaps the invention rather of poets than of priests; but being so well adapted to their purpose, the priests have artfully applied it to rivet the mental chains that, when the scriptures are concealed, they seldom fail to assist in the forging of mankind. (Moor, 1)

While Moor's language seems almost to echo "The mind-forg'd mana-
cles" (SE 46.8) of Blake's "London," the view of religion here most
likely derives from the Enlightenment critique made by Volney almost
twenty years earlier, except that Moor, like Blake, allows a greater place
for religion in the world when it is really mythology, "the invention
rather of poets than of priests." And Moor, also like Blake, explains
priestcraft as a conscious manipulation of poetry used to enslave the vulgar. Moor's division of Hinduism into religion and mythology is really
the same as Blake's separation of "forms of worship" and "poetic tales"
(MHH 11.Prose). Most important, the very fact that Moor ascribes
mythology to poets and sets them in opposition to the priests whose
province is organized religion puts the poet in a dissenting position.
Once again, Blake's mythological practice is historically homologous
with the British understanding of the Hindu system.

These observations on Blake's and Moor's shared attitudes regarding the subject of religion enforce the possibility that Blake was somehow drawn to Moor's book and saw in it a new kind of art that found
a place in his own work. In 1943 Anthony Blunt suggested that the
image of a female figure enthroned upon an open sunflower on plate 53
at the start of chapter 3 of Jerusalem (fig. 3) was most likely derived
from an image of a Devi in Moor's Hindu Pantheon (fig. 4).[28] Blunt says
the image from Moor was "known to Flaxman and therefore probably
to Blake."[29] We know that Flaxman was a lifelong friend of Blake who
might very well have conveyed Moor's book of Hindu mythology to the
poet. Blake's acquaintance with Joseph Johnson, the publisher of The
Hindu Pantheon, is another possible avenue for the poet's interest in the
book. Even though Johnson died when the book was in press, the probability that Blake would have taken an interest in it is enhanced because
his friend Fuseli would have had first-hand knowledge of the book as
well. Fuseli, like Blake, had been closely associated with Johnson for
many years, and Fuseli also employed the services of Moses Haughton
to engrave some of his own designs. In fact, Haughton was living in
Fuseli's house and working under his direct supervision on other projects while he was doing the engravings for The Hindu Pantheon.[30]

The design that opens chapter 3 of Jerusalem showing a seated
female figure perched atop an open sunflower does seem to be a pictorial
quotation of Haughton's drawing of a Devi seated upon a lotus blossom.
The principal reason for thinking this is simply that Blake's image is highly
unusual, so Haughton's drawing emerges as a logical explanation of a
design that is hardly within the medieval and Renaissance traditions that
Blake typically drew upon for artistic inspiration. Also, the tiered crown
on the head of Blake's figure is evidently derived from similar crowns that

Figure 3. Engraving of "Beulah," plate 53, William Blake, *Jerusalem, the emanation of the giant Albion,* copy D, London, 1804. Typ 6500 49F, Department of Printing and Graphic Arts, Houghton Library, Harvard College Library

adorn the heads of the Devi and other deities in the plates of Moor's book. These two details—the open flower and the tiered crown—argue strongly for Blake's use of the image from *The Hindu Pantheon* in some visually paraphrased form. The probability that Blake incorporates a visual component of Indian myth into a pictorial representation of his own mythology by quoting Haughton's Devi increases if the female figure seated on the sunflower in *Jerusalem* is understood as a personified image of the state of easeful repose that the poet called "Beulah."

There seems to be some dispute in Blake scholarship as to the identity of the figure, who has also been identified as Blake's nature goddess, Vala; as Albion's emanation, Jerusalem; as Jerusalem's enemy, Rahab; or as some kind of composite version of all of these female deities.[31] The text of plate 53, however, refers to Beulah three times but does not mention Vala, Jerusalem, or Rahab. The text also describes Los performing the creative task of "build[ing] Golgonooza . . . beneath Beulah" (*J* 53.15–16). The prophet-artificer Los is often identified with the poet-artist Blake, an identification that is especially relevant here if the figure at the top of the page is understood as a representation of Beulah. The

Figure 4. Drawing of a Pedma-Devi from Edward Moor's *The Hindu Pantheon*

plate itself, in other words, puts Blake's creative work in the same position as that of Los—literally "beneath Beulah." Also, the sunflower appears to float on water, like the lotus, possibly in illustration of "the rivers of Beulah; pleasant river! soft, mild, parent stream" (*J* 53.3).

Beulah is almost always glossed in Blake criticism as an intermediate state or condition between the two contrary states that Blake terms Eternity and Ulro. Eternity (also known as Eden) is a unified and unfallen state in which Humanity and Divinity are synonyms; Ulro is a divided and divisive state marked by morality, rationality, and the mechanistic natural philosophy Blake called, alternatively, Deism and Druidism. The intermediate state of Beulah—"where Contrarieties are equally True" (*M* 30.1)—is a refuge for fallen man from both the intensity of Eternity and the drudgery of Ulro. The general function of Beulah as a protective or preservative condition quite logically corresponds to the state of sleep that preserves the health of the body and also gives rise to dreams. The dream state, in turn, allows for the further association of Beulah with imagination or creation, hence making the "Daughters of Beulah" Blake's equivalent of the classical muses who inspire poetic song. The creative role of the Daughters of Beulah is partly the result of sexual satisfaction, consistent with the Biblical meaning of Beulah as a place of delight, comfort, refuge, and companionship—that is, of marriage: "Thou shalt no more be termed Forsaken; neither shall thy land any more be termed Desolate: but . . . shalt be called . . . Beulah: for the Lord delighteth in thee, and thy land shall be married" (Isaiah 62:4). Beulah, in short, is associated with sleep, dream, creativity, and married love.

Several of these features can also be found in the descriptions of the Devi in Moor's *Hindu Pantheon*. First of all, a Devi is a female deity who is especially alluring when associated with the lotus, an "emblem of female beauty" (Moor, 10). The Devi illustrated on Moor's plate 33 is termed a "Pedma-Devi" or "goddess of the lotus" (Moor, 160). The connection of female beauty with flowers and blossoms is also basic to Beulah, for obvious reasons. For equally obvious reasons the lotus flower in Moor is "a symbol of humidity, and marks an aquatic relation in its bearer" (Moor, 29). The lotus blossom is also associated with sleep, as in the myth of Vishnu that Moor recounts:

> It is related, in the *Scanda Purana*, that, when the whole earth was covered with water, and Vishnu lay extended asleep on the bosom of Devi, a lotus arose from his navel, and its ascending flower soon reached the surface of the flood; that Brahma sprang from that flower, and, looking around without seeing any creature on the boundless expanse, imagined himself to be the first born, and entitled to rank above all future beings; yet resolved to investigate the deep, and to ascertain whether any being existed in it who could controvert his claim to preeminence, he glided, therefore, down the stalk of the lotus, and finding Vishnu asleep, asked loudly who he was? "I am the first born," answered Vishnu; and when Brahma denied his primogeniture, they had an obstinate battle. . . . (Moor, 17–18)

Vishnu here has a certain general resemblance to Blake's androgynous Eternals, since the male god effectively gives birth to Brahma through the agency of the lotus that sprouts from his navel. Moor supports the argument for androgyny when he observes that "the *navel* of Vishnu . . . is worshipped as one and the same with the sacred *Yoni*" (Moor, 387, n.). In addition, the birth of Brahma from the body of Vishnu is not that far removed from the birth of Urizen from the side of Los (see *U* 6.2–4). Of course, the birth of Urizen out of Los also recalls the creation of Eve from Adam's rib, but it is worth noting that the Hindu myth has the "advantage," for Blake, of explaining the birth of one male god out of the body of another—precisely the situation in

Blake's myth but not in the book of Genesis. These general resemblances, however, are secondary to the particular similitude of the Hindu deity and the Devi upon whom he sleeps to the Daughters of Beulah, who likewise provide a place of easeful repose that leads to some act of creation. What is most striking, perhaps, is that the references to Beulah on plate 53 of *Jerusalem* beneath the image of the figure on a sunflower floating atop the waves add water or stream imagery to the constellation of attributes Blake uses to signify the state of Beulah. There is no water-imagery connected with Beulah in *The Four Zoas* or in *Milton*, or elsewhere in *Jerusalem*. Plate 53 is unique in this respect, thereby increasing the likelihood that the image of Beulah was inspired by the Pedma-Devi or lotus goddess in Moor's *Hindu Pantheon*. This means that Blake did not simply model the figure after the Devi for reasons of pictorial design alone; rather, he must have understood what the Devi meant in Hindu myth and recognized that his own conception of Beulah had certain things in common with that meaning.

If we accept Blake's pictorial quotation of the Devi in *The Hindu Pantheon* as fact, then it stands to reason that other images from Moor's book might have inspired other plates in *Jerusalem*. Take, for instance, the curious image that appears on the same page of Moor's book as the Pedma-Devi atop the lotus blossom (fig. 5). The fantastic scene represented here is described by Moor as "[t]he contest between Vice, personified under the name of MAHISHASUR, and Active Virtue, under that of DURGA, will" (Moor, 56). Moor explains that Durga (also called Bhavani) is one of the consorts of Siva who rides a lion (although Haughton's illustration suggests a tiger) in her combat with Mahishasur, a monster with the ability to assume many forms. In Haughton's drawing, the personified figure of vice is defeated in the form of a buffalo when Durga cuts off the head with a sword. The monster Mahishasur emerges from the neck of the slain beast, only to be dispatched at last by the spear of Durga (Moor, 153). The details of the story are less important than the design itself, which illustrates Durga at the moment of triumph with several different weapons held in the hands of her numerous arms. Blake seems to have imitated the design motif of the multiple arms in his representation of the three accusers of Socrates that tops plate 93 of *Jerusalem* (fig. 6). The artist has superimposed the three figures so that their six arms appear almost to emerge from a single torso. Like the sunflower-sitter of plate 53, the design here is so unusual in relation to the bulk of Blake's designs—which typically show the human figure reclining, standing, or flying—that it begs comparison with the multi-armed figure so common to Indian iconography. The superimposition of three figures with their arms arrayed in an arc before them at least creates the

Figure 5. Drawing of Mahishasur and Durga from Edward Moor's *The Hindu Pantheon*

impression of a single figure with multiple arms. The similarity of the design may also include a thematic reversal of the meaning of the image from *The Hindu Pantheon,* in that the Indian design sets a multi-armed figure of virtue against vice, whereas Blake has his figures point their accusing fingers at the virtuous presence of Socrates.

Thematic resemblances between *Jerusalem* plate 93 and the image of Durga from Moor are, once again, less important than the basic similarities of design. The same might be said of the strange figure that appears on plate 78 of *Jerusalem* (fig. 7). The human figure with the head of a bird may represent one of the "Spectres of Albions Twelve Sons" described in the text of this plate. The spectre in Blake is not an outright negation of humanity, but is, rather, a fallen or distorted version of some Eternal form. Here, the spectres are said to be "ravning to devour / The Sleeping Humanity" (*J* 78.1–3), and so the creature may be depicted with the head of a bird of prey for that reason, consistent with its ravening or devouring function. The pose of the seated figure, resting its head in its left hand, has been compared to *Melancholie I,* a print by Albrecht Dürer that Blake owned, and has been interpreted as "a portrait of Los as a melancholy prophet of apocalypse, rendered in a fusion

Figure 6. Engraving of the accusers of Socrates, plate 93, William Blake, *Jerusalem, the emanation of the giant Albion,* copy D, London, 1804. Typ 6500 49F, Department of Printing and Graphic Arts, Houghton Library, Harvard College Library

of Christian iconography, Renaissance humor theory, and classical mythology."[32] Perhaps so, but the figure in the Dürer print has the head of a man, whereas the figure in Blake's plate has the head of a bird. In fact, the head of Blake's bird-man bears a strong resemblance to that of a winged creature in one of the plates from *The Hindu Pantheon* (fig. 8). The creature is Garuda, who serves as the vehicle on which Vishnu and his consort ride and which Moor describes as "an eagle, or rather an animal composed of the eagle and the man" (Moor, 16). Those who wish to interpret Blake's beaked figure as a version of Los can find support in Houghton's plate because of the pictorial logic that links the great preserver of Hindu myth to Blake's conservator of humanity. If the figure is read as Los, then Urthona's "Vehicular Form" (*J* 53.1) and the form of Vishnu's vehicle look strikingly alike. Moreover, the interpretation of the figure as Los can be reconciled with the interpretation of the figure as Spectre if Los is understood to react here as he does in *Milton:* "he became what he beheld" (*M* 3.29). Here again, if Blake did model a version of Los on an image taken from Haughton's drawing of Garuda, then the choice shows that a conscious connection was made between one of his own mythic figures and a god from the Hindu pantheon. In this case, the connection is the function of preservation that both Vishnu and Urthona perform.

Both Garuda and Blake's composite creature bear the head of a bird featuring the hooked beak of an eagle or a hawk, but, strangely, both heads also seem to have the coxcombs and wattles more familiar on chickens, turkeys, or vultures. The most obvious similarity, however,

Figure 7. Engraving of a spectre, plate 78, William Blake, *Jerusalem, the emanation of the giant Albion,* copy D, London, 1804. Typ 6500 49F, Department of Printing and Graphic Arts, Houghton Library, Harvard College Library

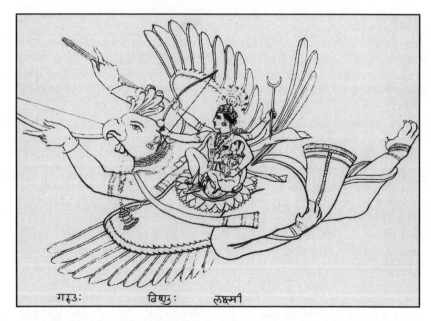

Figure 8. Drawing of Garuda from Edward Moor's *The Hindu Pantheon*

is the combination of bird and human, and this motif combining human
and animal forms is not so unusual in Indian iconography. One of the
more familiar of such figures is the Indian god Ganessa, featured on the
frontispiece of *The Hindu Pantheon* (fig. 9). Although the work is now
lost and exists only in a copy by William Bell Scott (fig. 10), Blake is said
to have done a drawing of two elephant-headed figures that might have
been modeled after the Indian god.[33] Blake's evident interest in Indian
images manifested in his *Jerusalem* designs and possibly in a lost drawing of Ganessa is not that surprising in view of his *Descriptive Catalogue*
of 1809. In addition to his description of the drawing of Charles Wilkins
translating the *Bhagavad Gita,* Blake also explains the compositional
method of two other pictures in a way that suggests his familiarity with
Indic images: "The two Pictures of Nelson and Pitt are compositions of
a mythological cast, similar to those Apotheoses of Persian, Hindoo, and
Egyptian Antiquity, which are still preserved on rude monuments, being
copies from some stupendous originals now lost or perhaps buried till
some happier age." Blake claims to have seen these "wonderful originals" of Persian, Hindu, and Egyptian antiquity as a result of "having
been taken in vision into the ancient republics, monarchies, and patriar-
chates of Asia" (*E* 530–31). The conclusion is inevitable that Blake's
visionary itinerary into Asian antiquity was made easier by the material
existence of such books as Edward Moor's *The Hindu Pantheon*.

The "mythological cast" that Blake tried to give to his pictorial compositions in 1809 belies, to some extent, the meaning of mythology that
operates in his poetic compositions. Likewise, the images in Moor's *Hindu
Pantheon* are more curious than controversial, largely because they *are*
images and, as such, do not convey the complexity of the Hindu system so
fully as the mythographic discourses of the 1790s did. Then, the atmosphere of dissent and the possibility of religious persecution made the initial presentation of Hindu mythology charged with theological meaning
that challenged the views of the established church. In 1790, confronted
with evidence of the astonishing antiquity of the Hindu myths, William
Jones was prompted to ask questions about the authority of the Bible with
some far-reaching consequences: "Either the first eleven chapters of *Genesis* . . . are true; or the whole fabric of our national religion is false" (*AR*
6 [Jan.–April 1790]: 313). When this remark appeared in the *Analytical
Review* Jones's courage to question the authority of the Bible and his
desire for truth came up for comment: "It is not, however, the truth of our
national religion, as such, that Sir William professes to have at heart; but
truth itself; and if any one can convince him that *Moses* drew his narrative through Egyptian conduits, from the primeval fountains of Indian literature, he will esteem him as a friend" (*AR* 6: 314).

श्री गणेश:

Figure 9. Engraving of Ganesa from Edward Moor's *The Hindu Pantheon*

Indian literature, then, had theological implications that ramified all the way from ancient Egypt to modern England, and so posed a problem for Anglican orthodoxy. A sense of just how high the Hindu gods had raised the theological stakes in Blake's age can be gained by taking another glance at Thomas Maurice. Writing around 1793, Maurice observes in his *Indian Antiquities* (1794) that the "unfathomable antiquity" of the Hindus had led such eminent Frenchmen as Voltaire and Bailly to found "those false and impious systems which have plunged a great nation into the abyss of atheism, and all its consequent excesses and miseries."[34] The superior antiquity of the Hindus and the resem-

Figure 10. William Bell Scott. Untitled reproduction of a drawing by William Blake for *William Blake, etchings from his works*, London, 1878

blances between their system and the Christian one were enough, for some, to invalidate revelation and prompt the question Blake had asked: why would some antiquities and scriptures come to be "neglected and disbelieved" while others were "collected and arranged" (*E* 543)? The great status conferred on Hindu mythology by the power and prestige of origins meant that its "primeval theology" had to be taken seriously.[35] After all, the gods of Hindostan had already destroyed one nation (or so Maurice thought), and their presence was, if anything, more evident in England during the 1790s than it had ever been in France. Theological concerns of this sort were obviously registered in one way by Maurice, the orthodox churchman, and in a fundamentally different way by

Blake, whose beliefs were not to be circumscribed by the established church. But Blake the poet was no different from an "antiquary" like Maurice in understanding ancient mythology in theological terms. The modern ability to detach a myth from its theological meaning and so construct an alternative rationale for its existence had barely begun in Blake's time. Then, there was no Frasier around to say that the gods embodied ceremonies of vegetation and rites of fertility, nor was there a Levi-Strauss available to elevate the primitive language of native gods into an elegant structuralist discourse that made complicated meaning out of basic distinctions and simple similitudes. Blake's contemporaries, by contrast, understood Indian mythology as a matter of great theological power: Thomas Maurice believed that Hinduism had already had a hand in destroying a French king, and William Jones felt that the Eastern faith might one day undermine the English church. If the ancient mythology of the Hindus offered a theological challenge to Church and King, and Blake knew about it, he would have been more than merely interested—he would have been inspired.

CHAPTER 3

Theology

The profusion of mythographic accounts of world religions in the latter half of the eighteenth century climaxed in the last decade of that century with the learned addresses and informed translations made by members of the Asiatic Society and their successors or imitators. These newly detailed explanations of Hindu religion would have found a ready audience among members of London's dissenting community, for several reasons. First, the antiquity of the Hindu scriptures challenged the authority of the Bible by raising the possibility that the Hebrew faith might have been derived from an earlier Indic source, as in, for example, the speculation that Moses had based his commandments on the Hindu laws of Menu. Second, the division of the Hindu faith into pure, primeval belief and empty, priestly ritual confirmed dissenting criticism of the established Church: the Brahmin priests were not unlike their Anglican counterparts in requiring conformity to ceremony and moral law. Third, the Hindu myths contained so many parallels with Christianity that they could be construed not only as a challenge to authority or a criticism of conformity, but also as an alternative version—a mythic retelling—of the Everlasting Gospel that all dissenters followed. As we have seen, Blake was in an unusually privileged position to take advantage of the Oriental Renaissance and acquaint himself with what he called "[t]he philosophy of the east" (*MHH* 12.Prose). And while there was much in this philosophy that was new and strange, British expositors of Hinduism often presented it in such a way as to make it accord with certain strains of Christian theology that Blake would have found immediately meaningful.

Although much of Blake's theology remains obscure, critics have come a long way since J. G. Davies concluded in 1948 that the poet's religious beliefs could be summed up by the Apostle's Creed.[1] This rather remarkable assertion does not provide much of an explanation as to why so orthodox a Christian should feel the need to express his beliefs in so unorthodox a form. More recent critics understand Blake as a latter-day saint of the English Civil War, a holdover from the days of the Ranters, Levelers, and other sectaries most active in the age of Cromwell. Indeed, it is hard not to think of Blake when one reads accounts of the Seekers and the Ranters, and even those who came before them. The consistently heretical John Everard (1575–c. 1650), for example, sounds like a precursor of Blake on a number of theological points: "He thought God was in man and nature, located heaven and hell in the hearts of men, and allegorized the Bible. 'The dead letter is not the Word, but Christ is the Word,' he said. 'Sticking to the letter' has been 'the bane of all growth in religion,' the cause of controversies and persecution. God's kingdom is come, and his will done, 'when Christ is come into thy flesh.' Miracles have not ceased, 'but our eyes are blinded and we cannot see them.'"[2]

Blake belongs to this kind of sectarian tradition, although it seems wrong to place him too securely within a particular sect. As long as the notion of sectarianism remains general, it is fairly easy to see Blake as a product of the dissenting tradition. This approach to the question of Blake's religious conviction originates in 1958 with A. L. Morton's study of Blake's sources, *The Everlasting Gospel*. In 1992, Jon Mee's *Dangerous Enthusiasm,* in the spirit of E. P. Thompson's *The Making of the English Working Class,* showed how amenable the new radicalism of the 1790s was with the older, underground tradition of religious dissent. In 1993, Thompson's *Witness against the Beast* made specific A. L. Morton's earlier, general identification of Blake as a sectarian dissenter by locating Blake within a particular antinomian tradition, that of Muggletonianism. More recently, A. D. Nuthall has described Blake's theological opposition of Son and Father as a composite of antinomianism and Gnosticism.[3] Finally, G. E. Bentley, Jr. begins the latest biography of Blake by placing the poet squarely within the tradition of "radical religious Dissent," which he learned "at the knees of Dissenting parents" and maintained throughout his life, while belonging to no church or sect as yet conclusively identified.[4] The theological consensus, then, is that Blake belonged to some indeterminate antinomian species of a definite Dissenting genus.

Blake's religious leanings put him in a good position to appreciate sympathetic explanations of the Hindu system at the end of the eighteenth century. British expositors of Brahmanism emphasized, quite sensibly, theological comparisons with Christianity and so fueled existing controversies about the origin of religion and the authenticity of the scriptures. Blake's reference to Charles Wilkins's translation of the *Bhagavad Gita* as "the Hindoo Scriptures" (*E* 548) shows that the poet understood the Hindu classic in theological terms as a kind of bible or sacred code. As such, the Hindu bible could take its place beside the Hebrew and Christian testaments as yet another collection of poetic truths subject to manipulation by priests for the manufacture of moral law. This antinomian attitude may not have been fully shared by Wilkins, but the preface to his translation is careful to make the point that the pure faith of the Hindus has been corrupted by priestly machinations. Moreover, parts of the final chapter of the *Gita* in Wilkins's rendering inflect Hindu beliefs with an antinomian accent that Blake would have been certain to hear. This curious fact may account for Blake's interest in Wilkins's translation in the first place.

In addition to Wilkins's "antinomian" version of the *Bhagavad Gita,* William Jones's scholarly investigations provided another assessment of the Hindu system that accorded with Blake's theological leanings. Like Wilkins, Jones separated the Hindu faith into theological purity and ritualistic practice. This division made it possible for the great comparatist to put the ceremonies of religious worship to one side and focus on the philosophical core of Hinduism, which Jones understood in highly Platonic terms. For Jones, the polytheistic world of the Hindus was reducible to a sublime but deeply dynamic unity. He explained that the numerous gods of the Hindu pantheon and the multiform universe itself were all created of the same material, or rather, created by the same energy—for divine energy can only appear in the form of matter to the mortal, deluded eyes of men. Because individual human participation in this divine energy is possible for the believer, Jones's idea of Hinduism is shaded more with Neoplatonic thinking than with traditional Platonic thought. The general outlines of this Neoplatonized Hinduism conform to the theological dimensions of Blake's myth, and, as we shall see, may have furnished the poet with some of the key details of that myth. This is not to say that Blake derived his Neoplatonism from William Jones, because Blake was exposed to Neoplatonic ideas well before Jones's work in the *Asiatick Researches* appeared in England. Blake did not need Jones to incorporate Neoplatonism into his creative mythography any more than he needed Wilkins to inject the myth with antinomian meaning. But the antinomian and Neoplatonic threads that were woven into the accounts of Hindu theology that circulated in Blake's time would surely have aroused the interest of one so attuned to the dissenting tradition, for it is precisely antinomianism and Neoplatonism that go furthest to explain the theological dimensions of Blake's myth.

Along with Wilkins and Jones, other contemporaries of Blake responded to Hinduism in theological terms that are curiously akin to the poet's mythic imaginings. The most curious case is that of Thomas Maurice, the Anglican churchman who believed that Hinduism had somehow helped to unhinge the security of the French state and propelled that great country into ruinous revolution (see Chapter 2). No doubt because of the assumed political threat, the orthodox Maurice

went to great pains to discredit the theology of the Brahmin faith. In one
of the stranger theological applications of mythographic investigation,
Maurice demonstrated what were, for him, perfectly evident connections between Hinduism and Druidism on the one hand, and between
Hinduism and Catholicism on the other. At the same time, because Maurice saw himself as the successor of the great William Jones, he also
sought to strip away the "Druid" and "Catholic" corruptions of Hinduism in order to communicate the philosophical purity of the Indian
faith, which he, like Jones, understood to be a variant of Neoplatonism.
Wilkins, Jones, and Maurice emphasized, respectively, the Antinomian,
Neoplatonic, and Druidic strains of Hinduism as they understood it, and
the strange composite theology that these British expositors of Brahmanism concocted bears comparison with Blake's creative mythography.
In a sense, where his contemporaries decoded mythology as theology,
Blake encoded his system with myth. As one commentator has it, while
others "were demythologizing Christianity, Blake sought to remytholo-
gize it."[5] Thus the theological interpretations of Indian myth that prolif-
erated in Blake's age help us to understand Blake's poetic enterprise for
what, in large part, it really is: a mythological representation of the conditions of religion as he found them at the end of the eighteenth century.
The argument here is that the mythic representations of religion created
by Blake received some of their impetus and much of their meaning from
the theological interpretations of Hinduism that so many of his contemporaries made.

I

The *Bhagavad Gita* arrived in England packed with a good deal
of sectarian baggage, including the translator's claim that the Brahmins were Unitarians. Connections between Brahminism and dissenting sects may seem far-fetched, but that connection was in fact made
in the late eighteenth century. In its review of Wilkins's *Gita* in 1785
The Gentleman's Magazine compared the Brahmins to the sect of dissenters who followed Jacob Boehme, whom Blake also admired (see
MHH 22.*Prose*):

> [T]he spiritual discipline of the Bramins [is] not unknown to some of
> the religious orders of Christians in the Romish church; in short, that
> of the ancient Ascetics or modern Behmenists: a total abstraction of the
> mind from every object but the contemplation of the Deity, his perfec-
> tions, or even his name.[6]

This strange comparison of the Brahmins to both the "Romish church" and contemporary Dissenters is only one of many instances of the paradoxical analysis of Hinduism produced by apologists for Anglican orthodoxy. Another instance is Thomas Maurice's comparison, made in his *Indian Antiquities,* of "the greater mysteries of Eleusis" to the Brahmin faith: the churchman claims that such ancient authors as Apuleius and Dion Chrysostomos speak of those mysteries "exactly as the Brahmins do of the divine raptures of *absorption* in the Deity, as the modern sect of Swedenborgh of those of their imagined Elysium."[7] These references to contemporary dissenting sects inspired by Boehme and Swedenborg, together with the antinomian tone that runs through parts of Wilkins's version of the *Bhagavad Gita,* help to explain the theological context in which Hinduism was placed; such placement would surely have excited Blake's interest.

Blake's first and only comment on Wilkins's translation of the *Bhagavad Gita* is made in 1809, but the poet's connections with Joseph Johnson could have led him to the Hindu classic much earlier than that. In the edition of Volney's *Ruins of Empire* that Johnson published in 1792 the author mentions Wilkins's translation in a long discussion of "the Hindoo system" and comments on its wide availability.[8] An even earlier reference to the *Bhagavad Gita* appears in the May 1790 issue of Johnson's *Analytical Review* in a summary of an article "On the Literature of the Hindoos" that concludes with a quotation from Sir William Jones in praise of Wilkins's translation:

> Since Europeans are indebted to the Dutch for almost all they know of Arabic, and to the French for all they know of Chinese, let them now receive from our nation the first accurate knowledge of Sanscrit, and of the valuable works composed in it; but if they wish to form a correct idea of Indian religion and literature, let them begin with forgetting all that has been written on the subject, by ancients or moderns, before the publication of the Gita. (*AR* 7 [May–August 1790]: 211)

Thus, in 1790 Blake could easily have become aware, for the first time, of the lone example of Hindu literature he mentions by name almost twenty years later.

When the *Gita* first appeared in London in 1785, however, Blake was an ordinary shopkeeper vending other artists' engravings. He was also developing an interest in Swedenborg and the New Jerusalem Church, especially after the death of his brother Robert in 1787.[9] In 1788 he engraved *All Religions are One,* a manifesto of his belief in the unerring power of poetic inspiration as the source from which all religion and philosophy originated. "[A]ll sects of Philosophy are from the

Poetic Genius adapted," he writes, from which it follows that "[t]he Religions of all Nations are derived from each Nations different reception of the Poetic Genius" (*E* 1). The elevation of Poetic Genius as the origin of the world's religions argues in favor of Blake's eventual receptivity to the Hinduism in the *Gita* as a religious representation of poetic truth, but Blake's religious interests were no doubt much closer to home in the late 1780s. Indeed, in 1789 Blake and his wife Catherine attended the first London meeting of the Swedenborgian New Jerusalem Church but soon rejected its tenets when it became evident that the congregation had become caught up in the rituals and ceremonies that constitute the institutionalization of faith.[10] The chances are that Blake would have become aware of the *Gita* after the break with the Swedenborgians, perhaps in 1790, when many events conspired to point the way to Wilkins: the arrival of the *Asiatick Researches* in London, Fuseli's reviews in Johnson's journal, Pitt's intolerance of dissent, and Burke's indictment of Warren Hastings. These last two events may seem removed from the *Bhagavad Gita*—and they were in 1785—but five years later they were not: the embattled Hastings had introduced the *Gita* to the West, and, in doing so, he had claimed for Hinduism a theology in common with Christianity. The claim was compromised, to be sure, but compromised in a way that accorded with Blake's understanding of the way religion worked. Whether this understanding was partially prompted by the representation of religion in the *Gita* we cannot know, but at the very least Hastings's preface and Wilkins's translation validated the view of faith that Blake had begun to form around 1788. Both Hastings and Wilkins urged the view that the theological truth of the *Bhagavad Gita* was separable from the superstition, ceremony, and mystery that accompanied it.

The only *Bhagavad Gita* available to Blake begins with a letter from Warren Hastings to Nathaniel Smith, the London director of the East India Company and a strong supporter of William Pitt. The letter was written from Benaris and dated 4 October 1784, after Pitt's India Bill had gone into effect. Thus, Governor-General Hastings writes as someone in a position of reduced authority who now has to factor home politics into the commercial operations of the Company in India. The letter is basically an appeal for greater patronage, though not for Hastings himself or even for the Company at large, but for Wilkins and others who might follow Wilkins's example. Hastings first urges Smith to peruse Wilkins's manuscript of the *Bhagavad Gita* and requests that he "present it to the Court of Directors, for publication by their authority," provided Smith "shall judge it worthy of so honorable a patronage" (*BG*

13). Hastings then makes a remarkable appeal for the founding of special projects in Indic literature solely on the basis of their cultural value, since no hope of commercial reward is possible. The publication of Wilkins's translation, he says:

> [M]ay . . . clear the way to a wide and unexplored field of fruitful knowledge; and suggest, to the generosity of his honorable employers, a desire to encourage the first persevering adventurer in a service in which his example will have few followers, and most probably none, if it is to be performed with the gratuitous labor of years lost to the provision of future subsistence: for the study of Sănskrēēt cannot, like the Persian language, be applied to official profit, and improved with the official exercise of it. It can only derive its reward, beyond the breath of fame, in a fixed endowment. (*BG* 13–14)

A cynical reading would have the embattled Hastings using "Mr. Wilkins's performance" (*BG* 13) merely to shore up his own weakened position in the new world of home politics in which the Company found itself for the first time. To some extent this must be the case. At the same time, however, there is no mistaking Hastings's earnest support of projects such as Wilkins's and his own evident interest in Indian literature. Such interest is manifest in the informed exposition Hastings gives Smith of the background of the *Gita*—its probable date of composition, its putative author, its relation to the rest of the *Mahabaratha,* and so on[11]—as well as in his summary of the antecedent action of the epic:

> The Mănābhārăt contains the genealogy and general history of the house of Bhaurut, so called from Bhurrut its founder; the epithet Mahă, or Great, being prefixed by token of distinction: but its more particular object is to relate the dissentions and wars of the two great collateral branches of it, called Kooroos and Pandoos; both lineally descended in the second degree from Veĕcheĕtrăveĕrya, their common ancestor, by their respective fathers Dreetrarashtra and Pandoo. (*BG* 6)

Hastings's letter, in short, gives us no reason to believe that his interest in the *Gita* was anything other than genuine, notwithstanding the possibility that promotion of the poem might also have been politically advantageous to Hastings himself.

Hastings made clear to Smith that the *Bhagavad Gita* was an important product of Indian tradition and promoted the poem on its own merits, but he also made the curious argument that the Hindu theology of the poem was consistent with Christianity. Once allowances are made for "obscurity, absurdity, barbarous habits, and a perverted morality," Hastings says, the reader will find little "which will shock either our religious faith or moral sentiments" (*BG* 7). This rather compromised assessment becomes less so as the letter proceeds, until finally the Hinduism of the *Gita* is pronounced "a single exception, among all the known religions of mankind, of a theology accurately corresponding with the Christian dispensation, and most powerfully illustrating its fundamental doctrines" (*BG* 10). How Blake would have reacted to this assertion is difficult to say, since the poet's eccentric brand of Christianity hardly comprised dispensations and doctrines. Yet there are parts of Hastings's account of the *Gita* that relate in general terms to theological elements in Blake's evolving mythology.

On the same page where Hastings claims the correspondence of the *Gita* with Christian doctrine, he points out "[o]ne blemish" that will surely be noticed by "every correct mind": "I mean, the attempt to describe spiritual existences by terms and images which appertain to corporeal forms" (*BG* 10). This so-called blemish is one that Blake sought to emulate in his own work, as when in *The Marriage of Heaven and Hell* he represents through the sea-serpent Leviathan one effect of religious orthodoxy. The fearsome Leviathan advances on the poet "with all the fury of a spiritual existence" until the creature is revealed to be nothing more than one of those "reptiles of the mind" that results from "[t]he man who never alters his opinion" (*MHH* 19.*Prose*). A verbal echo of Hastings's phrase "spiritual existences" in Blake's description of Leviathan's fury is possible, but the larger point is that Hastings has singled out an aspect of the *Gita* that is fully consistent with Blake's poetic practice of avoiding abstract terms in favor of concrete images. Hastings, on the other hand, construes the capacity for abstraction as a more sophisticated way of dealing with "a doctrine so elevated above common perception" as Hindu theology. He supposes that "corporeal forms" are a necessary first step to lead the mind "by a gradual advance to the pure and abstract comprehension of the subject" (*BG* 10). Hastings's attitude is certainly of a piece with Blake's statement in *The Song of Los* that has a British "Rintrah" conveying "Abstract Philosophy to Brama in the East" (*SL* 3.11). As for "Brama" himself, Hastings credits the author of the *Gita,* said to be "Krĕĕshnă Dwypayen Veiâs, a learned Bramin" (*BG* 5), with "the invention of the religion itself" since he "reduced the gross and scattered tenets of [the] faith into a scientific and allegorical system" (*BG* 5–6). Blake might have rankled at the word *scientific,* but not at the notion of an ancient figure creating a faith by means of an "allegorical system," mainly because he understood "Allegory addressed to the Intellectual powers" as "the Most Sublime Poetry" (*E* 730).

Hastings's letter to Nathaniel Smith is followed by a second letter from Wilkins to Hastings that briefly expresses the gratitude of "a pupil to his preceptor and patron" (*BG* 20). A "Translator's Preface" follows, in which Wilkins first credits Hastings with creating the conditions that made the learned Brahmans of Bengal comfortable and trusting enough to assist in the translation of their sacred literature. Next, Wilkins explains the theological purpose of the *Bhagavad Gita* as he understands it, that is, as an assertion of "the unity of the Godhead, in opposition to [the] idolatrous sacrifices . . . inculcated by the *Vēds*" (*BG* 24). Here Wilkins, like William Jones after him, dissociates the pure faith of Hinduism from the vulgar practice of rituals and ceremonies. The description of religion that Wilkins offers accords with Blake's understanding of the way priests choose "forms of worship from poetic tales" and use ritual and mystery to "enslav[e] the vulgar" (*MHH* 11.*Prose*). In Blakean terms, Krishna as described by Wilkins is not unlike those "ancient Poets" (*MHH* 11.*Prose*) who provide the original, energetic vision of the world that is subsequently systematized into religion for the purpose of priestly gain:

> The most learned *Brahmăns* of the present times are Unitarians according to the doctrines of *Krĕĕshnă*; but, at the same time that they believe but in one God, an universal spirit, they so far comply with the prejudices of the vulgar, as outwardly to perform all the ceremonies inculcated by the *Vēds,* such as sacrifices, ablutions, &c. They do this, probably, more for the support of their own consequence, which could only arise from the great ignorance of the people, than in compliance with the dictates of *Krĕĕshnă:* indeed, this ignorance, and these ceremonies, are as much the bread of the *Brahmăns,* as the superstition of the vulgar is the support of the priesthood in many other countries. (*BG* 24)

The connections that Wilkins draws between the priesthood and the vulgar are conceptually identical to those that Blake describes in *The Marriage of Heaven and Hell:* only minor differences of phrasing separate Wilkins's claim that the vulgar support the priests from Blake's assertion that the priests enslave the vulgar. As for Wilkins's understanding of the Brahmins as Unitarians, a kind of corollary belief emerges out of Blake's poetry, for his myth does construe the fall as a collapse of unity into multiplicity. Moreover, since it is not man but God who falls, Blake's myth repeats, in a way, the theological problem Wilkins ascribes to the author of the *Gita*—that of recovering divine unity from polytheistic proliferation.[12]

The nod to Unitarian Dissenters in his preface notwithstanding, in the text of Wilkins's translation there is much that seems incompatible with Blake's thought, and some account needs to be given of the ways in which the *Bhagavad Gita* and Blake diverge. This sense of divergence is especially evident on the topic of pleasure and passion. The *Gita* repeatedly cautions against the pleasures of the senses, as when Krishna counsels Arjuna to restrain desire: "A man is said to be confirmed in wisdom when he foresaketh every desire which entereth into his heart, and of himself is happy, and contented in himself" (*BG* 41). In *The Marriage of Heaven and Hell*, Blake claims that "[t]hose who restrain desire, do so because theirs is weak enough to be restrained" (*MHH* 5.*Prose*). The aphorism encourages the liberation of desire and suggests that its limits be tested, as in one of the better-known of the "Proverbs of Hell": "You never know what is enough unless you know what is more than enough" (*MHH* 9.46). The *Gita* in Wilkins's translation sets up an interrelationship between pleasure and wisdom, as Blake does in the *Marriage* ("The road of excess leads to the palace of wisdom" [*MHH* 7.3]), but it propounds the un-Blakean position that wisdom is perfected only when passion is subjugated: "The tumultuous senses hurry away, by force, the heart even of the wise man who striveth to restrain them" (*BG* 42). Wilkins's translation puts reason in the position of governing the senses and makes such government a condition of enjoyment:

> The man who attendeth to the inclinations of the senses, in them hath a concern; from this concern is created passion, from passion anger, from anger is produced folly, from folly a deprivation of memory, from the loss of memory the loss of reason, and from the loss of reason the loss of all! A man of a governable mind, enjoying the objects of his senses, with all his faculties rendered obedient to his will, and freed from pride and malice, obtaineth happiness supreme. (*BG* 42)

The relation of reason and the senses here is presented in language that mixes biblical diction with rationalistic philosophy, but the dynamic itself—reversed in favor of desire—turns up in *The Marriage of Heaven and Hell*: "Those who restrain desire, do so because theirs is weak enough to be restrained; and the restrainer or reasons usurps its place & governs the unwilling. And being restrained it by degrees becomes passive till it is only the shadow of desire" (*MHH* 5.*Prose*). Blake celebrates the senses rather than reason in this contest of contraries, but the terms he uses are not dissimilar to those in the *Gita*. Wilkins offers a step-by-step analysis of the loss of reason to the senses; Blake explains what happens when desire is "restrained . . . by degrees." Wilkins presents pleasure as the product of "a governable mind" and a will obedient to reason; Blake puts will on the side of desire as the contrary of the reason that "governs the unwilling." Blake's language is so close to Wilkins's but, at the same time, so contrary to Wilkins's meaning that it may very well be a deliberate, diabolical gloss on the translation. Even though Krishna says, at one point, "I am the prolific *Kăndărp* the God of love" (*BG* 86), the sense that Blake and the *Bhagavad Gita* make different if not wholly divergent assertions on the value of desire is inescapable.

The basic problem posed by Wilkins's translation as far as its probable effect on Blake is concerned is the incompatibility between Krishna's repeated admonitions to devotion and sacrifice and Blake's antinomian inclinations to run in the opposite direction of obedience to anything other than his own imagination. A poet who was opposed to moral codes on principle would hardly accept the morality of the *Bhagavad Gita*. Blake counters moral injunctions of all kinds wherever they appear, whether in the Bible or the *Bhagavad Gita* or in Bishop Watson's writings. But the *Bhagavad Gita* as Wilkins presents it contains many passages that undercut the presumed value of morality, and it differs from the Bible or Bishop Watson in that it often understands morality as a dynamic system rather than a static code. In the *Gita*, morality emerges from a set of complex relationships that is really self-perpetuating but ultimately meaningless. The grades of goodness or levels of morality described in chapter 14 of Wilkins's translation are called "three *Gŏŏn* or qualities arising from *Prăkrĕĕtĕĕ* or nature," namely, "*Sătwă* truth, *Răjă* passion, and *Tămă* darkness" (107).[13] These three qualities condition one another in various ways: "The *Sătwă-Gŏŏn* prevaileth in felicity, the *Răjă* in action, and the *Tămă*, having possessed the soul, prevaileth in intoxication. When the *Tămă* and the *Răjă* have been overcome, then the *Sătwă* appeareth; when the *Răjă* and the *Sătwă*, the *Tămă*; and when the *Tămă* and the *Sătwă*, the *Răjă*" (*BG* 108).

The way a single *guna* emerges as a dominant quality after the other two have been overcome suggests the basic synthesis described in *The Marriage of Heaven and Hell*: "Without Contraries is no progression" (*MHH* 3.*Prose*). The three *gunas* of the *Gita* also suggest Blake's classification of men into the Elect, the Redeemed, and the Reprobate:

> . . . under pretence to benevolence the Elect Subdud All
> From the Foundation of the World. The Elect is one Class . . .
> . . . they cannot Believe in Eternal Life
> Except by Miracle & a New Birth. The other two Classes;
> The Reprobate who never cease to Believe, and the Redeemd,
> Who live in doubts & fears perpetually tormented by the
>   Elect

(*M* 25.31–36)

Blake's language makes clear that the three classes relate to one another in theological terms, in accordance with the way *belief* is defined.[14] At first glance the only possible analogy of Wilkins's *gunas* with Blake's classification of humankind into Elect, Reprobate, and Redeemed appears to be the shared passion of the Reprobates and *Răjă*. If one reads further in Wilkins, however, "the *Sătwă-Gŏŏn*," a "pure and holy" quality associated with "those immaculate beings who are acquainted with the most high" (*BG* 109, 108), start to look more like Blake's Elect. Likewise, the passionate quality of the *Răjă-Gŏŏn* is called "inordinate desire," a quality also of Blake's Reprobate devils. And those ironically named "the Redeemd" seem to participate in the *Tămă-Gŏŏn* because their innocence and goodness are not unlike the "ignorance" and "idleness" (*BG* 108–9) described in the *Bhagavad Gita.* Making Blake's categories match up with the *gunas* of the *Gita* is less important, however, than the general idea that such categories are common to all mankind because they are forced upon humanity by the existence of morality. The values that Blake and the author of the *Gita* attach to the categories differ, but they both speak in a language informed by moral law.

The moral law that runs through the *Gita* is far from uniform, and, in fact, the Hindu text promotes certain theological points that Blake would have found compatible with his own antinomian orientation. Krishna tells Arjuna that "[a] man's own religion, though contrary to, is better than the faith of another, let it be ever so well followed" (*BG* 48). The reference may be to religious systems that are inherited rather than created, but Blake could have understood Krishna's observation as a validation of his own theological independence from the established church, especially in light of the further observation that "the wise man . . . seeketh for that which is homogeneous to his own nature" (*BG* 48). Blake's antinomian nature would have been alternately outraged and gratified by the last chapter of Wilkins's *Gita.* At the outset of this chapter, Krishna reminds Arjuna that the religious truths he is recounting have their origins in some remote poetic past, for he is merely passing on something that "[t]he bards conceive." What the bards are said to have conceived, however, are "deeds of worship," including "[s]acrifices, charity, and mortifications" that make up "the purifiers of the philosopher" (*BG* 124). Blake would almost certainly have read this passage as yet another demonstration of the way priestcraft operates: by perverting the original bardic pronouncements of the Poetic Genius into worship. Wilkins, in fact, provides a note to the passage containing the learned commentary of "one Srēē-dhăr Swāmĕĕ" to show that "the commentators of India are not less fond of searching for mystery, and wandering from the simple path of their author into a labyrinth of scholastic jargon, than some of those of more enlightened nations" (*BG* 154n. 114). What Wilkins does not see, however, is that—from a Blakean perspective—the *Bhagavad Gita* has already wandered into the labyrinth of mystery by requiring regulated worship of a deity in place of poetic understanding of humanity. Given his sense of the way religion operated, Blake could have picked his way through the *Bhagavad Gita* as he did every other religious text (including the Bible), choosing poetic tales from forms of worship. Thus, the *Gita* is of value to the student of Blake because we can be sure that he would have read it not merely as the medium of poetic truths that harmonized with the positive points of his own system, but as a repository of mystery and ritual to be overcome through energy and imagination.

The final chapter—or "lecture"—of the *Gita* is titled, "Of the Forsaking the Fruits of Action for Obtaining Eternal Salvation" (*BG* 124). The language that Wilkins uses here is heavily freighted with Christian meaning, and the idea that action is unrelated to salvation is perfectly in tune with Blake's antinomianism; in fact, it harmonizes with antinomian theology in general. As E. P. Thompson has pointed out, the theological distinction between salvation by works and salvation by faith bore a great deal of ideological weight in Blake's time:

> [F]or much of the eighteenth century, the doctrine of justification by faith was—and was seen to be—[a] "dangerous" heresy. All this was because it could . . . challenge very radically the authority of the ruling ideology and the cultural hegemony of Church, Schools, Law and even of "common-sense" Morality. In its essence it was exactly that: *anti*-hegemonic. It displaced the authority of institutions and of received worldly wisdom with that of the individual's inner light—faith, conscience, personal understanding of the scriptures or (for Blake) "the Poetic Genius"—and allowed to the individual a stubborn skepticism in the face of the established culture, a fortitude in the face of its seductions or persecutions.[15]

One of Blake's most consistent beliefs throughout his career is that conscience, not law, is the basis for morality: "If Conscience is not a Criterion of Moral Rectitude What is it?" (*E* 613). It follows that "The Gospel is Forgiveness of Sin & has No Moral Precepts" (*E* 619), and, further, that man is not saved by good works any more than he can be condemned by sinful actions.

If Blake read the final section of the *Bhagavad Gita* with an antinomian eye he would have found a lot to like, because Krishna stresses the ultimate irrelevance of the fruits of human action: "Works affect not me, nor have I any expectations from the fruits of works. He who believeth me to be even so, is not bound by works" (*BG* 52). If the Gospel was, for Blake, the forgiveness of sin, he would have found that Gospel in abundance in the *Bhagavad Gita:* "Although thou wert the greatest of offenders, thou shalt be able to cross the gulf of sin with the bark of wisdom. As the natural fire, O *Ărjŏŏn,* reduceth the wood to ashes, so may the fire of wisdom reduce all moral actions to ashes" (*BG* 55). Elsewhere Krishna encourages Arjuna to become like "some learned *Yōgēē*" who is "superior to those who are attached to moral works" (*BG* 67–68). Obviously, the Hindu meaning of "a perfection unconnected with works" (*BG* 131) is not precisely the same as a dissenting Christian's sense of salvation unrelated to works, but it is easy to see how Blake might have layered his own antinomian meaning over Wilkins's words in the *Gita.* This possibility is enhanced by the words that Wilkins actually uses, for he clearly draws on the theological vocabulary of his times. This point becomes obvious when Wilkins's translation is compared to the *Bhagavad Gita* as it is understood in English today. For example, where Wilkins writes "[a] man's own religion, though contrary to, is better than the faith of another, let it be ever so well followed" (*BG* 48), a modern translation reads: "Better one's own duty, though imperfect, than the duty of another well performed."[16] Surely it makes a difference to replace those loaded words *religion* and *faith* with the less-charged term *duty* as a translation of the Sanskrit noun *svadharmas* (a word that refers to a sense of obligation to one's own caste), not to mention the substitution of *imperfect* for the Blakean phrase *contrary to.*

Wilkins's translation is also remarkable for those passages that resemble broad, conceptual features of Blake's myth, which are not cognate with Christian theology. For example, when Arjuna asks Krishna for an explanation of Karma, not only the concept but the language itself suggests components of Blake's myth, in which the world of natural generation is said to be the product of the emanation Vala: "*Kărmă* is that emanation from which proceedeth the generation of natural beings" (73). The Sanskrit word *karma* means both "fate" and "works," and implies that one creates one's own fate through individual actions undertaken on earth. One of the clearest features of Blake's myth is the passage from Eternity to Generation, together with the sense that the sojourn in this vegetable world is temporary: "The Souls descending to the Body, wail on the right hand / Of Los; & those deliverd from the Body, on the left hand" (*M* 26.16–17). In book 16 of the *Gita* souls are said to be "doomed . . . from birth to birth" because of "lust, anger, and avarice" (*BG* 117–18), while "meer passion & appetite" (*M* 26.29) cause or at least contribute to a soul's rebirth in Blake. On this point the poet's theology and mythology seem to diverge. When he writes of "Souls descending to the Body" and subsequently being delivered from it, the language he uses betrays a belief in pre-existence.

This theological nuance of Blake's system derives from the Platonized Christianity of his day, and there is no reason to invoke the Hindu concept of reincarnation as a source for the idea; his letters, for instance, provide no evidence that Blake believed in reincarnation as a theological principle applicable to human reality. Blake's mythology, however, does employ the concept of reincarnation, as the successive forms of Orc in *The Book of Urizen* and *The Four Zoas* show: "Many forms of fish, bird & beast / Brought forth an Infant form / Where was a worm before" (*U* 19.34–36). In the seventh "Night" of *The Four Zoas* the energetic spirit of Orc seems fairly clearly to be incarnated in the form of Napoléon, when "The dragons of the North put on their armour" and vow to "Stop . . . the rising of the glorious King" (*FZ* 7.91.27, 30). The only evidence outside the poetry for Blake's evident interest in reincarnation is a "curious hypothesis" about Napoléon recorded by Blake's nineteenth-century biographer Alexander Gilchrist in a paragraph about the poet's "daring heterodoxy on religious topics." According to Gilchrist, Blake is supposed to have claimed that "the Bonaparte of Italy was killed, and that another was somehow substituted from the evident want of the name, who was the Bonaparte of the Empire!"[17] The anecdote is so odd as to be believable, and if it is true that Blake made the strange remark Gilchrist attributes to him, then the substitution of one Bonaparte for another might very well represent a bizarre Blakean attempt to explain reincarnation to some baffled auditor.

Blake may also have considered the possibility of reincarnation in animal form, but in a metaphorical, not a literal sense. Kathleen Raine has made the observation that Blake probably did not actually believe "that degenerate souls pass into the bodies of animals," but that he may echo the "Hindu teaching of metempsychosis in the suggestion that men may become animal incarnations in a symbolical sense."[18] Passages from *The Four Zoas* can be used to support this interpretation:

> Troop by troop the beastial droves rend one another sounding
>   loud
> The instruments of sound & troop by troop in human forms
>   they urge
> The dire confusion till the battle faints those that remain

> Return in pangs & horrible convulsions to their beastial
>   state
> For the monsters of the Elements Lions or Tygers or Wolves
>
> (*FZ* 8.101.47–48;102.1–3)

Raine says that these lines "may possibly echo a passage in the Gita," but unfortunately cites a 1935 translation in evidence. The relevant passage from Wilkins's translation has Krishna condemning "ignorant men . . . entangled in the net of folly" who "place all their trust in pride, power, ostentation, lust, and anger": "wherefore I cast down upon the earth those furious abject wretches, those evil beings who thus despise me, into the wombs of evil spirits and unclean beasts" (*BG* 117). Rebirth through the womb of an unclean beast is not unlike the "pangs and horrible convulsions" that Blake evokes to mark the metaphorical return to a "beastial state." The argument for metaphorical metempsychosis in *The Four Zoas* becomes stronger with the observation that "Animal forms of wisdom" (*FZ* 9.138.31) replace the furious beasts of prey when peace and regeneration descend at the close of the poem. In this connection the ending of *Jerusalem* is also noteworthy, as "Lion, Tyger, Horse, Elephant, Eagle Dove, Fly, Worm, / . . . Humanize / In the Forgiveness of Sins" (*J* 98.43–45). The fact that two creatures in this list are closely identified with India may be further reason for supposing that Blake put the Hindu notion of reincarnation to his own poetic purpose.

In short, the poetic application of a theological concept as alien to Christianity as reincarnation is a detail of Blake's myth that is likely derived from the *Bhagavad Gita*. Additional details of a similar non-Christian order include the notion of something "incorruptible and infinite in all things finite" (*BG* 127), which compares with Blake's conception of the "infinite / Shut up in finite revolutions" (*EP* 10.21–22). Blake's sense of cyclical rather than linear time may also have its source in Wilkins's *Gita,* which speaks of "all things . . . mounted upon the universal wheel of time" (*BG* 133). In more general terms, the four Zoas themselves do not seem so different from what the *Gita* describes as "various and manifold principles prevailing in the natural world of created beings" (*BG* 127). There is also something oddly Blakean about Krishna's description of his own "creative spirit": "I plant myself on my own nature, and create, again and again, this assemblage of beings" (*BG* 127).

Blake's ability to produce his mythic assemblage of beings out of the Poetic Genius does have something in common with Krishna's power to create out of his own nature. The conditions under which Blake's myth and Krishna's creation occur are also similar in that Blake and the *Bhagavad Gita* both present an intense theological drama in the context of a great war. In the *Gita* of Wilkins, the drama consists almost exclusively of Krishna's explanations of the value of "forsaking the fruits of action for obtaining eternal salvation" (*BG* 124). The theology imparted to Arjuna allows him to overcome his reluctance to enter the great battle between the sons of Pāndu and the sons of Kuru because he finally understands how unreal and insignificant individual action is in relation to the great round of existence that cycles through eternity.

In *The Four Zoas*, the collapse that occurs in Eternity parallels the chaos caused by the French Revolution and the Napoleonic campaigns, and it is easy to see how Blake would have been as distraught over the endless hostilities between the British and the French as Arjuna was over the ongoing hatred between the house of Kuru and the house of Pāndu. The war that furnishes the backdrop of the *Bhagavad Gita* is really a civil war, a war between brothers, but so, in a way, is any war, at least from the perspective of Blake's sublime Eternals: "Man liveth not by Self alone but in his brothers face" (*FZ* 9.133.25). At the end of *The Four Zoas*, it can hardly be said that Blake is reconciled to war so fully as Arjuna is at the close of the *Gita;* but, on the other hand, the way that Blake simply wishes away "The war of swords" and imagines the guardian Zoa Urthona girded "For intellectual War" instead (*FZ* 139.9) is nothing short of remarkable. As does the *Gita*, Blake offers a theological resolution to the problem of war. A faith informed by antinomianism requires rebellion against the moral law, but it also insists on forgiveness, and that is the simple triumph that appears at the end of *The Four Zoas:* all enemies are overcome through the power of forgiveness. For someone as ardently revolutionary as Blake had been earlier (when he composed *America*, for instance) the pacifist attitude toward the war of swords expressed at the end of *The Four Zoas* marks a great change indeed. In this respect Blake also follows his bardic mentor John Milton, whose *Paradise Lost* can likewise be read as a theological drama in the context of a great war that finds its resolution in resignation. The war in heaven as Milton describes it has something in common with the English Civil War,[19] but—whether celestial or civil—all sense of struggle is overcome at the close of the poem: Adam and Eve are at peace as they walk out of Paradise toward an uncertain but deeply human future, resigned to a fate informed by faith. The example of Milton is reason to suppose that Blake would have seen a similar pattern in the *Bhagavad Gita* and then imagined his own version of eternal events to match the Eastern and Western models.

What I mean to suggest by this last comparison of Blake and Milton is that whatever influence the *Bhagavad Gita* may have exercised on Blake's creative mythography occurred in the context of both familiar traditions and contemporary events. The end of *Paradise Lost* made the quiescent acceptance of human limitations known to Blake well before Wilkins rendered the story of Arjuna's resignation into English prose, but the Napoleonic wars would have given such resignation particular resonance for the disillusioned republican poet looking to find a way to close the *Zoas*. Likewise, Blake did not need Charles Wilkins to point out the irrelevance of human action because he already understood that salvation was obtained by faith, not works. Nor did he require William Jones to explain the theological value of Intellect. But the poet could well have found some valuable instruction in the way that Wilkins and Jones communicated familiar theological concepts through the medium of an entirely new and politically charged system of mythology. The language that Wilkins used in his translation of the *Bhagavad Gita* turned Arjuna into a kind of antinomian hero, forsaking the fruits of action. Likewise, William Jones drew on an established Neoplatonic tradition in his exposition of Hinduism that made it appear that the Brahmins had been waging "Intellectual War" centuries before Blake dressed the Zoa Urthona out for similar metaphysical combat. The fact that contemporary English writers employed both antinomian and Neoplatonic theology in their expositions of Hinduism could only have made the Indian system all the more compelling for Blake. But the Hindu theology imparted to Great Britain by the likes of Wilkins and Jones was not conveyed solely in the form of theological treatises. The *Bhagavad Gita* is an epic narrative, and "The Hymn to Narayena" is a mythographic poem. Theology took mythic form in the British representations of Hinduism well before Blake presented Dissenting theology in the mythic form of his own elaborate imaginings.

II

The argument that Blake's attraction to Hindu myth occurred because of some sense of shared belief becomes more compelling when we realize that the British understanding of Hindu theology includes a pronounced Neoplatonic strain that runs through Blake as well. As we shall see, the antinomian points of Wilkins's *Gita* have a kind of theological complement in William Jones's Neoplatonic explanations of the Hindu system. The revival of Neoplatonism in Blake's age means that he received an introduction to the philosophy a few years before Jones began to explain Hindu theology to the West in Neoplatonic terms. As early as Augustine, Neoplatonic philosophy had been adapted to Christianity to explain, in part, the relationship between the ideal or divine realm and the material or earthly sphere. The Christian variant of classical Neoplatonism puts Christ in the position of *nous* or Intellect as the means of mediation between matter and spirit, body and soul.[20] It is easy to see how this tradition might be reconciled to Dissenting theology, with its all-important emphasis on the believer's ability to communicate directly with divinity, without the aid of church or priest. Thus, Blake's exposure to Neoplatonism could well have prepared the ground for a sympathetic understanding of the Hindu system because that system was couched in terms already familiar to him. For this reason it should be useful to know what those terms were and to understand the context in which they appeared to him just prior to their appearance in the work of Jones.

Blake got his Neoplatonism mainly by way of Thomas Taylor, an important translator of Plato in the England of Blake's time. In the 1780s Blake made the acquaintance of Taylor, who, like Blake, was the son of a dissenting tradesman using his literary talents to work his way into the fringes of genteel society. Unlike Blake, Taylor developed a stronger allegiance to that society than to his radical background, so that by the early 1790s he was using his hard-earned erudition to mock the revolutionary rhetoric of Paine and Wollstonecraft that Blake responded to with such sympathy.[21] Some have taken Taylor's reactionary politics (he authored a satire of Wollstonecraft titled *A Vindication of the Rights of Brutes*) as proof against the possibility that Blake might have picked up some Neoplatonic notions from Taylor, who is said to "stand . . . at an opposite pole to Blake" so that he "touches at no point on Blake's central stance" (Thompson, 49). The problem, I think, is rooted in the conflict between the antinomian tendency to merge the human and the divine and the Platonic impetus to locate those categories in separate material and ideal realms. Neoplatonism, however, differs from Platonism on precisely this point: that it allows a route for the human to reach the divine. Blake's acquaintance with Taylor, therefore, may be more important to the development of the poet than Thompson, for one, allows. When Blake says "put off Holiness And put on Intellect" (*J* 91.55–56) he counters the moral law with the Neoplatonic means of reaching the divinity within that is the Everlasting Gospel of antinomian theology. Blake, in other words, set antinomianism and Neoplatonism in a reciprocal theological relationship and made them reinforce one another.

The agency that allows the merely mortal human being to apprehend his divine essence is known as *nous* in Greek texts by Plotinus and

other classical authors now called "Neoplatonic." Among English Neoplatonists *nous* translates as "intellect," which becomes the medium
whereby soul and body are unified, a point that Taylor makes in his
introduction to *The Hymns of Orpheus* (1787): "intellect is the first
recipient of a divine nature; and soul is divine, so far as it requires an
intellectual medium. But the body which participates a soul of this kind
is divine, in as great a degree as the nature of body will admit."[22] In
Blake, this kind of nuanced philosophical thinking becomes more of a
theological assertion: "Man has no Body distinct from his Soul for that
calld Body is a portion of Soul discerned by the five Senses, the chief
inlets of Soul in this age" (*MHH* 4.*Prose*). There is ample evidence to
support the claim that Blake valued intellect as the means of mediating
the separation of soul and body and of reconciling both into the composite entity he called "the human form divine" (*SI* 18.11). In *Jerusalem*,
God is called "the intellectual fountain of Humanity" (*J* 91.10). In *Milton*, the character Ololon descends from Eden or Eternity "to Felphams
Vale . . . with dreadful thunderings / Into the Fires of Intellect" (*M*
42.7–9), that is, into the mind of Blake. In the description of his painting of *The Last Judgment*, Blake explains that Jesus is pictured in
"Beams of Glory in which are . . . Infants emanating from him" because
"these represent the Eternal Births of Intellect from the divine Humanity" (*E* 562). Blake understood his own art to be one of those "Intellectual Gifts" that descend from "the Holy Ghost" (*E* 554), so that when
he describes his own creative process as a condition of being "drunk
with intellectual vision" (*E* 757) he means that his visions of Eternity are
made possible by intellect. Thus, the Neoplatonic notion of intellect as
the mechanism of mediation between Eternity and generation was of
considerable use to Blake, not only as an explanation of his own visionary mythology, but also as material for the myth itself.

Theologically, Blake's Neoplatonism meshes with Dissent because
it provides an intellectual basis for ideological removal from the temporal regimes of Church and King. Blake says as much when he censures
Holiness and attributes political ambition to absence of Intellect: "The
Fool shall not enter into Heaven let him be ever so Holy. Holiness is not
The Price of Enterance into Heaven Those who are cast out Are All
Those who having no Passions of their own because No Intellect. Have
spent their lives in Curbing & Governing other Peoples" (*E* 564). Neoplatonism can be reconciled with antinomianism because the philosophy
provides one more justification for the believer's removal from any
obligation to the moral law. Indeed, it provides more than a justification—it provides a mechanism, for Intellect can be used to measure
morality and record its errors. Conflicts and inconsistencies are plentiful

in Blake's system, but the relationship of Neoplatonic theology and Protestant Dissent is not among them. Intellect is also useful to the man who wants to gauge the worth of those who spend their lives "Governing other Peoples," so Neoplatonism contains a political component that complements republicanism along with antinomianism. Neoplatonism so configured may be curious and eccentric, but it would have equipped Blake in an oddly appropriate way to understand Hinduism in England at the end of the eighteenth century.

Accounts of Hinduism by Jones and others that pointed out the analogies between Brahminism and Platonism appeared in London at a decisive moment in Blake's poetic development. These accounts confirmed the Platonized explanations of Hinduism that had appeared as early as 1768, with Alexander Dow's *History of Hindostan*:

> God seeing the earth in full bloom called forth *intellect*, which he endued with various organs and shapes, to form a diversity of animals upon the earth. Intellect is a portion of the great *soul of the universe*, breathed into all creatures, to animate them for a certain time. After death it animates other bodies, or returns like a drop into that unbounded ocean from which it first rose. . . .[23]

In this example, the Neoplatonic notion of intellect is employed to explain the Hindu concept of reincarnation. The Neoplatonic tradition was so much a part of the eighteenth-century understanding of Hinduism that at least one theologian tried to play Brahma and Plato off against one another in an effort to show the hazards of their shared idealism.

In a study of *The Influence of Philosophy on Christianity* (a treatise appended to *Disquisitions Relating to Matter and Spirit* [1777]), Joseph Priestley regards Hinduism and other heathen systems as the source of certain doctrines that have corrupted Christianity in various ways. He is chiefly concerned to show that Christian criticism of materialism has its origins in paganism, and is therefore suspect. The argument from design that Priestley promotes makes the materiality of matter crucial to the proof of the mechanical perfection of a universe set into motion by the First Cause; the argument also guarantees the predictability of natural phenomena and ensures the reliability of the experimental method. Thus, Priestley had both a theological and an empirical stake in debunking the tradition of philosophical idealism in favor of his own system of scientific materialism. According to Priestley, the belief that matter is ultimately insubstantial and also evil is the mistaken heritage of Greek and Indian philosophy:

> That the leaven of this Oriental philosophy was mixed with christian-
> ity, in a very early period, even in the times of the apostles, all antiq-
> uity, and even their own writings, sufficiently testify; and it is far from
> being wholly purged out even at this day. But whether the first intro-
> duction of it was directly from the East, or by the medium of the Greek
> philosophy, is not quite clear. (*Disquisitions*, 277)

Examples of the "Oriental philosophy" Priestley has collected are interesting because they show that Neoplatonic ideas had permeated the
European understanding of Hinduism well before the work of William
Jones. For Priestley the authority of Dow—soon to be surpassed by that
of Jones—was sufficient to his purpose of showing the *theological* superiority of materialist philosophy. He used what Dow said about Hindostan to argue that Brahminism was idealism, and that it had contributed to a larger tradition of idealist philosophy that was merely a
pagan corruption of Christianity. Blake, by contrast, understood materialist philosophy, such as Deism, as a rationalistic reduction of the
Christian vision that was animated by intellect. Clearly, the Neoplatonic
context for Hinduism provided by sympathetic Indologists like Jones
could only have made Brahma attractive to Blake as a theological para-
digm for mythic proliferation.

When Sir William Jones introduced English readers to the similarities in the myths of many nations in his essay "On the Gods of
Greece, Italy, and India," he did so within an established Platonic tradition that reached back to antiquity. Likewise, in his essay "On the
Mystical Poetry of the Persians and the Hindus," he explained the theology at work in the Eastern tradition by pointing out that the tradition
was also represented in the classical West: "'PLATO travelled into *Italy*
and *Egypt*,' says CLAUDE FLEURY [1640–1725], 'to learn the Theology
of the Pagans at its fountain head': its true fountain, however, was neither in *Italy* or in *Egypt* . . . but in *Persia* and *India*."[24] If the Brahmins
were "Platonists," so much the better for Blake, because his dissenting
brand of Neoplatonism would have allowed him to see the theological
relevance of the Hindu system to his own evolving mythology. In this
respect, Blake was in the right place at the right time to see something
that many of his contemporaries could not. In *India and the Romantic
Imagination,* John Drew remarks that, "contemporaneously with
Jones, Thomas Taylor could labor to make the Neoplatonists known to
the English in their own language with as little reference to India as
Jones made to Plotinus and Porphyry in his exposition of the
Vedanta."[25] A couple of generations later the belief that Neoplatonism
and Hinduism were interrelated was commonplace. In 1836, an obitu-

ary of Thomas Taylor supplemented the philosopher's observations on the origins of Neoplatonism in Alexandria by claiming that "the disciples of Brahma . . . mingled in the throng . . . of nations, religions, and sects" in the ancient Egyptian city.[26] Blake, for one, was in a position to see the connection between the Neoplatonism of Taylor and the Platonized Brahminism of Jones well before the idea became commonplace. And given the purposes to which Blake put his Plato, that some of Blake's contemporaries understood Brahminism as an Asian cognate of English Dissent makes it that much more likely that Blake did, in fact, see the connection.

William Jones's essay "On the Gods of Greece, Italy and India" from the *Asiatick Researches* is replete with references to Plato and comparisons of Hindu mythology with Greek philosophy. Blake's familiarity with this famous exercise in comparative religion, though not assured, can be fairly assumed because his friend Fuseli apparently possessed a copy of the first volume of the *Asiatick Researches* at a time when he and Blake had a close working relationship and were seeing each other on a regular basis. As we have seen in Chapter 1, Blake's basic mythographic formulation in *The Marriage of Heaven and Hell*—that religion originates with poetic explanations of nature—bears comparison with Jones's analysis of the sources of all mythology. These sources are said to include "[t]he metaphors and allegories of moralists and metaphysicians" that are "very fertile in Deities; of which a thousand examples might be adduced from PLATO" and other classical authors (Jones, 2: 322). Jones offers "the charming philosophical tale of PSYCHE, or the *Progress of the Soul*" as a classical example of a mythological allegory with a theological meaning, and follows this Neoplatonic example with an instance from Hinduism that likewise illustrates the interrelationship of mythic allegory and theology proper. The example is "the *Indian* MA'YA', or, as the word is explained by some *Hindu* scholars, 'the first inclination of the Godhead to diversify himself . . . by creating worlds,' [which] is feigned to be the mother of universal nature and of all the inferior Gods" (Jones 2: 322). The concept of Maya in its allegorical form can be compared to the fall of Albion, who does "diversify himself" into variegated generation through the agency of Vala, personified as nature herself. Such similarities make it is easy to see how a Blakean (mis)reading of Jones's essay might lend support to a poetic synthesis of Platonism, Hinduism, and Sectarianism, even though Jones quite deliberately comes up shy of forming such a synthesis himself.

Often it is difficult to tell whether Jones's reluctance to explore the full ramifications of his observations about religion is due to his own piety or to concerns about the piety of his audience, which would have

included some of his powerful patrons in England. Time and again Jones
employs his methodical comparative approach to religion in such a way
as to put the authority of Christianity into question, only to assert that
authority afresh on the basis of orthodox dogma. Near the end of his
essay "On the Gods of Greece, Italy, and India" Jones assures his readers that "the adamantine pillars of our *Christian* faith [cannot] be
moved by the results of any debates on the comparative antiquity of the
Hindus and *Egyptians,* or on any inquiries into the *Indian* Theology"
(Jones 2: 392), only to offer a succession of analogies to suggest that the
Christian faith is not unique on a number of theological points. The
Christian trinity is compared to the Indian triad of Brahma, Vishnu, and
Siva, the implicit analogy being that the creative power of Brahma has
something in common with that of the first person of the trinity, while
the preservative power of Vishnu suggests the saving agency of the second. As for Siva, the reader is left to ponder the association of that deity
with fire, a connection that prompts comparison with the tongues of
flame through which the Holy Ghost becomes manifest at Pentecost.

Jones's ambivalence about biblical authority comes through in a
remarkable passage that combines commentary about the Christian, Platonic, and Hindu triads with some liberal allowance for the possibility
of Dissent:

> [T]he *Indian* Triad, and that of PLATO, which he calls the Supreme
> Good, the Reason, and the Soul, are infinitely removed from the holi-
> ness and sublimity of the doctrine, which pious *Christians* have
> deduced from texts in the Gospel, though other *Christians,* as pious,
> openly profess their dissent from them. Each sect must be justified by
> its own faith and good intentions. . . . (Jones 2: 393)

Having just stated, in a roundabout way, that some pious, dissenting
Christians might find holiness and sublimity in the Platonic triad after
all, Jones then presents an extensive account of the life "of CHRISHNA"
filled with events that resemble the life of Christ: like Jesus in Bethlehem,
"the incarnate deity of the *Sanscrit* romance was cradled . . . among
Herdsmen"; just as Herod did in the case of Jesus, "a tyrant, at the time
of his birth, ordered all new-born males to be slain"; and Krishna, like
Jesus, "performed . . . miracles [and] raised the dead" (Jones 2: 393–94).
Jones's explicit purpose in pointing out these analogies is apparently to
show that, because of the evident resemblance between "our church
[and] that of the *Hindus*" (Jones 2: 393), "[t]he *Hindus* . . . would readily admit the truth of the Gospel" (Jones 2: 396). The superior antiquity
of the Hindu account, however, makes a modern reader come away

from Jones's essay with the sense that the theological authority of "our church" is not absolute; a Dissenting reader like Blake at the end of the eighteenth century would have come to a similar conclusion, especially given Blake's diabolical ability to read his beliefs into the prose of other writers quite unlike himself.

Blake's capacities as an aggressive reader, however, would not have been necessary for him to see the similarities in his own system and the one attributed to the Hindus in Jones's essay "On the Mystical Poetry of the Persians and Hindus." This essay—published in the third volume of the *Asiatick Researches* in 1792 and summarized in the *Analytical Review* in 1794—makes a number of theological points that seem remarkably close to Blake's expressed beliefs. This is the piece that opens with the proviso that the true fountain of Plato's theology can be located in Persia or India. But Jones is also at pains to show how the theology of some of his more enlightened contemporaries also seems to draw substance from that same Asian fountain, albeit indirectly, through Plato. Jones quotes copiously from the French theologian Jacques Necker, whose authoritative study of comparative religion, *Sur L'Importance des opinions religieuses* (1788), made him a celebrated figure during the Revolution.[27] Necker's Neoplatonism is evident in his admonition for men "to respect the intellectual power, with which they are adorned" (Jones 2:216). Blake's respect is evident in his belief that "Allegory addressed to the Intellectual powers" is "the Most Sublime Poetry . . . in the same manner defind by Plato" (*E* 730). Necker also says that intellect makes it possible for men to "*consider . . . themselves as an emanation from* [the] *infinite Being*" and even to hear "the Supreme Intelligence . . . give this commission to the spirits, which emaned from him: . . . *seek not to remove the veil spread over the secret of your existence: your nature is composed of those divine particles, which, at an infinite distance, constitute my own essence*" (Jones 2: 217, 219). Blake's diction is hardly as conventional as this, but the Neoplatonic conceptions described here can all be identified as components of Blake's theology: humanity as an emanation of God; eternal truth veiled from temporal apprehension; human multiplicity comprising divine unity. Blake comes close to Necker's notion that the divine particles of human existence appear unified from a great distance when he explains how "the States Signified by . . . the Individuals" in the Bible, such as Moses or Abraham, are only so when viewed from a distance: "these various States I have seen in my Imagination when distant they appear as One Man but as you approach they appear Multitudes of Nations" (*E* 556–57). Blake's formulation is more concrete than Necker's, but the same Neoplatonic logic governs them both.

The Platonic point is also evident when Jones compares Necker's theology to that of the Persians and Hindus: "the beauties of nature are faint resemblances, like images in a mirror, of the divine charms" (Jones 2: 220). Blake says the same thing when he claims that "[t]here Exist in that Eternal World the Permanent Realities of Every Thing which we see reflected in this Vegetable Glass of Nature" (*E* 555). This standard Platonic formulation becomes more important when it is understood as Blake's basis for both theological belief and poetic method. Indeed, the poetic method of "Allegory addressed to the Intellectual powers . . . hidden from the Corporeal Understanding" (*E* 730) results in a textual embodiment of Neoplatonic theology, not just a description of it. Jones expresses a similar conception when he discusses "a singular species of poetry, which consists almost wholly of a mystical religious allegory." The poetry of the Hindus, he says, sometimes "seems on a transient view to contain only the sentiments of a wild and voluptuous libertinism" (Jones 2: 212). Such sentiments Blake would ascribe to the "Corporeal Understanding"; for Jones, they form the mythological allegory that obscures the theology: "an ardently grateful piety is congenial to the undepraved nature of man, whose mind, sinking under the magnitude of the subject, has recourse to metaphors and allegories, which it sometimes extends beyond the bounds of cool reason" (Jones 2: 212). Blake would have had no patience with this last remark, but he would have agreed with the general point that theological truths can be conveyed by means of an allegorical system.

Jones assumes that theological truths are best imparted directly, by means of reason and straightforward prose; Blake, by contrast, recognizes that there is something about the theological truths to be imparted that makes them better suited to imagination and allegorical poetry. This is so because imaginative allegory is addressed to those same intellectual powers that make the mediation of nature and spirit possible and allow for human participation in divine energy. Intellect, in other words, makes true perception possible, so that "every thing [can] appear to man as it is: infinite" (*MHH* 14.*Prose*). Despite this difference, it is still true that William Blake and William Jones are intent on conveying theological truths that are informed by some of the same Neoplatonic notions. The similarity can be made evident by a comparison of Jones's Hindu hymns to Blake's poetry. Jones wrote a series of hymns addressed to Hindu deities that are basically poetic exercises intended to introduce European readers to Hindu mythology through the medium of familiar verse forms. Jones described his "Hymn to Camdeo" (or Kama, the Indian god of love) as something "certainly new and quite original, except the form of the stanza, which is Milton's" (Pachori 49n. 1). The best known of these poems is "A Hymn to Narayena," a work that a contemporary Indian critic calls "his most poetical and profound explanation of Hinduism" (Pachori 51n. 1). The poem was first published in the *Asiatic Miscellany* of 1785 and then widely reprinted, in whole or in part, in a number of British periodicals (the *Gentleman's Magazine,* the *Critical Review,* and the *Monthly Review*—all in 1787) and in compilations of various Hindu translations and commentaries (Drew, 76). "A Hymn to Narayena" was, in short, the most widely circulated expression of Hindu mythology in England just prior to the appearance of the *Asiatick Researches.*

In his essay "On the Gods of Greece, Italy, and India," Jones explains the nature of the deity he addresses in the poem: "NA'RA'YAN, or *Moving on the Waters* . . . in the masculine gender" is the divine spirit of the "One Supreme Being," whom the Hindus "call BRAHME, or THE GREAT ONE, in the neuter gender." Narayena, in other words, is the means by which Brahme "manifest[s] his power" (Jones 2: 350). As Jones explains in the headnote to "A Hymn to Narayena," the Hindu divinity can be understood as energy personified:

> [T]he inextricable difficulties attending the *vulgar notion of material substances* . . . induced many of the wisest among the Ancients, and some of the most enlightened among the moderns, to believe, that the whole Creation was rather an *energy* than a *work,* by which the Infinite Being, who is present at all times in all places, exhibits to the minds of his creatures a set of perceptions, like a wonderful picture or piece of musick, always varied, yet always uniform; so that all bodies and their qualities exist, indeed, to every wise and useful purpose, but exist only in so far as they are *perceived.* . . . This *illusive operation* of the Deity the *Hindu* philosophers call Maya, or *Deception.*[28]

What is striking in Jones's headnote to the "Hymn to Narayena" is the contrast of the uniform perception of the world of appearances that is Maya and the suggestion of vigorous energy behind it in the form of an "Infinite Being." The Veil of Vala is a late addition to Blake's myth, but the general contrast of authentic energy and deceptive perception appears early on in *The Marriage of Heaven and Hell:* "If the doors of perception were cleansed every thing would appear to man as it is, infinite" (*MHH* 14.*Prose*). And in the same work, when Blake describes "the Antediluvians who are our Energies" he connects the original creation with an equally original energy:

> The Giants who formed this world into its sensual existence and now seem to live in it in chains; are in truth. the causes of its life & the

> sources of all activity, but the chains are, the cunning of weak and tame minds. which have power to resist energy. according to the proverb, the weak in courage is strong in cunning. (*MHH* 16.*Prose*)

As this passage shows, the failure to perceive the creation in its original, energetic form is due more to moral limitations than to beneficent illusion. Later on, however, the energetic artisan of the creation is Los, who rages at his forge to produce a world that preserves humanity by shielding it from the awful power of Eternity. Energy and illusion are paired off in Blake's mature myth much as they are in William Jones's early introduction to Hindu thought in the explanatory note to "A Hymn to Narayena."

True to his claims in the essay "On the Mystical Poetry of the Persians and Hindus," Jones separates theology and mythology in "A Hymn to Narayena," giving theological explanations in the prose headnote prior to the mythological presentation of the poem itself. Once allowances are made for the neoclassical idiom that Jones employs (a strategy to make the strange mythology of the Hindus accessible to English readers), a number of the details of Indian mythology that Jones presents can be seen to jibe with Blake's system. In *The Four Zoas,* the grand theme of the epic action is Albion's "fall into Division & his Resurrection to Unity" (*FZ* 1.4.4), with "fall" here being synonymous or, at least, synchronous with creation. In Jones's "A Hymn to Narayena," the god Brehm creates the universe at the moment when "[f]rom Unity diversified he sprang" (*AM* 10). In Albion's case, his fall can be explained as an erotic attraction to Vala, goddess of nature and generation: "Among the Flowers of Beulah walkd the Eternal Man & Saw / Vala the lilly of the desart. melting in high noon / Upon her bosom in sweet bliss he fainted" (*FZ* 7.83.7–9). The result of this blissful experience is generation: "Vala was pregnant & brought forth Urizen Prince of Light / First born of Generation" (*FZ* 7.83.12–13). Urizen, in turn, fabricates the natural world of generation into the mechanistic universe called the Ulro. A similar sequence of events begins in Jones's "A Hymn to Narayena" when Brehm looks upon the goddess Maya, who "with love divine inflam'd," inspires the Hindu god to create "Unnumber'd worlds": "this gorgeous universe he fram'd" (*AM* 10). Blake uses the word *frame* in "The Tyger" to signify creation, a minor point perhaps, but other points in "A Hymn to Narayena" suggest more considerable analogies. The first evidence of creation in the Hindu myth is the movement of the waters, not unlike that of Tharmas, the "Parent power" (*FZ* 1.4.7) who takes watery form in Blake's myth. Also, when the neuter Brehm is diversified into the masculine "Brehma" in "A Hymn to Narayena" Jones invokes his muse to "say . . . what four-form'd Godhead came" (*AM* 11) into existence after the diversification of the original, uncreated being. The concept of a unified divinity subsequently composed of four forms certainly suggests Albion's division into the four Zoas, as does the proliferation of Hindu names that appears in Jones's poem as the creation itself proliferates: Narayen, Venamaly, Peitamber, Pedmanabha, Kytabh, Medha. The names themselves do not resemble the names that Blake gives to his mythic figures, but both sets of names are alike in that they are *unlike* anything else in the European canon of Christian and classical mythology. More important, however, is the evidence such lists of names give to the argument that Jones and Blake both present the same theological situation of divinity diversified into the cosmos.

Further points of cosmology are common to Jones's hymn and Blake's poetry, such as the myth of the mundane egg and the conception of the creation as a mechanistic universe separated from Eternity. In "A Hymn to Narayena," Jones's account of the myth of the mundane egg is well removed from Blake's language but not from Blake's myth: "Then o'er the vast expanse primordial wind / Breath'd gently, till a lucid bubble rose, / Which grew in perfect shape an Egg refin'd" (*AM* 10). The world that the egg contains is dismissed as "[d]elusive" and "unsubstantial" (*AM* 14), having been described in terms not quite as mechanistic as those used to describe the Ulro of Urizen perhaps, but mechanistic nonetheless, as such technical terms as *elemental* and *pensile* suggest:

> Blue crystal vault, and elemental fires,
> That in th'ethereal fluid blaze and breathe;
> Thou, tossing main, whose snaky branches wreathe
> This pensile orb with intertwisted gyres;
> Mountains, whose radiant spires
> Presumptuous rear their summits to the skies
> . . .
>
> Hence! vanish from my sight. . . .
>
> (*AM* 13–14)

Natural images are dismissed as delusive because "all perceptions" are inferior to the "One abundant source / Whence ev'ry object ev'ry moment flows," that is, the original energy from which "Suns . . . derive their force" and "planets learn their course" (*AM* 14).

The inferiority of perception is explained earlier in the poem as due to mere "emanations" of the senses, a product of the power of Narayena that "[b]ids from each sense bright emanations beam" (*AM* 12), so that divine energy may appear as material form to human beings through the mediation of Maya. In theological writings, the word *emanation* usually refers to the creation of one god by another, and that is the sense in which Blake uses the word when he describes the production of female emanations out of male Zoas. Jones's usage in "A Hymn to Narayena" is epistemological, but so, in a way, is Blake's: once the Emanations become separated from the Zoas the senses are likewise divided—Tharmas is largely confined to taste, Urizen to sight, Luvah to smell, and Urthona to hearing.[29] Blake's myth and Jones's poem, then, have a number of theological and mythological points in common, similarities that can easily be overlooked because of differences in diction and form, for Jones merely declaims his static version of Hindu myth where Blake sets his system into turbulent narrative motion. But the differences recede when the main points of the Hindu and the Blakean myths are understood in the light of their common theological basis in Neoplatonic thought.

The value of William Jones's exposition of Hinduism for someone like Blake is that it provides a model of a complex mythology with a theological meaning that might be understood both in terms of ancient truth and contemporary validity. For Jones, those terms are mainly Platonic and Neoplatonic, and they provide a means of making the new literature from the East accessible to the West by framing it within an existing theological tradition. Blake understood this tradition in a special way, to be sure, and what makes his understanding special is the addition of Dissent. For Jones, the veil of Maya was a beneficent illusion that he could reconcile to an idealist epistemology; for Blake, the veil of Vala was also a kind of scrim that reduced perception and limited human vision of divine forms, but the sense of epistemological limitation is further compounded by the intrusion of the moral law. Jones could separate theology from mythology and find the philosophical purity of the Vedanta in the involved mythology of the Hindu allegories. Blake, on the other hand, was constitutionally incapable of making this kind of separation: to do so would have been to accede to reason, which was, after all, the method of morality—the negation, in turn, of intellect and imagination. As expressed in his poetry, Blake's theology is inseparable from his mythology because his beliefs have their intellectual being in those creatures of the imagination he called the Zoas. The word *zoa* itself is etymologically related to the Greek word for "creature" or "animal," and Blake's world is indeed animated, alive with many gods that in the aggregate add up to God.

The kind of polytheistic unity that drives Blake's myth is closely akin to the teeming universe of Hindu divinities that Jones describes—

gods with strange names who war among themselves and diversify into the creation, pairing off with their consorts and emanations. Blake's myth also ramifies into history, for the wars of Eternity carried out by the gods are endlessly repeated and recycled in the generated world of time and space, populated by men and women who live, suffer, and die. Blake saw this world around him and tried to give a mythological accounting of it, and the two expositors of Hindu myth so celebrated by his contemporaries would have certainly aided in the endeavor. Charles Wilkins and William Jones supplied a familiar template for the Hindu system in their theological and philosophical commentary upon it. In addition, Jones's essays and Wilkins's *Gita,* taken together, provide glimpses of a mythic vision that conforms to Blake's: Jones presents a model of mythic action before the world begins, while Wilkins helps to bring the myth into the world itself to show what happens afterwards, when "Gods combine against Man" (*FZ* 9.126.9) in the wars that men wage against one another. Blake may have located the origins of contemporary events in an ancient myth of his own creation, but history provided a model for that myth in the work of Wilkins and William Jones.

III

The examples of Charles Wilkins's translation of the *Bhagavad Gita* and William Jones's copious accounts of Indic myth show that the most important expositions of Brahminism to appear in Blake's time aligned the ancient Hindu faith with certain key theological principles that were compatible with Christianity. The points of comparison that Wilkins and Jones emphasized, however, were not always in accord with the institutionalized faith of the Church of England. On the contrary, the "antinomian" points that appeared in Wilkins's *Gita* and the Neoplatonic claims that Jones made were more readily reconciled to Dissent. The theological circumstances under which Hinduism was introduced to the West, combined with Blake's generous inclination to believe that all religions are one at the mythic level of poetic origins, argue in favor of Blake's receptivity to the mythological material that accompanied contemporary theological explanations of the Brahmin faith. Not all of Blake's contemporaries, however, were as sympathetic to Brahma in the East as Blake was. As we have seen, Joseph Priestley employed Hinduism mainly as a foil to show the superiority of both materialist philosophy and Unitarian theology. Clearly, Blake stands at some remove from Priestley and other contemporary witnesses to the Oriental Renaissance.

Blake differs from these contemporaries chiefly in his evident ability to dissolve the Hindu system into his own without subjecting it to Christian bias. With the exception of enlightened scholars like Sir William Jones— who seems to have raised Christian objections to Hindu theology for form's sake alone—a number of Blake's contemporaries understood Indian religion as a mass of confused theological precepts that combined only the worst points of both paganism and versions of Christian faith outside the pale of the Anglican establishment.

One of the oddest critiques of the Hindu system is the one presented by the churchman Thomas Maurice in his *Indian Antiquities*, the subtitle of which reads, in part, *Dissertations relative to . . . The Pure System of Primeval Theology . . . and the Various and Profound Literature of Hindostan*. Maurice relies on the authority of William Jones for his exposition of the positive pole of the Hindu faith, the primeval theology of which is virtually identical to Neoplatonic philosophy. As we have seen, Blake's system is likewise dependent on such Neoplatonic notions as intellect and energy, for Blake imagines a world in which human intellect is empowered by the energy of its divine origins to see beyond natural forms and witness the visions of Eternity. The dark side of Hinduism in Maurice's *Indian Antiquities* is also closely akin to that terrible negation of humanity that Blake called "Druidical" (E 542), so that, in the larger analysis, it can be said that the contrary poles of Blake's system—the intellectual unity of humanity and God versus the idolatrous worship of inhuman matter—correspond to the British understanding of Hinduism at the end of the eighteenth century.

We have already shown in some detail how fully Neoplatonic philosophy informed the enlightened interpretation of Hindu theology. Thomas Maurice recapitulates this interpretation in his exposition of the primeval purity of the Indian system, but the churchman has a much greater stake in exploring the deterioration of primeval theology into senseless ritual. He does this by devoting a great deal of attention to a demonstration of the strange thesis that "the Druids were Brahmins."[30] In a lengthy "Dissertation on the Origins of the Druids," Maurice cites one Reuben Burrow for affirmation that the Druids were "a race of emigrated Indian philosophers" (*IA* 6: viii–ix). This emigration is part of Maurice's post-deluvian history of the world involving the dispersion of the three sons of Noah and their families: "the progeny of Shem" are diffused over southern Asia, "the family of Ham" over Africa, and "the descendents of Japhet" over "the East and West quarters of that northern district," that is, India and northern Europe. Maurice explains how "a colony of priests, professing the Brahmin religion, and educated in the great school of Babylon, actually emigrated, in the most early periods, from Asia, with the Japhetic tribes who established themselves in Europe" (*IA* 6: 193). These Brahmins, "gradually mingling with the great body of Celtic tribes who pursued their journey to the extremity of Europe, finally established the Druid, that is, Brahmin system of superstition in ancient Britain" (*IA* 6: 197). Maurice has all kinds of linguistic proof for the infiltration of Brahmin priests into Celtic tribes. The term *Druid* itself, "derived from Celtic Dru, or Deru, an oak," together with other Welsh terms, "direct our attention to the Sanscreet name of the old Brahmins," which is "DERVASAS." Thus, Maurice reasons, "[t]he Dervish of the East . . . and the Druid of the West, are the same character, under names but little varied" (*IA* 6: 24–25). Further proof of the connection comes by way of one Colonel Grant, who is said to be able to decipher "Tibetan characters . . . solely by his knowledge of the old Irish language" (*IA* 6: 24).

Having established his argument on such foundations as these (which would not have seemed so absurd in Blake's day as they do in our own), Maurice begins to make the unstated purpose of his Brahmin-Druid comparison clear. It turns out that the "Brahminism" of the Druids furnishes a perfect explanation for the origins of Catholicism, another corruption of the primeval theology that the Church of England has evidently succeeded in recovering:

> At the entrance of all the Eastern temples were placed vessels filled with consecrated water, with which the votaries at their entrance besprinkled themselves; and this custom, there can scarcely be any doubt, originated in India, where large tanks for the ablution of a people . . . to this day remain invariably placed in the fount of their pagodas. . . . The antiquity . . . and universality of this practice, as well as that of using consecrated *beads* in their worship of the Deity, common to the Brahmins not less than the Druids, apparently demonstrate from what primæval source the votaries of modern superstition in Rome, have borrowed this Asiatic rite. (*IA* 6: 166)

Maurice also comments on the "sanguinary sacrifices" celebrated by the British Druids that took the form of "inclosing men, women, and children, in one vast wicker image, in the form of a man," and then setting fire "to the huge colossus" (*IA* 6: 105). The author is a bit fuzzy on the question of whether the wicker man originated with the Brahmins or was an innovation devised by the ancient Britons, but the larger point that idolatry and ritual can lead to the horrors of human sacrifice is clear. Maurice, then, sees the Druid superstition inspired by the Brahmin priests coming to rest in Rome. At one point in *Jerusalem* Blake cautions against making "Rome thy patriarch Druid" (*J* 61.50), but usually Blake is more general in his ascription of any dehumanizing system to the realm of Druidism, and he never equates the Druids with the Brahmins. Nonetheless, Blake's theological division of Christian faith into intellectual vision and Druid idolatry repeats precisely Thomas Maurice's contradictory exposition of Brahminism.

Blake eventually avers that "Albion was the Parent of the Druids" (*J* 27.*Prose*), or, more precisely, the anti-Albion—the spectre that is the origin of sacrificial moral law: "the Tree of Good & Evil [is] rooted beneath the cruel heel / Of Albions Spectre the Patriarch Druid" (*J* 98.47–48). The myth that ensues from Albion's fall from unity and his spectrous division into Druidism contains many points that resemble Hindu mythology, and given all the mythographic and theological material at Blake's disposal we should not be surprised that this is so. Blake may very well have understood the Druids in the same general terms that Maurice did, and so deployed his myth accordingly. Maurice, after all, is not an original writer and merely conveys the details of a strange tradition that evidently existed well before he tried to consolidate them. For example, in William Hurd's encyclopedic *History of the Religious Rites, Ceremonies, and Customs of the Whole World* (1774), certain elements of Druid theology are described that are also common to the Hindu system, such as the belief that "the souls of men . . . passed from one body to another," and that "human souls might have inhabited animal bodies."[31] Also, the first fable in Paul Henri Mallet's prose *Edda* (translated into English in 1770) concerns the "great respect" the Scandinavians show "to the New-comers from Asia" because of the "divine power resident in them."[32] With this type of theological and mythic material for a background, as the understanding of the Hindu system grew it could easily be adapted as an explanation for the traditional understanding of Druidism. Thus, when we find Maurice explaining that "[t]he four heads [of Brahma] are symbols of the four elements and four quarters of the world" and find a similar symbolic system attached to the four Zoas—the Druid progeny of Albion—the similarity can be attributed to Hindu influence on a native British tradition. The English understanding of the "double conduct" of the Brahmin priests also accords with Blake's division of religion into poetic truth and empty ritual. Likewise, Blake's system comprehends the same contrast of primeval theology and human sacrifice that his contemporaries found in the Hindu faith, which they understood as either sublimely intellectual and Neoplatonic or grossly idolatrous and Druidic.

Whether the points of similarity in Blake's mythic system and the one attributed to the Hindus by the likes of Thomas Maurice result from direct influence or from a more general kind of cultural transaction is difficult to determine. The writings of Maurice were, in fact, widely available; they were also extensively summarized in the *Analytical Review*, so Blake could have come across the *Indian Antiquities* in his dealings with Joseph Johnson. What is certain, at least, is that the similarities exist, and exist in such a way as to clarify some of the theological obscurities in Blake's poetry. For example, the concept of divine energy dispersed into the creation while simultaneously remaining sublimely apart from it is not one that conforms to Christian doctrine in Blake's time. Such an idea, however, is consistent with eighteenth-century explanations of Hindu theology and with Blake's mature myth. To try and make sense of Blake without the occasional reference to Hinduism results in some genuine theological difficulties. Consider, for example, how Hindu thought might have helped this frustrated commentator: "Obscurities can arise in the later prophetic books, not just because Blake was managing his art badly, but because he was attempting to reconcile doctrines that could not be logically reconciled. The books plunge into obscurity at exactly those points (of which the problem of the unity and dispersal of the godhead is one) where Blake was involved in actual doctrinal or philosophical contradictions."[33] To my mind, the theological problem of the unity and dispersal of the godhead in Blake's prophetic books is better understood not as a case of bad art or shoddy logic, but as a creative response to an Indian idea. This is not to say that Blake's beliefs are any less Christian for his incorporation of elements outside of Christianity into his mythic system, so long as those elements perform their allegorical function of showing that the separation of humanity and God can be overcome, and that Jesus is the medium for the reconciliation of man and God as the human form divine. That sublime concept of incarnation is not contradicted by occasional accounts of reincarnation that reduce humanity to the likes of tigers or wolves. On the contrary, Blake's allegorical use of Hindu myth helps to enforce the Christian image by making the separation of man from his own divine humanity appear all the more acute.

In *The Marriage of Heaven and Hell*, Blake puts "the philosophy of the east" ahead of the Hebrew prophecy. Later, in *The Song of Los*, Brahma comes before Moses in Blake's poetic genealogy of world religions. What is significant, however, is not so much that Blake supports the possibility that Eastern mythology is of greater antiquity than Hebrew religion, but that no single religion is authorized by antiquity. Moreover, if religion is really mythology—"poetic tales" inspired by the Poetic Genius—then any inspired poet can create his own individual system, his own set of poetic tales that might have the same sublime authority as those on which other religions are based. In Blake's case, the capacity to create such a system was surely aided by the explosion of mythographic studies of world religions that appeared in his lifetime. Among those studies, the ones describing the mythology of the Hindus would have been particularly compelling for someone like Blake. The antiquity of the Eastern faith challenged the authority of Western orthodoxy and so accorded, in a general sense, with the tradition of Protestant Dissent. At the same time, because the Hindus were clearly the victims of empire, they attracted republican sympathy as well. The political and theological contexts in which the Hindu myths were first communicated to English readers would have been quite conducive to their favorable reception by the Neoplatonic poet who wrote *The Book of Thel* and by the radical, antinomian author of *The Marriage of Heaven and Hell*. That such a reception did, in fact, occur is suggested by particular similarities in the myth that Blake created and the Hindu myths that his contemporaries recounted.

In every case, contemporary responses to the Oriental Renaissance include theological components that also appear in Blake's creative mythography. Wilkins's rendering of the *Bhagavad Gita* infuses the Hindu epic with antinomian meanings that also ramify through Blake's mythology. Likewise, William Jones's philosophical explanations of Hinduism rely on some of the same Neoplatonic formulations that Blake engaged to overcome holiness and morality with intellect and energy. Joseph Priestley and Thomas Maurice, Unitarian Dissenter and Anglican Churchman, could not be more different from one another, yet they are alike in understanding the Hindu system as either a theological or a political threat, and so they both help to show how charged with meaning mythology was felt to be in the crucial decade when Blake created his mythological system. The conclusion that follows is at once simple and involved: Blake's system has a point of historical origin in common with the heightened awareness of the Hindu system. Every other system, whether classical or biblical, belonged to the distant past, but the myths of Hindostan were new, in a sense, because their discovery was so recent. At the same time, their astonishing antiquity made the Hindu myths that much closer to the sublime condition Blake called Eternity. And while other mythologies were certainly available to Blake, none of those systems (the Scandinavian, say) carried so much political and theological meaning as the myths of India did. Here at last was a "new system" (in Jacob Bryant's phrase) that involved ancient myths with contemporary affairs. The combination of politics, mythography, and theology that emerged was specific to the historical conditions under which the Hindu system came to light. Had the translation of the Hindu texts taken place a hundred years later a different set of meanings would have resulted. But the fact is that the transmission of Indic myth to English culture occurred under conditions of great theological uncertainty and tremendous political upheaval. Given these circumstances, the Hindu system could certainly serve as one important model for Blake's creative mythography, which tries to describe the mythic origins of current crises and makes modern events emerge from great primordial moments. The system that Blake created was even newer than the Hindu one, but somehow older, for Blake's mythology belongs, all at once, to Eternity and history together.

Postscript

The order of the topics presented in this study represents a reduction of a set of cultural events that must have occurred almost simultaneously to a certain historical sequence: politics, mythography, theology. Blake's career can be easily mapped onto this sequence because he gave expression to his feelings for radical politics rather early on, and he was not alone in imagining a republican London as a real alternative to the institutions of monarchy and state religion. But, in Blake's case, the radical alternative was only imagined, and imagined in so florid a form as to effectively compromise any intended political position. From the outset Blake's creative mythography was better suited to the transfer of theological rather than political meaning, even though the myth is given greater political inflection earlier rather than later. In "A Song of Liberty" that ends *The Marriage of Heaven and Hell* and then again in *America a Prophecy* Blake declares that "Empire is no more" (*MHH* 27.*Prose; AP* 6.15). In both instances, however, the political wish for the removal of empire is already involved with antinomian theology and mythic machinery. With *The Four Zoas,* the myth becomes much more elaborate, with the result that political meaning either becomes more densely coded or is crowded out altogether, so that now the libertarian declaration that once abolished empire is revised to announce, instead, that "Mystery is no more" (*FZ* 9.134.29). With the substitution of "Mystery" for the earlier "Empire" the elevation of theological meaning over political meaning is evident. But regardless of whether politics or theology is more heavily inflected, the medium for both is Blake's composite mythography, a system created out of many sources.

In principle there is no reason why Hindu mythology should receive greater emphasis than any other source that was available to Blake as he began to create his own composite system. My emphasis here has proceeded from the belief that the poet's relationship to Hinduism has been mishandled by earlier critics who neglect to discuss the historical circumstances under which Eastern mythology was most likely conveyed to Blake. Those circumstances put Blake in the extraordinarily serendipitous position of being at the right place at the right time with the right political and religious attitudes to experience the Oriental

Renaissance in an artistically rewarding way. Around 1790, as the publications of the Asiatic Society in Bengal began to arrive in London,
Blake was in the midst of a religious reevaluation of his Christian beliefs,
having only recently removed himself from the Swedenborgian New
Jerusalem Church. He was also energized by reports of the French Revolution and excited by the prospect of political revolution in England as
well. The Indian materials that arrived from Bengal were immediately
politicized by a radical ideology that questioned the operations of
empire in distant dominions. At the same time, some establishment figures construed the Hindu myths as a threat to the interconnected stabil-
ity of Church and State. Because of his dissenting religious heritage and
his new republican politics, Blake was well equipped to understand the
Hindu myths as they were presented and interpreted by his contemporaries. He clearly had opportunity for exposure to Hindu tradition in the
1790s by way of the few friends and patrons he had at the time: Fuseli,
Johnson, Flaxman, Hayley, and Humphry were all involved in the great
Asiatic awakening of late eighteenth-century London. Blake also had the
opportunity to acquaint himself with Hindu myth by means of the
mythographic work of Volney, Jones, Mickle, and Maurice. As a popularizer of antiquarian matters, Maurice's investigations are particularly
useful to illustrate the impetus to myth that the Hindu discoveries com-
pelled. The presence in Indian myth of so many motifs known from
other systems—the mundane egg, a great flood, a triad of gods, and so
on—urged a thorough reexamination of all religious systems and incited
a great many controversies about the relationship of Hindu myth and
Christian belief.

There are two interrelated reasons for thinking that Blake participated in these controversies and took advantage of the opportunities
available to him. These reasons I have called the "polemical" and the
"poetic." The polemics of religious controversy stimulated by the Hindu
discoveries insisted that the Indian system be divided into theological
purity and vulgar practice. This division is consistently maintained,
without exception, by all the English expositors of Hinduism in Blake's
time, from Charles Wilkins and William Jones to Thomas Maurice and
Edward Moor. The division attributed to the Hindu system is relevant
to Blake because he believed that the religious practices of his age were
corrupt and vulgar forms of original poetic vision. British expositions of
Hinduism, then, either confirmed or contributed to Blake's understanding of the way religions worked. So Blake espoused some of the same
theological premises that allowed his contemporaries to separate sublimity from ritual and—depending on what aspect of the system received
the emphasis—to either celebrate the Brahmin faith for its theological

purity or excoriate it for its superstitious corruption. As we have seen, Blake's myth also imagines a system that is likewise divided, between Neoplatonic purity on the one hand and Druidic practice on the other. But Blake was a poet and not a polemicist, and he created a great poetic myth where his countrymen could merely reason and compare. Thus, a second justification for thinking that Blake modeled his myth on the Hindu system is the evident similarity of that system to his own: Brahma and Albion are both four-fold giants existing ages before the beginning of the world who create the universe by diversifying their own unified being into it. The variegated generation of nature that ensues from the creative act is really divine energy masked as material form. The transformation of the god's energy occurs in the context of slumber and deluge, and the creation itself is figured both as a mundane egg and also as a female emanation, called "Maya" in one case, "Vala" in the other. In both cases, however, the emanation is an agent of delusion who casts a veil over human vision and narrows perception down to matter. As the four-fold god sleeps, another god preserves a portion of the divine energy during a contest of contrary powers that, strangely, draw their own adversarial energy from each other: Luvah's destructive power is largely derived from Urizen, and Vishnu frequently takes over the role of destroyer from Siva. In both the Blakean and the Hindu systems human history reenacts the patterns of the past: the infinite is shut up in finite revolutions, and everything turns upon the wheel of time. Release from the round of existence is possible, at times, simply through some act of heightened perception: Krishna opens the window of vision that allows Arjuna to see how little action matters; Jesus provides imagination and intellect to show how far removed the moral law is from the human form divine.

As this last point of comparison shows, resemblances between the Hindu and the Blakean systems do not mean that Blake was a Hindu; instead, he deployed the Hindu system—or, rather, his own modified version of a British representation of it—to convey a Christian meaning. As we have seen, Hinduism was mediated through more familiar traditions in Blake's time. William Jones and other enlightened Indologists remarked on the correspondences of Hinduism to Platonism. The less-enlightened perspective of Thomas Maurice emphasized an actual emigration of Brahmans to Britain to explain the sacrifices and rituals of the ancient Druids. Finally, some of Blake's contemporaries understood the Hindus in terms of dissenting Protestant sects, and so compared them to the Unitarians, Swedenborgians, and Behemists that they knew already. As strange as all of this seems, the British understanding of Hinduism, in which an ancient Eastern culture is mediated by several strands of the

Western tradition, may be an early instance of a type of cultural transaction that has occurred many times since and is especially prevalent in our own age. Indeed, it may very well be that the "discovery" of one culture by another always requires a traditional idiom to make the foreign familiar and the Other understandable. The way the otherness of Indic culture was maintained within a set of existing traditions in the eighteenth century suggests a dynamic that is not so much multicultural as intercultural, for the transmission of one culture through another never results in an intact transfer of cultural ideas and values. This is not to say, however, that "something is lost in the translation"; on the contrary, a great deal is gained, because what results from any intercultural transaction is an entirely new configuration, a hybrid creation that comes alive with new and startling correspondences of the familiar and the foreign. Blake's creative mythography is the product of precisely this kind of intercultural condition in which familiar traditions are remade into the myth of their own origins. In the cultural exchange that occurred at the end of the eighteenth century, abstract philosophy is all that is given to Brahma in the East, but Brahma returned so much more in the form of Hindu mythology, and Blake was among the first to benefit from that generous tradition. In the end, the sleep of Albion owes a great deal to the Asiatic awakening that Blake and his associates experienced at the end of the eighteenth century. As subtly as the spirit of Narayena moves upon the water in the Brahmin story of creation, the spirit of Hindu mythology moves within the creative mythography of William Blake.

Mythographic Material from Joseph Priestley's *Comparison of the Institutions of Moses with those of the Hindoos*

The front matter of Joseph Priestley's *Comparison of the Institutions of Moses with those of the Hindoos and other Ancient Nations* (Northumberland: A. Kennedy, 1799) includes a list of "Synonyms of Hindoo Names and Deities" (xvi–xvii) and "The Titles of some of the books quoted in this Work" (xvii–xix). The first list is reproduced because the sheer profusion of names demonstrates a certain mythographic richness that suggests a similar superfluity of names and deities in Blake's mythology. In addition, the inclusion of the biblical figures Adam and Noah in a list of "Hindoo" deities shows that Blake's linkage of Adam, Noah, and Brahma in *The Song of Los* is not so unique or idiosyncratic as it seems. The second list also shows how wide-ranging mythographic comparisons were in the last decade of the eighteenth century: the list makes evident that Priestley's study of Hindu religion cannot be complete without a parallel investigation of Persian, Arabic, and Scandinavian mythology as well.

Synonyms of Hindoo Names and Dieties

Hindoo, Gentoo.
Veda, Ved, Beda, Bhade.
Vedam, Bedang.
Shastah, Shaster, Sastra.
Caliougam, Cal Jug.
Mahabad, Menu, Mouni, Adam, Noah.
Satyavarman, Satiavarto, Sattiavattna, Satyavarman, Noah.
Brahma, Birma, Burmha, Brumma.
Vichnou, Bistnoo, Kistna, Kissen, Chrishnou, Christen, Narayen,
    Jaggernat, Rhaam.

Siva, Seid, Chib, Chiven, Tchiven, Mahadeva, Moideb, Mahadeo,
    Moisoor, Isuren, Routren, Ruddery.
Budda, Bod, Pout, Boutta, Fo, Odin, Xaca.
Bramin, Brahmen.
Chatariya, Cheteree.
Vaissya, Bice.
Sudra, Sooder, Choutre.
Muni, Menu.
Beass, Biache, Vyasa.
Gayatri, Goitre.
Gebre, Parsi.
Faquir, Joguis.

The Titles of some of the books quoted in this Work

*Dissertations and Miscellaneous pieces relating to the history, and antiq-
    uities, the arts, sciences, and literature of Asia.* 3 vols. 1792, &c.
Ezourvedam, ou Ancien Commentaire du Vedam. Iverdun, 1778.
Histoire du Christianisme des Indes, par La Croze. 2 vols. 1758.
*Sketches chiefly relating to the History, Religion, Learning, and Man-
    ners, of the Hindoos.* 2 vols. 1792.
*A Code of Gentoo Laws, or Ordinations of the Pundits, from a Persian
    Translation, made from the original written in the Shanscrit lan-
    guage.* 1777.
Northern Antiquities, translated from Mr. Mallet by Dr. Percy. 2 vols.
    1770.
*The Agreement of the Customs of the East-Indians with those of the
    Jews and other antient People.* 1705.
*An Account of the Religion, Manners, and Learning of Malabar, in sev-
    eral Letters written by some of the most learned Men of that
    Country to the Danish Missionaries.* By Mr. Philips, 1717.
Histoire de la Religion des Banians, &c. traduit de l'Anglois, de Henry
    Lord, 1667.
*The Ceremonies and Religious Customs of the various nations of the
    known World.* By B. Picart, abridged from the French Original,
    1741.
*A Relation of the Voyage to Siam performed by six Jesuits, sent by the
    French King in 1685.* London, 1688.
*A Dissertation on the Languages, Literature, and Manners, of Eastern
    Nations,* by John Richardson, 1778.
Voyage de Niebuhr en Arabie. 2 vols. 1780.

A new Account of the East-Indies, by Alexander Hamilton. 2 vols.
   1727.
A Journey over Land to the East Indies, by Donald Campbell of Bar-
   bree, Philadelphia, 1797.
Oeuvres de Boulanger. 8 vols. 1778.

Synopsis of *The Four Zoas*

N.B.: Seasoned students of Blake will not require recourse to the following summary, which is intended mainly for novice readers who need a rough guide to the poem. As with all such summaries, it is no substitute for close, careful, and repeated reading of the poem itself.

The Four Zoas is a nightmare epic (cf. Enitharmon's dream of history in *EP* 9.1–5) that details the fall/sleep/death of Albion. The allegory requires that Albion have at least two identities: a political allegory makes Albion England, separated from his emanation Jerusalem, a symbol for a just society based on liberty; a psychosexual allegory makes Albion Everyman, or any human being in a state of psychic fragmentation. Keep in mind the Blakean fact that Albion is also Atlantis, or the "<patriarch of the Atlantic Continent> whose History Preceded that of the Hebrews <& in whose Sleep <or Chaos> Creation began" (*E* 558). Note the curious identification of sleep, chaos, and creation in Blake's own comment on his completed myth. In *The Four Zoas*, Albion is asleep through most of the poem (hence the artistic license for dreamlike or nightmarish effects). The first four numbered sections (or "Nights") describe a condition of chaos attending the fall of Albion's four component elements, or Zoas (i.e., Tharmas, Luvah, Urizen, and Urthona—in their order of collapse); the second four sections describe the creation of a limited, fallen world by the prophet Los and its six-thousand years of iron-age history—succeeding Orc cycles of revolution and repression (or the cycling of Orc into Urizen). The last section imagines a powerful apocalypse of terrifying renewal, wrought by a transformed Los, in which Albion is resurrected into unity and the four Zoas are restored to their original, unfallen state.

Night the First

The poem announces its general subject as the fall of Albion. The particular subject of Night I is the fall of Tharmas, the Zoa or component of Albion that unifies and integrates the other three components (i.e., reason/Urizen, imagination/Urthona, emotion/Luvah). In his fallen state, however, Tharmas becomes chaos, a raging sea that overwhelms Albion (cf. the Atlantis myth). When a Zoa is in Eternity or Eden, "he" is androgynous. When a Zoa falls, the female portion, or Emanation, separates from the male. The Emanation of Tharmas is Enion, an earth-mother in jealous contest with Tharmas the sea-father. In a psychosexual sense, "emanations" can also be understood as erotic thoughts or male fantasies about women, a meaning that seems to apply to Enion's jealousy over Tharmas's capacity to produce rival female emanations. Enion's moral severity and insistence on the purity of Tharmas result in the further breakdown of Tharmas's unity: something called the Spectre of Tharmas separates from Tharmas proper. This Spectre is, ironically, exactly what Enion thinks she wants: a moralistic, pure being who is obedient to the dictates of duty and law. The appearance of the Spectre, which certifies the Zoa's disunity, causes a crisis in Beulah (a reposeful, married state necessary to creation), and the Daughters of Beulah make the typical (in Blake) error of trying to limit or control the Spectre. They do this by creating a containing space called Ulro and by closing the Gate of the Tongue. This act announces the constriction of the sense of taste, which is one of the things that happens as the distance from Eternity increases: the multiple senses of the Eternals are limited and diminished in the Ulro of nature. In any case, under these newly constrained conditions Enion and the Spectre of Tharmas "unite" to produce "two little Infants" (*FZ* 1.8.2), soon to be named Los and Enitharmon (the name *Los* is evidently meant to recall "loss," while *Enitharmon* combines the names Enion and Tharmas). Los is Urthona in temporal or generated form, and Enitharmon is the emanation of Los/Urthona. Los and Enitharmon are also, respectively, time and space, or, at least, the managers thereof. As the boy Los matures, he gains in prophetic power. Enitharmon, also, seems capable of prophecy, since she declaims "a Song of Death" (*FZ* 1.10.9) about Luvah's theft of Urizen's light. In her account, when Urizen is deprived of light he descends as the grim reasoner and angry sky-god of the Lambeth prophecies. He suggests to Luvah that they carry out an assault on Albion's now-vulnerable supremacy, but Luvah has plans of his own to usurp Albion's place in Eden and to attack Urizen as well. The discord requires that the Daughters of Beulah protect Albion's emanation Jerusalem, the spirit of Liberty, and so she is "lulld into silent rest" (*FZ* 1.20.11). The first night ends with Urizen and Luvah locked "in the wars of Eternal Death" (*FZ* 1.20.15).

Night the Second

The second night describes the fall of Luvah, which is necessarily conditioned by the ascent of Urizen to the heights of moral law. Albion abdicates his power to Urizen at the opening of this section, which can only portend ill for Luvah. Urizen's first task is that of Architect of Ulro, creating a measured, mechanistic world—nature from the perspective of the Druid worshiper or the Deist philosopher. Such a world is a dark, satanic mill, here called the "Furnaces of affliction" (FZ 2.25.40), within which the emotional and sexual power of Luvah is contained. As Luvah is consumed in Urizen's furnace, Vala is reduced to ashes, a world void of vision that can merely be measured but never understood. Urizen supervises the highly geometric construction of this world, now called the "Mundane Shell" (FZ 2.24.8). Urizen retires from his labors and returns to his emanation Ahania for comfort and renewal (such services are provided in Beulah as relief from the Ulro, but the benefits of Beulah are largely denied Urizen). Finding his emanation now separate, the inevitable torments of jealousy ensue. Los and Enitharmon appear, and the latter is particularly delighted with the alienation of Ahania from Urizen (here Enitharmon takes on the features she had in *Europe*, delighting in the sinister dominion of female over male). At this point Enion appears and recites a beautiful song of Experience, bewailing the selfish, cynical limitations of that state. These developments seem to have something to do with the loss of Luvah: his confinement by Urizen precipitates or aggravates the alienation of Ahania and the bitterness of Enitharmon. In other words, the Luvah or love element in all these mythic characters is lost when Luvah is limited. The section ends with Ahania leaving Urizen completely, and thus presaging the fall of Urizen in the next Night.

Night the Third

This part of the poem opens with Urizen's rejection of Ahania as Sin, when her true identity is Wisdom (cf. Athena). Urizen fears the revenge of Luvah in the form of Orc, even though the fiery form of Orc has not yet been revealed. Ahania tries to console Urizen by pointing out that his salvation is within his grasp if he will resume his eternal role as the wise reasoner, rather than that of the abstract rationalist or the vengeful Jehovah. Despite Ahania's plaintive, nostalgic pleadings, Urizen hurls her from him, and so ensures absolute separation of reason from wisdom and his own catastrophic fall. Sure enough, the mathematically correct world measured out in the previous Night comes crashing down, and chaos reappears in the "form" of the Spectre of Tharmas. Blake gives voice to chaos in a great speech that sends Enion, earlier on the verge of an enlightened Experience capable of reorganization into Innocence, fleeing and withering away into a state that Blake calls "Entuthon Benithon" (*FZ* 3.45.13), the extreme of negation or non-entity. With this brief Night the fall of the Zoas is complete (with, again, the partial exception of Urthona), and the stage is set for the growth of Los as the poet-smith whose task it is to rebuild the fallen world and awaken Albion from his sleep of death.

Night the Fourth

Night IV begins with the chaotic Tharmas's pleas to Los to rebuild the universe, but Los is not quick to cooperate, allying himself temporarily with Urizen. Los at this point is far from being a rationalistic geometer or architect *like* Urizen, but he is equally far from being a fully mature imaginative artist or poet-prophet. Tharmas coerces Los into cooperation by wrenching Enitharmon apart from him and delivering her to the Spectre of Urthona, a shadow of Los's true self. With the artificer separate from his inspiring Emanation, Los—driven by jealousy—can only create a world of time and space by commanding his spectral, blind will. So the Spectre obeys the voice of Los, and mans the furnaces of iron as Los rebuilds the fallen universe of Urizen. The resultant creation is only a slight improvement over the rocky wasteland of Ulro: the world is now a vegetative universe that Blake calls "a Human polypus of Death" (*FZ* 4.56.16). At this point a divine (i.e., truly human and imaginative) principle intercedes and sets limits beyond which Man/Albion cannot fall: one boundary is called "the Limit of Opacity" (*FZ* 4.56.19), or Satan (that is, Urizen in his totally fallen, temporal form); the other is named the "Limit of Contraction" (*FZ* 4.56.21), or Adam. Los is completely confused (he goes mad, in fact) by this turn of events, as his first effort at creation has gone awry. Los at the end of this Night must literally collect himself and start over. When he does, he and Enitharmon animate the Ulro or Polypus with the demon of energy known as Orc, and the cycles of history begin—the subject of the Nights to come.

Night the Fifth

Night the Fifth opens with the madness of Los. Because of the events that have so disturbed Eternity, Los and Enitharmon begin to shrink "into fixed space" (*FZ* 5.57.12). To protect against the absolute diminution of the Divine Humanity, Los builds the protective city of art called Golgonooza. Within this protected space the demon Orc begins to mature; Los feels threatened when the "ruddy boy" reaches fourteen (*FZ* 5.60.6–7; cf. *AP* 1.2). Los's binding of Orc is then recounted, much as it was in *The Book of Urizen,* chapter VII. Here, Los and Enitharmon sorrow over the binding of the child and return to liberate him, only to find that his limbs have vegetated and taken root in the rocks, becoming interwoven with "the Chain of Jealousy" (*FZ* 5.62.23). Los and Enitharmon faint, revive, and return to Golgonooza, leaving Orc to howl away in pain. "[T]he rendings of fierce howling Orc" (*FZ* 5.63.16) reach down into the deep dens of Urizen and disturb that fallen Zoa, awakening in him memories of Eternity. Urizen rouses and begins to explore his caverns as this brief Night ends.

Night the Sixth

Urizen's attempt to satisfy his thirst by drinking from a river is stayed by "three terrific women" (*FZ* 6.67.5) who turn out to be his fallen daughters (Blake is probably alluding to the aged King Lear and his three daughters). Urizen curses them and they, in turn, curse Tharmas (the logic seems to be that the curse directed at Tharmas in his role as god of water prevents the satisfaction of Urizen's desire). Tharmas appears with his waves frozen upright and expresses his wish to die; he also asks Urizen to enter into a kind of contract to guarantee their mutual annihilation: "Withhold thy light from me for ever & I will withhold / From thee thy food so we shall cease to be" (*FZ* 6.69.15–16). Urizen opts out of this arrangement and begins to explore his ruined world. The ruin has something to do with the changed language of nature, no longer "Vocal as in Climes of happy Eternity" (*FZ* 6.71.5). At last he begins to rebuild his mechanistic world and gets it running again before making his way to the rival world of Golgonooza built by Los. In the caves of Orc he finds the horses of light stolen by Luvah (Orc's eternal form). He spins the web of religion and plants the Tree of Mystery.

Night the Seventh

N.B.: Because Night VII exists in two separate manuscripts, conventionally labeled VIIa and VIIb, no easy summary of the action of this Night is possible, as the reader sometimes has the sense that the same events are narrated twice. For the textual problem of integrating VIIa and VIIb, see *E* 836.

Urizen descends into the caves of Orc where he finds the horses of light (v. end of Night VI). Orc remains bound, but his spirit soars into "the shrine of Enitharmon" (*FZ* 7.77.22), making Los envious of Orc's intimacy with his own emanation. The envy evidently originates somehow with Urizen, who seems to be the source of most negative emotions. What is clear, at any rate, is that Urizen is the source of all morality and superstition, a deadly combination symbolized by the Tree of Mystery. Urizen causes the Tree to take root in the caves of Orc and extend its branches up "into the heaven of Los" (*FZ* 7.78.6). Then, in what seems a grotesque parody of the temptation of Christ in the wilderness, Urizen expresses pity for the enchained Orc, but Orc will have none of this: "Thy Pity I contemn" (*FZ* 7.78.43). Urizen responds with admonitions to keep the commandments of duty and law, and then summons his three daughters—Eleth, Uveth, and Ona—to knead the "bread of Sorrow" (*FZ* 7.79.23), which is a symbol of religious hypocrisy, food that pretends to nourish but, instead, starves humanity. Urizen's insistence on moral duty causes Orc to take the form of a serpent that negates the commandment to obey: Orc in serpent form wreathed about the Tree of Mystery is Blake's explanation of the antecedent action of the book of Genesis. Similarly, when "the Shadow of Enitharmon" (*FZ* 7.81.12) leaves Los out of pity for Orc and then returns, Blake is replaying Eve's fall in his own terms (borrowed more from Milton's *Paradise Lost* than from the Bible, however). To further explain the genesis of Genesis, the Shadow of Enitharmon tells the Spectre of Urthona "Secrets of Eternity" (*FZ* 7.83.5): It seems that the Eternal Man (Albion) coupled with Vala to produce Urizen, making him "First born of Generation" (*FZ* 7.83.13). The logic seems to be that since Vala is nature, any creature born of her would be natural—which may explain Urizen's role as architect of Ulro. The really strange part of the Shadow's creation story is how, after the birth of Urizen, Vala doubles into herself and Luvah. The allegory may be an attempt to explain the belief that once an act of generation takes place, humanity divides into the sexes: birth gives birth to the necessity of parents of opposite sex. Continuing her account of these primal events, the Shadow claims that Luvah "assumd the Place / Of the Eternal Man & smote him" (*FZ* 7.83.31–32). This would account for the sleep of Albion that opens the poem in Night I. To simplify, the Shadow of Enitharmon and the Spectre of Urthona can be thought of as roughly analogous to Eve and Adam after the fall; that is, they are the negation of the kind of humanity represented by Los and Enitharmon proper. The proof of this assertion comes when the Shadow and the Spectre, under the shadow of the Tree of Mystery, embrace and produce "male forms without female counterparts or Emanations" (*FZ* 7.85.19).

These creatures become Urizen's warriors, and under his supervision carry on trade, commerce, religion, and war. Still rewriting Genesis, Blake explains the reason for the division in Genesis of day and night: "The day for war the night for secret religion in [Urizen's] temple" (*FZ* 7.96.18). The intense imagery of carnage that dominates for several pages is undoubtedly inspired by the Napoleonic Wars. Even Los seems to succumb to the compulsion to follow war, a development that causes Enitharmon to cry out for his awakening. Finally, in what seems an act of desperation to end the Urizenic wars, the Shadow (of Urthona?) embraces the fire of Orc and sets his revolutionary energy free: "The hairy shoulders rend the links free are the wrists of fire" (*FZ* 7.91.17; cf. *AP* 2.2). Orc might be identified here as Napoleon, an interpretation consistent with the efforts of "[t]he dragons of the North" to put down "the rising of the glorious King" (*FZ* 7.91.27, 30). The effort succeeds, as Luvah is crucified and the British/Roman empire of Urizen goes on to celebrate the wonders of conquest. All that is left of Orc is the serpent form about the Tree of Mystery, which is, at the same time, the cross of Jesus and the fatal tree in Eden. The Tree of Mystery takes root in Los's world, but then a turning point occurs in the poem as Los puts an end to the torments of love and jealousy in the spirit of forgiveness: "I will quell my fury & teach / Peace to the Soul of dark revenge & repentance to Cruelty" (*FZ* 7.86.11–12). At the end of Night 7, Los bears a close resemblance to William Blake as he literally remakes his enemy Urizen, whereupon Los is surprised "that he felt love & not hate" (*FZ* 7.90.65).

Night the Eighth

The Council of God meets in the form of Jesus "to create the fallen Man" (*FZ* 8.99.3), that is, to awaken Albion. The process is evidently a gradual one, since Albion is not fully awake until Night 9. The action in Eternity is enough, however, to inspire Los and Enitharmon with "the Divine Vision" (*FZ* 8.99.15), and so they begin to rehumanize the spectral victims of Urizen's wars. Meanwhile, Orc remains perverted into serpent form by mystery and moral law, and Urizen continues to use Orc's energy for his own ends, trying "[t]o undermine the World of Los" (*FZ* 8.100.34). In other words, Blake sets up a competition between human and inhuman forces as the conditions of Los's world, with the full horror of war and religion being mitigated by humanity. Urizen's power is compromised when "the Shadowy Female" (*FZ* 8.102.26) urges the "King of Light [to] relent" (*FZ* 8.103.12). Her tears saturate the "Web of Religion" and cause it to collapse, whereupon Urizen becomes "tangled in his own net" (*FZ* 8.103.26, 31). Los and Enitharmon continue the work of creative humanity and form a "Vast family" (*FZ* 8.103.37) in female form: this is Jerusalem, or liberty, the basis for redemption from the kind of world perpetuated by Urizen. There follows an important passage (*FZ* 8.113.1–104.18) describing Golgonooza, Ulro, and Beulah from the perspective of Eternity. In Golgonooza, Los and Enitharmon create humanity, and Satan tries to destroy it. In Ulro, the scene is one of torment and mystery due to Urizen's laws. In Beulah, the end or purpose (of Beulah itself) is seen as redemption. After this explanatory interlude, the narrative returns to Jerusalem, around which (or about whom) an enormous war rages, out of which emerges Satan himself as a kind of reverse emanation—"[a] male without a female counterpart" (*FZ* 8.104.25). Jerusalem here is not so much the emanation of the giant Albion as the site of the crucifixion of Jesus. The death of the "Lamb of God" gives birth to "Mystery" (*FZ* 8.105.6, 15), the name written on Vala's forehead as she assumes the role of Rahab, or whore of Babylon (see *FZ* 8.105.13–30). "Thus was the Lamb of God condemnd to Death" (*FZ* 8.106.1) by Mystery (a.k.a. Rahab, Tirzah, Amalek). Los, in the role of Joseph of Arimathea, takes the body down from the cross and protects it in the sepulcher. He then admonishes Rahab to repent, as he has, so that Jerusalem can be set free. Urizen, who is, after all, the source of all mystery, hears Los's admonition and becomes stupefied. His weakness is Orc's strength, which is still, evidently, the negative energy of iconoclastic power, or revolution for revolution's sake. Tharmas and Urthona empower Los to protect Enitharmon during the rage of Orc when Urizen "repentant forgets his wisdom" (*FZ* 8.107.17). Urizen's forgotten wisdom is personified as Ahania, who appears and sings a pessimistic song of death (*FZ* 8.108.9–109.12). Her song is countered by a reply from Enion, who offers an optimistic song of death that looks forward to the day when "[t]he Eternal Man . . . reassumes his ancient bliss" (*FZ* 8.110.27–28). When this resumption of eternal bliss will occur is indicated by the length of time that the Lamb of God resides in the sepulcher. In the traditional biblical version of events, Jesus rises after three days; in Blake's millenarian version, the period of entombment is two thousand years. During this time, Rahab holds Jerusalem captive. Toward the end of the period, however, Rahab communes with Orc and ceases to be Mystery; or, rather, Mystery is reformed into Deism: "so now anew began / Babylon again in Infancy Calld Natural Religion" (*FZ* 8.115.23–24). Thus, Blake brings his fantastic narrative up to his own times by the end of the eighth night.

Night the Ninth

"Night the Ninth," subtitled "The Last Judgment," begins with Los and Enitharmon building Jerusalem while Jesus stands beside them in spirit even though the body of the lamb is still in the sepulcher (cf. Orc's capacity to maintain an active spirit while his body is bound). If Jerusalem is the new world of liberty, then the old world of mystery must be destroyed to ensure the survival of liberty. Los commences the apocalypse when he seizes the sun and moon and rips the firmament apart, whereupon we find that the last judgment is a political judgment against "[t]he thrones of Kings" and the oppressors of the poor, who "awake up to the harvest" (*FZ* 9.117.18–19). Mystery and moral law (respectively, Rahab/Tirzah and the books of Urizen) are consumed by the fires of Orc, which action makes possible "bright visions of Eternity" (*FZ* 9.118.19). As mystery ends, "intellect/And Reason" begin (*FZ* 9.119.19–20), so Albion, awakening, calls on Urizen to "[c]ome forth" from the "slumbers of . . . cold abstraction" (*FZ* 9.120.19). Albion threatens to cast out Urizen if he does not repent of religion, "first author of this war" (*FZ* 9.120.43). Urizen repents and arises, and Ahania dies—but Urizen can expect to find her reborn "in the spring" once he assumes his proper role as cultivator of humanity (*FZ* 9.122.10–12). Urizen's repentance is a momentous event that makes "[a]ll things reversd" (*FZ* 9.122.27): evidence of this reversal comes when tyrants, priests, warriors, and merchants are seized by those whom, formerly, they oppressed. Humanity begins to be remade when Urizen and his sons beat guns and other weapons into plowshares. Urizen drives "the Plow of ages" and replants "the Seed of Men" into "their own appointed places" (*FZ* 9.124.26, 30; 9.125.7); significantly, the seeds of "Kings & Princes" fall on "unproducing sands" and "hardend rocks" (*FZ* 9.125.10–11). Then, "watered" by the fires of Orc, the harvest of humanity begins to ripen, and Ahania awakens from death. In one of the most important passages in the poem, Albion orders Luvah and Vala to return to their proper place in the loins and warns against the chaos that ensues "[i]f Gods combine against Man Setting their Dominion above / The Human form Divine" (*FZ* 9.126.9–10). With Luvah and Vala restored to the loins, Blake presents a dialogue between them to represent the earthly paradise of healthy, human sexual love (compare this section, from 126.18 to 129.18, to *The Book of Thel*). With Luvah and Vala reconciled, and Urizen and Ahania meaningfully related, Tharmas calls on Enion to return and rejoin him. Through the intercession of Vala, Tharmas and Enion are "renewd" in the form of childhood innocence: "Thou little Boy art Tharmas & thou bright Girl Enion"

(*FZ* 9.130.7–8). Perhaps because the Zoas are now all rehabilitated, Urizen shouts "Times are Ended" and begins to reap the harvest of humanity he has sown (*FZ* 9.131.31, 9.132.5–7). The valley of dry bones begins to animate and gives off the voice of Enion, who celebrates the "human form" and the "joys of existence" (*FZ* 9.132.18, 28). Albion arises, but the other Eternals observe that he is a changed Man— his female form is now separate, which makes generation both possible and necessary. The changed form of Albion prompts one of the Eternals to deliver a speech describing the conditions of human existence that begins with mortality ("Man is a Worm") but ends with love and community: "Man liveth not by Self alone but in his brothers face" (*FZ* 9.133.11, 25). At last, Mystery is declared a thing of the past, and a song of liberty follows in which the end of Mystery is celebrated in language almost identical to that of *America* (6.6–15), except for the substitution of "Mystery" for the earlier "Empire." Blake's imaginary apocalypse of political freedom is given expression by another song of liberty "[c]omposed by an African Black" (*FZ* 9.134.35–135.1–3) and by an effective epigram delivered by Luvah: "Attempting to be more than Man We become less" (*FZ* 9.135.21). After Urizen threshes out the nations and the "Legions of Mystery" run through "the wine presses of Luvah" (*FZ* 9.135.34–38), Albion calls for Tharmas and Urthona to arise, and all the Zoas assume their proper places, restored to unity. The poem ends with Urthona, regenerate, putting off religion and putting on "the golden armour of science / For intellectual War" (*FZ* 9.139.8–9): "The war of swords departed now / The dark Religions are departed & sweet Science reigns" (*FZ* 9.139.9–10).

Notes

Introduction

1. E. P. Thompson, *The Making of the English Working Class* (New York: Vintage, 1966), 52: "Against the background of London Dissent, with its fringe of deists and earnest mystics, William Blake seems no longer the cranky untutored genius to those who know only the genteel culture of the time."

2. Raymond Schwab, *The Oriental Renaissance: Europe's Rediscovery of India and the East, 1680–1880,* trans. Gene Patterson-Black and Victor Reinking (New York: Columbia University Press, 1984), 11. According to Schwab, the phrase "La Renaissance oriental" first appears as a chapter title in Edgar Quinet's *Génie des religions* (1841).

3. G. E. Bentley, Jr., in *The Stranger From Paradise: A Biography of William Blake* (New Haven: Yale University Press, 2001), notes that Basire was "the principal engraver to the Society of Antiquaries" and says that Blake most likely saw Bryant in Basire's shop (32, 38); he also says that Blake's engraving work for Basire "probably included some of the quarto plates in Jacob Bryant's *New System*" (66).

4. Jacob Bryant, *A New System, or, An Analysis of Ancient Mythology,* 2d ed., 3 vols. (1775–76; rpt. New York and London: Garland, 1979), 2: 251. Further references are cited parenthetically in the text as "Bryant."

5. The usual explanation for Blake's use of the term *Zoas* is that he picked it up from the Greek of the New Testament in the fourth chapter of Revelations, where the Greek plural *Zoa* is used to refer to "the four living creatures" of Ezekiel's vision in the first chapter of the Book of Ezekiel. See Harold Bloom's commentary in *E,* 948.

6. See Bryant, *A New System,* 2: 344, for Thamuz and Thaumus; 3: 2 for Luban. For discussion of these references see Kathleen Raine, *Blake and Tradition,* 2 vols. (Princeton: Princeton University Press, 1968), 1: 416 n.35.

7. Northrop Frye, *Fearful Symmetry: A Study of William Blake* (1947; Princeton: Princeton University Press, 1969), 108.

8. Jon Mee, *Dangerous Enthusiasm: William Blake and the Culture of Radicalism in the 1790s* (Oxford: Clarendon Press, 1992), 30, 20.

9. Blake's cycles are progressive, however—otherwise they could not point to apocalypse at all. This double sense of time as both cyclical and progressive, together with other elements of Blake's poetic system, can be accounted for more fully if religious traditions outside the Western canon come into play. The possibility that Blake drew on such traditions is heightened by his exposure to them, and also by his belief that those traditions were legitimated by inspiration. The dual nature of time as both cyclical and linear is apparently expressed in *The Four Zoas* when "[t]he Saviour mild and gentle" establishes the boundaries of human experience: "Then wondrously the Starry Wheels felt the divine hand. Limit / Was put to Eternal Death" (*FZ* 4.56.17, 23–24).

10. S. Foster Damon, *William Blake: His Philosophy and Symbols* (Boston and New York: Houghton Mifflin, 1924), 145.

11. Denis Saurat, *Blake and Modern Thought* ([New York]: Dial Press, 1929), 109.

12. Frye, *Fearful Symmetry*, 173, 442n. 4.

13. Editor's preface, Peter F. Fisher, *The Valley of Vision: Blake as Prophet and Revolutionary*, ed. Northrop Frye (Toronto: University of Toronto Press, 1961), v.

14. Raine, *Blake and Tradition*, 1:xxxi.

15. Charu Sheel Singh, *The Chariot of Fire: A Study of William Blake in the Light of Hindu Thought* (Salzburg: Institut für Anglistik und Amerikanistik, Universität salzburg, 1981), 25. Singh compares the common classical image of the sun in a chariot drawn by horses that appears in Blake's "To Summer" (*E* 409) to a passage from the *Rig Veda* taken from W. J. Wilkins, *Hindu Mythology* (New Delhi: Rupa & Co., 1978).

16. Kathryn S. Freeman, *Blake's Nostos: Fragmentation and Nondualism in "The Four Zoas"* (Albany: State University of New York Press, 1997), 32–33.

17. See, for example, Raine, *Blake and Tradition*, 1:xxvii.

18. The image of the Indian lingam is deemed obscene by the comte de Volney in *The Ruins; or, a Survey of the Revolutions of Empire*, 3d ed. (London: J. Johnson, 1796), 167; the "alluring forms" of the Devi are described in Edward Moor, *The Hindu Pantheon* (London: J. Johnson, 1810), 235.

19. An example of this competition is E. P. Thompson's commentary on Raine's *Blake and Tradition* in *Witness against the Beast: William Blake and the Moral Law* (Cambridge: Cambridge University Press, 1993), xviii: "Much of Raine's 'tradition' appears, at first sight, to say some of the things that Blake is saying, but it is saying them in a different way. It is genteel, other-worldly, elusive, whereas Blake—whether in poetic or in visual image—has a certain literalness of expression, robustness and concretion. . . . Raine's 'tradition' . . . lacks altogether the radical edge or bite of Blake's expression."

20. This condensed and partial history of Blake interpretation is represented by the following texts: Edwin John Ellis and William Butler Yeats, *The Works of William Blake*, 3 vols. (London: Bernard Quaritch, 1893); David V. Erdman, *Blake: Prophet Against Empire: A Poet's Interpretation of the History of His Own Times* (Princeton: Princeton University Press, 1954); Harold Bloom, *Blake's Apocalypse: A Study in Poetic Argument* (Garden City: Doubleday, 1963); Raine, *Blake and Tradition*; and Thompson, *Witness against the Beast*.

21. Thompson's *Witness against the Beast* and his antinomian interpretation of Blake may be the most substantial contribution to our historical understanding of the poet since Erdman's *Prophet against Empire*. But Thompson's earlier presentation of Blake as a radical writer (in *The Making of the English Working Class*) has been questioned on the basis of "the comparatively scant record of direct peer intersection" and on other grounds by Steve Clark and David Worrall in their introduction to *Historicizing Blake* (New York: St. Martin's, 1994), 4–11. Given this criticism, I must qualify my own use of the epithet *radical* in relation to Blake. Clearly, Blake is not a radical writer in the same sense that Paine is because he is a poet and not a pamphleteer. At the same time, *America* and the "Song of Liberty" appended to *The Marriage of Heaven and Hell* offer ample evidence of Blake's interest in republican ideology, a radical position by any measure in the England of the early 1790s. Thus Blake can be called a radical author for a span of five years or so (1790–95), but he cannot be understood as a radical activist: there is no real evidence to show that he ever acted on the radical sentiments he entertained in his poetry.

Chapter 1: Politics

1. Peter Ackroyd, *Blake* (New York: Knopf, 1996), 145.

2. Richard D. Altick, *The Shows of London* (Cambridge: Belknap Press of Harvard University Press, 1978), 299. Altick adds that public memory of the tiger attack against General Munro's son in 1792 helps to account for the popularity of a mechanical tiger that was first exhibited in 1808 and is still on view in the Victoria and Albert Museum. The Muslim potentate Tipu Sultan had the tiger built for his amusement; it was "captured" by the English after Tipu's defeat in 1799. When activated by a crank mechanism, the artificial tiger lets out a roar as it devours a prostrate English citizen who lies in terror under the beast.

3. The seeming inconsistency between poem and picture has been noted by, among others, Anne Kostelanetz Mellor, *Blake's Human Form Divine* (Berkeley: University of California Press, 1974), 65; Martin K. Nurmi, *William Blake* (1975; Kent: Kent State University Press, 1976), 64; and Henry Summerfield, *A Guide to the Books of William Blake for Innocent and Experienced Readers* (Gerrards Cross, Buckinghamshire: Colin Smythe, 1998), 95: "For all its greatness as a poem, 'The Tyger' has a feeble illustration. At the foot of a barren tree of Experience stands a beast looking rather like a child's stuffed animal."

4. For the identification of Rintrah as Pitt, see David V. Erdman, *Blake: Prophet Against Empire: A Poet's Interpretation of the History of His Own Times*, 3d ed. (Princeton: Princeton University Press, 1977), 201–2, 210, 212, 218.

5. R. J. Macintosh, ed., *The Memoires of Sir James Macintosh*, 2 vols. (1836), 1: 212. Sir James Mackintosh coined the terms "Sultanised" and "Brahmanised." Quoted by Pamela Nightingale, *Trade and Empire in Western India* (Cambridge: Cambridge University Press, 1970), 137n. 2. Further references are cited parenthetically in the text as "Nightingale."

6. Eudo C. Mason, introduction to *The Mind of Henry Fuseli: Selections from his Writings* ([London]: Routledge & Paul, [1951]), 45.

7. G. S. Misra, *British Foreign Policy and Indian Affairs, 1783–1815* (London: Asia Publishing House, 1963), 1. Further references are cited parenthetically in the text as "Misra."

8. Rudolph Robert, *Chartered Companies and their Role in the Development of Overseas Trade* (London: G. Bell, 1969), 73. Further references are cited parenthetically in the text as "Robert."

9. Lucy S. Sutherland, *The East India Company in Eighteenth-century Politics* (Oxford: Clarendon Press, 1952), 365. Further references are cited parenthetically in the text as "Sutherland."

10. George D. Bearce, *British Attitudes towards India, 1784–1858* (London and New York: Oxford University Press, 1961), 11–12. Further references are cited parenthetically in the text as "Bearce."

11. J. L. Brockington, "Warren Hastings and Orientalism," *The Impeachment of Warren Hastings: Papers from a Bicentenary Commemoration*, ed. Geoffrey Carnall and Colin Nicholson (Edinburgh: Edinburgh University Press, 1989), 92–93.

12. Another example is *A Defense of the political and parliamentary Conduct of the Right Honorable Edmund Burke* (1794). According to the *Analytical Review*, the author of the pamphlet offers an "ironical defense" of Burke in which "[t]he unprecedented length of Mr. Hastings's trial is thus pleasantly vindicated," as this quotation shows: "It has been said, that the unprecedented length of the impeachment was a disgrace to the jurisprudence of the country, and an intolerable grievance to Mr. Hastings. That it has been attended with some *slight* inconvenience to that gentleman I am ready to admit: but is the inconvenience of an individual to be regarded, when so much *pleasure* and *satisfaction* arise to the whole nation, from its curiosity being gratified in beholding the novel and superb spectacle occasioned by the trial of Warren Hastings?" (*AR* 20 [Sept.–Dec. 1794]: 83).

13. Brian Gardner, *The East India Company: A History* (New York: McCall, 1972), 133. Further references are cited parenthetically in the text as "Gardner."

14. A. Berriedale Keith, preface to *Speeches and Documents on Indian Policy, 1750–1921,* 2 vols. (London: Oxford University Press, 1922), 1: xv–xvi.

15. Blake's infernal interpretation of the same political and religious matters that Johnson chronicled through the relatively staid medium of the *Analytical Review* shows that the poet and the publisher were part of the same radical milieu. The extent of their actual contact with each other, however, remains a topic of conjecture. We do know that Blake's employment with Johnson intensified in the 1790s, when Johnson published 14 books with prints engraved by Blake. Several of these books were authored by some of the more radical members of the Johnson circle. For example, Blake did engravings for Mary Wollstonecraft's children's book, *Original Stories from Real Life* (1791), and for J. G. Stedman's *A Narrative, of a Five Years' expedition, against the Revolted Negroes of Surinam* (1796), a book detailing the horrors of slavery. See G. E. Bentley, Jr., *Blake Records* (Oxford: Clarendon Press, 1969), 609–19, for a list of the engraving projects on which Blake is known to have worked. The involvement with Johnson and Wollstonecraft argues that Blake was, at the very least, "on the periphery of the Johnson circle" (ibid., 41). E. P. Thompson believes Blake was "occasionally present" at the weekly dinner parties that Johnson held for his radical friends Paine, Priestley, Wollstonecraft, and Fuseli (Thompson, *Witness Against the Beast,* 127). It is certain that he dined with Johnson and some fellow engravers in June 1794 because the fact is so recorded in Stedman's journal, and also on 4 April 1797, according to an entry in William Godwin's diary (Erdman, *Blake: Prophet Against Empire,* 157). Although this diary has been called "the only consistent record of the Johnson circle," Godwin's failure to record Blake's presence more frequently should not be taken to mean that the poet was unaware of the political and cultural issues the circle discussed. For one thing, Godwin was not a regular member of the Johnson circle until January 1797 (ibid., 158 n.26), well after the most intense period of Blake's involvement with Johnson as his employer; for another, we should not assume that Johnson would have invited the eccentric engraver and the rationalistic philosopher to dine on the same evenings. Blake was probably party to some discussions at Johnson's dinner table off-and-on throughout the 1790s, and even when he was not he could have gotten second-hand reports from his friend Fuseli, who was much more involved with Johnson than Blake was because of his regular contributions to the *Analytical Review* (see Mason, *The Mind of Henry Fuseli,* 356–58, for a list of Fuseli's contributions to the *Analytical Review*). It is reasonable to suppose that the material that appeared in the *Analytical Review* was also discussed in the Johnson circle, and that Blake participated in some of those conversations, or that Blake occasionally saw issues of the journal when he went to Johnson on business related to his own engraving work. Blake's opportunity for exposure to the material discussed in Johnson's *Analytical Review* is crucial to the argument that the poet was also exposed to Eastern mythology at precisely the point when he was forming his own system of mythology. And while we cannot assume that Blake read all the articles about India that appeared in the *Analytical Review*—or, for that matter, that he read any of them—their mere

presence reveals the interest in Indian culture that had penetrated into the milieu of republican politics and dissenting theology where Blake circulated. The most recent assessment of Blake's relationship to Johnson affirms, in my view, that the two men were in regular contact during the period when new information about the myths of India appeared in the *Analytical Review*. In *The Stranger from Paradise: A Biography of William Blake* (New Haven: Yale University Press, 2001), G. E. Bentley, Jr. says that "Johnson was one of the chief employers of Blake's graver" from 1779 to 1786, but that, "[b]eginning in 1787, when Blake met Fuseli, his commissions from Johnson became increasingly ambitious" (108). Reflecting on his relationship with Blake, Johnson in 1802 wrote to William Hayley: "Ever since I have had a connection with Mr Blake I have wished to serve him & on every occasion have endeavored to do so" (quoted by Bentley, *The Stranger from Paradise*, 108).

16. Gerald P. Tyson, *Joseph Johnson: A Liberal Publisher* (Iowa City: University of Iowa Press, 1979), 95.

17. For this reading of Blake's "London," see E. P. Thompson, *Witness against the Beast: William Blake and the Moral Law* (Cambridge: Cambridge University Press, 1993), 176 and 176n. 5.

18. William Jones, "The Preliminary Discourse," *Asiatick Researches*, 12 vols. (London: Vernor and Hood, 1798), 1: ix. Further references are cited parenthetically in the text as "Jones, *Asiatick Researches*."

19. William Jones, "The Third Anniversary Discourse," *Sir William Jones: A Reader*, ed. Satya S. Pachori (Delhi: Oxford University Press, 1993), 175.

20. Quoted by O. P. Kejariwal, *The Asiatic Society of Bengal and the Discovery of India's Past, 1784–1838* (Delhi: Oxford University Press, 1988), 64. Further references are cited parenthetically in the text as "Kejariwal."

21. Kejariwal, 14–15, claims that di Nobili was, in fact, the author of the *Ezour-Vedam*; Raymond Schwab, however, disputes di Nobili's authorship in his authoritative 1950 study, *The Oriental Renaissance: Europe's Rediscovery of India and the East, 1680–1880*, trans. Gene Patterson-Black and Victor Reinking (New York: Columbia University Press, 1984), 155. What is clear, in any case, is that the *Ezour-Vedam* "reflects the ordinary learning of the missionary circles rather than Brahmanic sources" (Schwab, 155).

22. The year before this first review of the *Asiatick Researches* was published, Fuseli had developed a close working relationship with Johnson as the translator of J. C. Lavater's *Aphorisms on Man* (1788), and he continued to work for the publisher on a variety of projects. John Knowles, Fuseli's nineteenth-century biographer and literary executor, says Fuseli wrote "upwards of eighty articles" for the *Analytical Review*, "some of which were long and laboured criticisms, while others were only brief notices of the contents of the books" (John Knowles, *The Life and Writings of Henry Fuseli*, 3 vols. [London: Colburn and Bentley, 1831], 1: 80). In his study of Joseph Johnson, Gerald P.

Tyson comments that, "[i]n addition to his own writings, Fuseli performed humbler tasks for Johnson, the full extent of which will probably never be known" (Tyson, *Joseph Johnson,* 62). One task was that of part-time editor of Johnson's edition of William Cowper's translation of Homer. This project began in 1786 and continued into 1789, at which time Fuseli "restricted his contributions to a few textual notes [to the *Odyssey*] identified by the initial 'F.'" (Tyson, 63). Fuseli, then, was using his initial to identify himself as the author of his notes to Cowper's Homer in the same year that the initial "F." turns up at the end of the first review of the *Asiatick Researches.* In an appendix to *The Mind of Henry Fuseli,* Eudo C. Mason attempts to infer Fuseli's authorship of contributions to the *Analytical Review* based on his "peculiar style, his favourite phrases and quotations, themes and ideas." This method, says Mason, "make[s] it possible to determine [Fuseli's] authorship beyond reasonable doubt in most cases" (354). Mason also follows Knowles's observation that Fuseli's articles "generally have the initials Z.Z. affixed" (355). In addition to the initials Z.Z., Fuseli is said to have used the initials "Y.Y., U.U., V.V. and (pretty certainly) L.L." (356). Strangely, Mason does not list F. as one of Fuseli's shorthand signatures, even though that initial is both obvious in itself and obvious because it is clearly recorded as a sign of Fuseli's authorship elsewhere—in his notes to Cooper's Homer and in some of his letters (see, for example, a letter to William Roscoe dated November 1791 as reproduced in David H. Weinglass, ed., *The Collected Letters of Henry Fuseli* [Millwood, New York: Kraus, 1982], 76). This failure to consider F. as one of Fuseli's initial signatures is especially perplexing in view of the fact that some of the articles attributed to Fuseli on the basis of his "peculiar style . . . , themes and ideas" are comparable in style, theme, and idea to articles signed F. but not attributed to Fuseli. For example, Mason attributes a review of *Bell's New Pantheon* signed R.R. to Fuseli. This review observes that "[l]ess attention has been paid to orthography and correctness of spelling in general, than might have been expected" (*AR* 8 [Sept.–Dec. 1790]: 295). The preceding article, a review of Condorcet's *Life of Voltaire,* is signed F.; this F. also complains of "many mistakes in orthography" in the book under review (*AR* 8 [Sept.–Dec. 1790]: 291). Mason's method, then, leads to the conclusion that, if R.R. is Fuseli, then F. is also Fuseli because both express concerns about orthography. This logic is particularly useful in suggesting Fuseli's authorship of the second installment in the series of reviews of the first volume of the *Asiatick Researches,* the one that follows the initial notice signed F.: the second review is unsigned, but it summarizes William Jones's essay "On the Orthography of Asiatic Words in Roman Letters" and runs for more than seven pages (*AR* 5 [1789]: 334–41). If a concern with orthography was one of Fuseli's hobbyhorses, then Fuseli is most likely the F. who wrote the review of Condorcet as well as the anonymous reviewer of the essay on orthography from the *Asiatick Researches.*

23. Carol Louise Hall, *Blake and Fuseli: A Study in the Transmission of Ideas* (New York and London: Garland, 1985), 58. All told, Blake did engraving work for Johnson on at least six projects in the 1780s, but Lavater's *Aphorisms* requires special emphasis. Blake annotated his copy of Lavater closely and

also modeled his own "Proverbs of Hell" in *The Marriage of Heaven and Hell* partly on Lavater's aphoristic style, showing that Blake shared some of Fuseli's intellectual interests, and that Johnson's publications occasionally influenced the poet's own work. It follows, then, that Blake could easily have been the beneficiary of Fuseli's and Johnson's interest in the publications of the Asiatic Society, and that he could have put those publications to his own use, just as he did Lavater's *Aphorisms.*

24. Harold Bloom, "Commentary," *E* 897.

Chapter 2: Mythography

1. Alexander Gilchrist, *The Life of William Blake* (1907; rpt. Mineola, N.Y.: Dover, 1998), says that Humphry spent the years 1785–88 in India "and had reaped a golden harvest in Oude by painting miniatures of the native princes" (236).

2. *Asiatick Researches,* 12 vols. (London: Vernor and Hood, 1798), 1: 436–7. The name on the list is spelled Osias Humprys, but the variation in spelling is not sufficient evidence to suppose that the person Blake knew was not the same person who was a member of the Asiatic Society. It should be noted that the designation "Members of the Asiatic Society, From 15 January to 1784 to 15 January 1789" evidently refers to membership at any time over that period, not to membership from the inception of the Society. The original, founding members of the Asiatic Society numbered 13, and Humphry was clearly not of that number. The list with Humphry's name on it includes 86 other regular members, plus the Secretary, John Herbert Harington, and the President, Sir William Jones, who died in 1794.

3. Regarding the invitation to the 1809 exhibition, Blake writes to Humphry: "I inclose a ticket of admission if you should honour my Exhibition with a Visit" (*E* 770).

4. Robert D. Richardson, Jr., introduction to *A New Translation of Volney's Ruins,* 2 vols. (1802; rpt. New York and London: Garland, 1979), 1: v, vii; Gerald P. Tyson, *Joseph Johnson: A Liberal Publisher* (Iowa City: University of Iowa Press, 1979), 137.

5. E. P. Thompson, *Witness Against the Beast: William Blake and the Moral Law* (Cambridge: Cambridge University Press, 1993), 199, xvii.

6. G. E. Bentley, Jr., *Blake Records Supplement* (Oxford: Clarendon Press, 1988), xliv.

7. M. Volney, *The Ruins; or, a Survey of the Revolutions of Empires,* 3d ed. (London: J. Johnson, 1796), 72, 73–74. Further quotations from this edition are cited parenthetically in the text as *"Ruins."*

8. Thompson, *Witness Against the Beast,* 200.

9. Frank E. Manuel, *The Eighteenth Century Confronts the Gods* (Cambridge: Harvard University Press, 1959), 131.

10. Ibid., 134.

11. For the publication history of this and other translations of Indian texts in France, see Raymond Schwab, *The Oriental Renaissance: Europe's Rediscovery of India and the East,* 1680–1880 (New York: Columbia University Press, 1984), 51–52.

12. John Drew, *India and the Romantic Imagination* (Delhi and New York: Oxford University Press, 1987), 71n. 143.

13. Ibid., 78.

14. Flaxman had known Blake since 1779; Hayley may have been acquainted with Blake as early as 1784, when Flaxman sent him a copy of Blake's *Poetical Sketches,* although his patronage of Blake's engraving did not begin until 1800. For a discussion of Blake's friendship with Flaxman and Hayley, see Ackroyd, *Blake,* 70–72, 214, 220–22, and passim.

15. William Hayley, *An Elegy on the Death of the Honorable Sir William Jones* (London: Cadell and Davies, 1795), 35.

16. William Jones, *The Works of Sir William Jones,* 2 vols. (1807; rpt. New York and London: Garland, 1984), 319–20. Further references to this edition are cited parenthetically in the text as "Jones."

17. Drew calls Maurice "the most influential on literature of Jones's followers" and says that "the space given to him by the periodicals in the 1790s is as much as that given to the *Asiatic Researches.*" *India and the Romantic Imagination,* 80, 81n. 214.

18. Thomas Maurice, *The History of Hindostan,* 3 vols. (1795–98; rpt. New York and London: Garland, 1984), 2: vi. Further references are cited parenthetically in the text as *"HH."*

19. A. D. Nuttall, *The Alternative Trinity: Gnostic Heresy in Marlowe, Milton, and Blake* (Oxford: Clarendon Press, 1998), 11. In Kathleen Raine, *Blake and Tradition,* 2 vols. (Princeton: Princeton University Press, 1968), 2: 180, the image of the serpent-entwined egg from Bryant's *New System* is reproduced with the caption "The Orphic world egg." "Ophic" rather than "Orphic" would seem to be correct.

20. William Jones, "The Hymn to Narayena," *Sir William Jones: A Reader,* ed. Satya S. Pachori (Oxford: Oxford University Press, 1993), 51.

21. For a discussion of some of Blake's and Priestley's shared attitudes, see Jon Mee, *Dangerous Enthusiasm: William Blake and the Culture of Radicalism*

in the 1790s (Oxford: Clarendon Press, 1992), 176–77. In the early 1790s Priestley's dissenting views and republican politics put him and Blake in the same radical camp, and Blake would certainly have looked with favor upon Priestley's highly public support of the French Revolution. That support is sounded even in the unlikely forum of *A Comparison of the Institutions of Moses with those of the Hindoos,* where Priestley says, "I still trust that the consequences of that revolution will be great and happy" (*A Comparison of the Institutions of Moses with those of the Hindoos and other Ancient Nations* [Northumberland: A. Kennedy, 1799], xv. Further references are cited parenthetically in the text as "Priestley"). In the preface to *The Institutions of Moses* Priestley alludes to the "riots in Birmingham," a reference to the events of 1791 when William Pitt spurred reactionary patriots to loot Priestley's house, destroying many of his manuscripts and working papers. This attack and the atmosphere of intolerance led Priestley to immigrate to Philadelphia in 1794. The sense expressed in the preface to *The Institutions of Moses* that Priestley is getting back to interrupted mythographic work is clear. In other words, there is some evidence to indicate that the theological comparison of Mosaic and Hindu religion published in 1799 was the completion of a project formulated earlier in the decade when Priestley might have had some contact with Blake. The reason for suggesting this tortured connection is that some of the mythological references made in Priestley's book also appear in Blake's poetry. At the same time, Priestley's account of the original circumstances that gave rise to his 1799 book illustrate, once again, the intensity of interest in Indian affairs circa 1790, and, whereas Blake's association with Priestley in 1790 is uncertain, no uncertainty attaches to the fact that Blake was subject to the same historical circumstances that Priestley experienced.

22. The painter Samuel Palmer (1805–51) told Blake's first biographer Alexander Gilchrist (1828–61) that Blake "was no disciple of Priestley" (Gilchrist, *The Life of William Blake,* 321), a fairly meaningless remark because Blake can hardly be called a disciple of anyone at all. Also, Palmer was born the year after Priestley died and only knew Blake in his last years after he had already lumped Priestley in with those "Druid" rationalists Francis Bacon and Isaac Newton. Blake's "The Everlasting Gospel" (c. 1818) compares all three men to that arch-materialist, "Caesar himself": "Like dr Priestly & Bacon & Newton / Poor Spiritual Knowledge is not worth a button" (*E* 519).

23. Piloo Nanavutty, "William Blake and Hindu Creation Myths," *The Divine Vision: Studies in the Poetry and Art of William Blake* (1957; New York: Haskell House, 1968), 170; Raine, *Blake and Tradition,* 2: 51–52.

24. The composition of most of *The Four Zoas,* including "Night the Sixth," has been plausibly dated sometime after 1800. See *E* 718.

25. S. Foster Damon, *William Blake: His Philosophy and Symbols* (Boston and New York: Houghton Mifflin, 1924), 426.

26. William Julius Mickle, "Enquiry into the Religious Tenets and Philosophy of the Brahmins," in *The Lusiad: or, The Discovery of India,* 3d ed., 2 vols. (London: Cadell and Davies, 1798), 2: 202. Further references are cited parenthetically in the text as "Mickle."

27. See Edward Moor, *The Hindu Pantheon* (London: J. Johnson, 1810), x, for his warm acknowledgments of Wilkins's friendship. Further references to *The Hindu Pantheon* are cited parenthetically in the text as "Moor."

28. Anthony Blunt, "Blake's Pictorial Imagination," *Journal of the Warburg and Courtland Institutes* 6 (1943): 206. The image of the Devi that Blunt refers to appears at the top of plate 33 in Moor's *Hindu Pantheon.*

29. Ibid.

30. Eudo C. Mason, introduction to *The Mind of Henry Fuseli: Selections from his Writings* ([London]: Routledge & Paul, [1951]), 45: "[F]rom 1803 to 1819 [Fuseli] had Moses Haughton living in his home and working under his direction." While it is true that the middle-aged Blake and the elderly Fuseli were hardly as close in 1809 as they had been in their younger days when they collaborated on engraving projects, they were not necessarily estranged from one another during this period, as Peter Ackroyd claims in *Blake* (New York: Knopf, 1996), 287–88, 301. In fact, the public compliments exchanged between them— both before and after the appearance of *The Hindu Pantheon*—suggest a high degree of mutual respect. Blake defended Fuseli against his critics in a letter to the editor of the *Monthly Magazine* in 1806 (*E* 768), and Fuseli lauded Blake around 1815 (G. E. Bentley, Jr., *Blake Records* [Oxford: Clarendon Press, 1969], 238). In June 1810, the Repository of Arts, in a favorable notice of Blake's engravings for Blair's *Grave,* commented that "Blake has lately received much deserved commendation from Fuseli" (Bentley, *Blake Records Supplement,* 62). Thus it is not inconceivable that Fuseli might have pointed out Haughton's work to Blake.

31. David V. Erdman, *The Illuminated Blake* (Garden City: Anchor, 1974), 332, identifies the figure as "Vala dressed as Rahab." W. J. T. Mitchell, *Blake's Composite Art: A Study of the Illuminated Poetry* (Princeton: Princeton University Press, 1978), 206n. 46, gives a history of the interpretation of the figure and says that "the melancholy female of plate 53 . . . is a composite form of Vala and Jerusalem which intertwines the fallen and eternal perspectives" (207). It should be noted that the state of Beulah is itself a composite of "fallen and eternal perspectives."

32. Mitchell, *Blake's Composite Art,* 27.

33. The etching of the elephant-headed figures said to have been done after Blake by William Bell Scott reproduced in figure 10 is taken from Scott's *William Blake: Etchings from his Works* (London: Chatto and Windus, 1878). The etching is the third selection in the book of what are said to be "typical

examples of the beautiful inventions to be found in the master." Scott's note on the etching reads as follows: "The little drawing just mentioned [i.e., a drawing of ocean waves and storm clouds with the caption, "And the waters prevailed upon the earth an hundred and fifty days"] was presented to the present possessor by the late Kenny Meadows, the draughtsman and water-colour painter. On the back of it, till then covered up, he pointed out the exis-tence of a sketch which interested him much, as he considered it an example of Blake's comic style; perhaps the only one. I have thought it worth while to have this drawn on stone for the same reason. It is certainly highly curious. Kenny Meadows believed it was intended by Blake as a symbolic representa-tion of John Varley, who was in later life a man-mountain like Falstaff" (n.p.). Scott's autobiography gives similar information: "Kenny Meadows had given me a little sketch by Blake of a huge stout human figure with an elephant's head, dawdling on his foot a human child similarly equipped, which he explained as most probably a symbolical portrait of Varley, so I was prepared to find a 'mountain of a man'" (*Autobiographical Notes of the Life of William Bell Scott,* ed. W[illiam] Minto, 2 vols. [New York: Harper and Brothers, 1892], 1: 118). John Varley was a watercolorist and an astrologer whom Blake met in 1818. See Ackroyd, *Blake,* 328–32, for a discussion of Blake's and Varley's relationship.

34. Thomas Maurice, *Indian Antiquities* (London: Faulder, 1800), 4: vii–ix.

35. Maurice subtitles his *Indian Antiquities,* in part, *Dissertations relative to . . . The Pure System of Primeval Theology.*

Chapter 3: Theology

1. J. G. Davies, *The Theology of William Blake* (Oxford: Clarendon Press, 1948), 161. Davies adds: "To those who have glorified Blake as the great heresiarch this conclusion [that Blake's theology falls "within the general tradi-tion of Christianity"] may seem somewhat of an anti-climax, but to those whose experience of the Christian religion is as vital as was that of Blake [!], it is but further testimony to the compelling truth of the Gospel for all those who approach it in a spirit of adventure and with a thirst for that wisdom 'that resteth in the heart of him that hath understanding.'"

2. Christopher Hill, *The World Turned Upside Down: Radical Ideas dur-ing the English Revolution* (New York: Viking Press, 1972), 149. Hill quotes from Everard's *The Gospel Treasury Opened,* 2d ed. (1659), I, 221, II, 103, 254, 340.

3. See A. L. Morton, *The Everlasting Gospel: A Study in the Sources of William Blake* (London: Lawrence & Wishart, 1958); Jon Mee, *Dangerous Enthusiasm: William Blake and the Culture of Radicalism* (Oxford: Clarendon

Press, 1992); E. P. Thompson, *Witness against the Beast: William Blake and the Moral Law* (Cambridge: Cambridge University Press, 1993); and A. D. Nutthall, *The Alternative Trinity: Gnostic Heresy in Marlowe, Milton, and Blake* (Oxford: Clarendon Press, 1998).

4. G. E. Bentley, Jr., *The Stranger from Paradise: A Biography of William Blake* (New Haven: Yale University Press, 2001), xxiv, 7–12.

5. Leopold Damrosch, Jr., *Symbol and Truth in Blake's Myth* (Princeton: Princeton University Press, 1980), 70.

6. "Remarks on the Dialogues of Kreeshna and Arjoon," *The Gentleman's Magazine* 55, no. 12 (December 1785): 955.

7. Thomas Maurice, *Indian Antiquities* (London: W. Richardson, 1801), 5: 237, 240.

8. M. Volney, *The Ruins: or, a Survey of the Revolutions of Empire*, 3d ed. (London: J. Johnson, 1796), 350–1n. 31. See also discussion in Chapter 2.

9. Peter Ackroyd, *Blake* (New York: Knopf, 1996), 102.

10. Ibid., 147.

11. Hastings identifies the *Gita* as "an episodical poem from the 'Măhābhărăt,' a most voluminous poem, affirmed to have been written upwards of four thousand years ago, by Krĕĕshnă Dwypayen Veiâs, a learned Bramin; to whom is also attributed the compilation of 'The Four Vêdes, or Bêdes,' the only existing original scriptures of the religion of Brahmâ" (*BG* 5).

12. Wilkins says that the author of the *Bhagavad Gita* intends as his "principal design . . . to bring about the downfall of Polytheism; or, at least, to induce men to believe *God* present in every image before which they bent, and the object of all their ceremonies and sacrifices" (*BG* 24).

13. Northrop Frye was the first to suggest that Blake's moral categories "may come from the three 'Gunas' of the *Bhagavadgita*, XIV," but he does not elaborate on the resemblances at all. See *Fearful Symmetry: A Study of William Blake* (1947; Princeton: Princeton University Press, 1969), 442n. 4.

14. For a thorough discussion of Blake's three classes of men, see Peter F. Fisher, *The Valley of Vision: Blake as Prophet and Revolutionary*, ed. Northrop Frye (Toronto: University of Toronto Press, 1961), 5–16.

15. Thompson, *Witness against the Beast*, 5.

16. Winthdrop Sargeant, trans., *The Bhagavad Gītā* (Albany: State University of New York Press, 1994), 192.

17. Alexander Gilchrist, *The Life of William Blake* (1907; rpt. Mineola: Dover, 1998), 348–49.

18. Kathleen Raine, *Blake and Tradition,* 2 vols. (Princeton: Princeton University Press, 1968), 1: 252.

19. David Quint, *Epic and Empire: Politics and Generic Form from Virgil to Milton* (Princeton: Princeton University Press, 1993), 268–324.

20. John Rist, "Plotinus and Christian Philosophy," *The Cambridge Companion to Plotinus,* ed. Lloyd P. Gerson (Cambridge: Cambridge University Press, 1996), 407–8.

21. Ackroyd, *Blake,* 88–89. For a study of Blake's exposure to Thomas Taylor and Neoplatonism, see George Mills Harper, *The Neoplatonism of William Blake* (Chapel Hill: University of North Carolina Press, 1961).

22. Kathleen Raine and George Mills Harper, eds., *Thomas Taylor the Platonist: Selected Writings* (Princeton: Princeton University Press, 1969), 174.

23. Quoted in Joseph Priestley, *Disquisitions relating to Matter and Spirit* (1777; rpt. Kila, Montana: Kessinger, n.d.), 260. Further references to this edition are cited parenthetically in the text as *"Disquisitions."*

24. William Jones, *The Works of Sir William Jones,* 2 vols. (1807; rpt. New York and London: Garland, 1984), 2: 211–12. Further references to this edition are cited parenthetically in the text as "Jones."

25. John Drew, *India and the Romantic Imagination* (Oxford: Oxford University Press, 1987), 69. Further references are cited parenthetically in the text as "Drew."

26. Obituary of Thomas Taylor, *Gentleman's Magazine 5,* new series (Jan. 1836): 92.

27. Satya S. Pachori, ed., *Sir William Jones: A Reader* (Delhi: Oxford University Press, 1993), 146n. 6. Further references are cited parenthetically in the text as "Pachori."

28. William Jones, "A Hymn to Narayena," *The Asiatic Miscellany* (London: Wallis, 1787), 7. Further references to this edition are cited parenthetically in the text as *"AM."*

29. See S. Foster Damon, *A Blake Dictionary: Ideas and Symbols of William Blake* (Boulder: Shambhala, 1979), for identifications of sense correspondences under the headings of Luvah, Tharmas, Urizen, and Urthona.

30. Thomas Maurice, *Indian Antiquities* 6 (London: John White, 1801): xiv. Further references to this volume are cited parenthetically in the text as *"IA 6."*

31. William Hurd, *A New Universal History of the Religious Rites, Cere-*

monies, and Customs of the Whole World (Newcastle-upon-Tyne: K. Anderson, 1812), 35.

32. Paul Henri Mallet, *Northern Antiquities,* 2 vols. (1770; rpt. New York and London: Garland, 1979): 2: 1.

33. Thompson, *Witness against the Beast,* 159.

Selected Bibliography

Works Cited: Mythographic, Indic, and Other Studies Published during Blake's Age

Asiatick Researches, or, Transactions of the society instituted in Bengal, for inquiring into the history and antiquities, the arts and sciences, and literature of Asia. 12 vols. London: Vernor and Hood, 1798.

Bryant, Jacob. *A New System, or, An Analysis of Ancient Mythology.* 2d ed. 3 vols. 1775–76; rpt. New York and London: Garland, 1979.

Chambers, W., and Sir W[illiam] Jones. *The Asiatic Miscellany.* London: Wallis, 1787.

Hayley, William. *An Elegy on the Death of the Honorable Sir William Jones.* London: Cadell and Davies, 1795.

Hurd, William. *A New Universal History of the Religious Rites, Ceremonies, and Customs of the Whole World.* Newcastle-upon-Tyne: K. Anderson, 1812.

Johnson, Joseph, ed. Review of *Asiatic Researches, or Transactions of the Society Instituted in Bengal, for inquiring into the History and Antiquities, the Arts, Sciences, and Literature of Asia. Analytical Review* 5 (Sept.–Dec. 1789): 202–6.

———, ed. Review of *A Defense of the political and parliamentary Conduct of the Right Honorable Edmund Burke. Analytical Review* 20 (Sept.–Dec. 1794): 83–84.

———, ed. Review of *De l'Inde, &c. On India, or Thoughts on the Means which France ought to employ with Respect to its Possessions in Asia. Analytical Review* 8 (Sept.–Dec. 1790): 357–58.

———, ed. Review of *Dissertations and miscellaneous Pieces relating to the History and Antiquities, the Arts, Sciences, and Literature of Asia. Analytical Review* 18 (Jan.–April 1794): 112.

———, ed. Review of *The East India Charter considered,* by William Fox. *Analytical Review* 17 (Sept.–Dec. 1793): 334–35.

———, ed. Review of "Egypt and other countries adjacent to the Cali River or Nile of Ethiopia, from the ancient books of the hindus," by Francis Wilford. *Analytical Review* 19 (May–August 1794): 120–29.

———, ed. Review of *Heads of Mr. Francis's Speech, in Reply to Mr. Dundas, on the 23d of April, 1793, in a Committee of the whole House, to consider of the Government and Trade of India. Analytical Review* 17 (Sept.–Dec. 1793): 213–14.

———, ed. Review of *Letters, Political, Military, and Commercial, on the present State and Government of Oude and its Dependencies. Analytical Review* 24 (July–Dec. 1796): 424–25.

———, ed. Review of *A Letter to the Right Hon. Edmund Burke, in Reply to his "Reflections on the Revolution in France." Analytical Review* 8 (Sept.–Dec. 1790): 415.

———, ed. Review of *The Merits of Mr. Pitt and Mr. Hastings, as Ministers in War and Peace, impartially stated. Analytical Review* 18 (Jan.–April 1794): 212–14.

———, ed. Review of *"On the Gods of Greece, Italy, and India,"* by Sir William Jones. *Analytical Review* 6 (Jan.–April 1790): 313–17.

———, ed. Review of *Les Préjugés Detruits, &c. (Prejudices Destroyed),* by J. M. Lequinio. *Analytical Review* 17 (Sept.–Dec. 1793): 215–23.

———, ed. Review of *Substance of the Speech of the Right Honourable Henry Dundas, on the British Government and Trade in the East Indies, April 23, 1793. Analytical Review* 17 (Sept.–Dec. 1793): 210–13.

———, ed. Review of *The Theological Repository; consisting of original Essays, Hints, Queries, &c. calculated to promote religious Knowledge,* vols. 4–6. *Analytical Review* 2 (Sept.–Dec. 1788): 304–8.

———, ed. Review of *Translations of the Letters of a Hindoo Rajah; written previous to, and during the Period of his Residence in England. To which is prefixed a preliminary Dissertation on the History, Religion, and Manners of the Hindoos,* by Eliza Hamilton. *Analytical Review* 24 (July–Dec. 1796): 429–31.

Jones, William. *The Works of Sir William Jones.* 2 vols. 1807; rpt. New York and London: Garland, 1984.

Knowles, John. *The Life and Writings of Henry Fuseli.* 3 vols. London: Colburn and Bentley, 1831.

Mallet, Paul Henri. *Northern Antiquities.* 2 vols. 1770; rpt. New York and London: Garland, 1979.

Maurice, Thomas. *The History of Hindostan; its arts, and its sciences, as connected with the history of the other great empires of Asia, during the most ancient periods of the world.* 3 vols. 1795–98; rpt. New York and London: Garland, 1984.

———. *Indian Antiquities: or, Dissertations relative to the ancient geographical divisions, the pure system of primeval theology, the grand code of civil laws, the original form of government, the widely-extended commerce, and the various profound literature, of Hindostan: compared, throughout, with the religion, laws, government, and literature, of Persia, Egypt, and Greece. The whole intended as introductory to, and illustrative of, the history of Hindostan.* 1793; London: R. Faulder; W. Richardson; John White, 1800–01.

Mickle, William Julius. "Enquiry into the Religious Tenets and Philosophy of the Brahmins." *The Lusiad: or, The Discovery of India.* 3d ed. 2 vols. London: Cadell and Davies, 1798.

Moor, Edward. *The Hindu Pantheon.* London: J. Johnson, 1810.

Obituary of Thomas Taylor. *Gentleman's Magazine 5*, new series (Jan. 1836): 91–92.

Priestley, Joseph. *A Comparison of the Institutions of Moses with those of the Hindoos and other Ancient Nations.* Northumberland: A. Kennedy, 1799.

———. *Disquisitions relating to Matter and Spirit.* 1777; rpt. Kila, Montana: Kessinger, n.d.

"Remarks on the Dialogues of Kreeshna and Arjoon." *The Gentleman's Magazine 55*, no. 12 (December 1785): 955–57.

Volney, compte de. *A New Translation of Volney's Ruins.* 2 vols. 1802; rpt. New York and London: Garland, 1979.

———. *The Ruins; or, a Survey of the Revolutions of Empire.* 3d ed. London: J. Johnson, 1796.

Wilkins, Charles, trans. *The Bhăgvăt-Gēēta, or Dialogues of Krĕĕshnă and Ārjŏŏn.* 1785; rpt. Delmar: Scholars' Facsimiles & Reprints, 1959.

Works Cited: Modern Criticism

Ackroyd, Peter. *Blake.* New York: Knopf, 1996.

Altick, Richard D. *The Shows of London.* Cambridge: Belknap Press of Harvard University Press, 1978.

Bearce, George D. *British Attitudes towards India, 1784-1858.* London and New York: Oxford University Press, 1961.

Bentley, G. E., Jr. *Blake Records.* Oxford: Clarendon Press, 1969.

———. *Blake Records Supplement.* Oxford: Clarendon Press, 1988.

————. *The Stranger From Paradise: A Biography of William Blake.* New Haven: Yale University Press, 2001.

Bloom, Harold. *Blake's Apocalypse: A Study in Poetic Argument.* Garden City, N.Y.: Doubleday, 1963.

Blunt, Anthony. "Blake's Pictorial Imagination." *Journal of the Warburg and Courtland Institutes* 6 (1943): 190–212.

Brockington, J. L. "Warren Hastings and Orientalism." *The Impeachment of Warren Hastings: Papers from a Bicentenary Commemoration.* Ed. Geoffrey Carnall and Colin Nicholson. Edinburgh: Edinburgh University Press, 1989.

Clark, Steve, and David Worrall, eds. *Historicizing Blake.* New York: St. Martin's, 1994.

Damon, S. Foster. *A Blake Dictionary: Ideas and Symbols of William Blake.* Boulder, Co.: Shambhala, 1979.

————. *William Blake: His Philosophy and Symbols.* Boston and New York: Houghton Mifflin, 1924.

Damrosch, Jr., Leopold. *Symbol and Truth in Blake's Myth.* Princeton: Princeton University Press, 1980.

Davies, J. G. *The Theology of William Blake.* Oxford: Clarendon Press, 1948.

Drew, John. *India and the Romantic Imagination.* Delhi and New York: Oxford University Press, 1987.

Ellis, Edwin John, and William Butler Yeats. *The Works of William Blake.* 3 vols. London: Bernard Quaritch, 1893.

Erdman, David V. *Blake: Prophet Against Empire: A Poet's Interpretation of the History of His Own Times.* 3d ed. Princeton: Princeton University Press, 1977.

————, ed. *The Complete Poetry and Prose of William Blake.* Newly revised edition. Garden City: Anchor, 1982.

————. *The Illuminated Blake.* Garden City: Anchor, 1974.

Fisher, Peter F. *The Valley of Vision: Blake as Prophet and Revolutionary.* Ed. Northrop Frye. Toronto: University of Toronto Press, 1961.

Freeman, Kathryn S. *Blake's Nostos: Fragmentation and Nondualism in "The Four Zoas."* Albany: State University of New York Press, 1997.

Frye, Northrop. *Fearful Symmetry: A Study of William Blake.* 1947; Princeton: Princeton University Press, 1969.

Gardner, Brian. *The East India Company: A History.* New York: McCall, 1972.

Gilchrist, Alexander. *The Life of William Blake.* 1907; Mineola: Dover, 1998.

Hall, Carol Louise. *Blake and Fuseli: A Study in the Transmission of Ideas.* New York and London: Garland, 1985.

Harper, George Mills. *The Neoplatonism of William Blake.* Chapel Hill: University of North Carolina Press, 1961.

Hill, Christopher. *The World Turned Upside Down: Radical Ideas during the English Revolution.* New York: Viking Press, 1972.

Keith, A. Berriedale, ed. *Speeches and Documents on Indian Policy, 1750–1921.* 2 vols. London: Oxford University Press, 1922.

Kejariwal, O. P. *The Asiatic Society of Bengal and the Discovery of India's Past, 1784–1838.* Delhi: Oxford University Press, 1988.

Manuel, Frank E. *The Eighteenth Century Confronts the Gods.* Cambridge: Harvard University Press, 1959.

Mason, Eudo C., ed. *The Mind of Henry Fuseli: Selections from his Writings.* [London]: Routledge & Paul, [1951].

Mee, Jon. *Dangerous Enthusiasm: William Blake and the Culture of Radicalism in the 1790s.* Oxford: Clarendon Press, 1992.

Mellor, Anne Kostelanetz. *Blake's Human Form Divine.* Berkeley: University of California Press, 1974.

Misra, G. S. *British Foreign Policy and Indian Affairs, 1783–1815.* London: Asia Publishing House, 1963.

Mitchell, W. J. T. *Blake's Composite Art: A Study of the Illuminated Poetry.* Princeton: Princeton University Press, 1978.

Morton, A. L. *The Everlasting Gospel: A Study in the Sources of William Blake.* London: Lawrence & Wishart, 1958.

Nanavutty, Piloo. "William Blake and Hindu Creation Myths." *The Divine Vision: Studies in the Poetry and Art of William Blake.* 1957; New York: Haskell House, 1968.

Nightingale, Pamela. *Trade and Empire in Western India.* Cambridge: Cambridge University Press, 1970.

Nurmi, Martin K. *William Blake.* 1975; Kent: Kent State University Press, 1976.

Nuttall, A. D. *The Alternative Trinity: Gnostic Heresy in Marlowe, Milton, and Blake.* Oxford: Clarendon Press, 1998.

Pachori, Satya S., ed. *Sir William Jones: A Reader.* Delhi: Oxford University Press, 1993.

Quint, David. *Epic and Empire: Politics and Generic Form from Virgil to Milton.* Princeton: Princeton University Press, 1993.

Raine, Kathleen. *Blake and Tradition.* 2 vols. Princeton: Princeton University Press, 1968.

———, and George Mills Harper, eds. *Thomas Taylor the Platonist: Selected Writings.* Princeton: Princeton University Press, 1969.

Rist, John. "Plotinus and Christian Philosophy." *The Cambridge Companion to Plotinus.* Ed. Lloyd P. Gerson. Cambridge: Cambridge University Press, 1996.

Robert, Rudolph. *Chartered Companies and their Role in the Development of Overseas Trade.* London: G. Bell, 1969.

Sargeant, Winthdrop, trans. *The Bhagavad Gītā.* Albany: State University of New York Press, 1994.

Saurat, Denis. *Blake and Modern Thought.* [New York]: Dial Press, 1929.

Schwab, Raymond. *The Oriental Renaissance: Europe's Rediscovery of India and the East, 1680–1880.* Trans. Gene Patterson-Black and Victor Reinking. New York: Columbia University Press, 1984.

Scott, William Bell. *Autobiographical Notes of the Life of William Bell Scott.* Ed. W[illiam] Minto. 2 vols. New York: Harper and Brothers, 1892.

———. *William Blake: Etchings from his Works.* London: Chatto and Windus, 1878.

Singh, Charu Sheel. *The Chariot of Fire: A Study of William Blake in the Light of Hindu Thought.* Salzburg: Institut für Anglistik und Amerikanistik, Universität salzburg, 1981.

Summerfield, Henry. *A Guide to the Books of William Blake for Innocent and Experienced Readers.* Gerrards Cross, Buckinghamshire: Colin Smythe, 1998.

Sutherland, Lucy S. *The East India Company in Eighteenth-century Politics.* Oxford: Clarendon Press, 1952.

Thompson, E. P. *The Making of the English Working Class.* New York: Vintage, 1966.

———. *Witness against the Beast: William Blake and the Moral Law.* Cambridge: Cambridge University Press, 1993.

Tyson, Gerald P. *Joseph Johnson: A Liberal Publisher.* Iowa City: University of Iowa Press, 1979.

Weinglass, David H., ed. *The Collected Letters of Henry Fuseli.* Millwood: Kraus, 1982.

Wilkins, W. J. *Hindu Mythology.* New Delhi: Rupa & Co., 1978.

Index